NEITHER
SEPARATE
NOR EQUAL

D0709035

In the series

Women in the Political Economy

edited by Ronnie J. Steinberg

NEITHER SEPARATE NOR EQUAL

WOMEN, RACE, AND CLASS IN THE SOUTH

Edited by
Barbara Ellen Smith

 Temple University Press
PHILADELPHIA

PROPERTY OF
BAKER COLLEGE OF OWOSSO

Temple University Press, Philadelphia 19122
Copyright © 1999 by Temple University, except
Chapter 9 © Carol Stack and Chapter 13 © Mab Segrest.
All rights reserved
Published 1999
Printed in the United States of America

⊗ The paper used in this publication meets the requirements of the
American National Standard for Information Sciences—Permanence
of Paper for Printed Library Materials, ANSI Z39.48-1984

Library of Congress Cataloging-in-Publication-Data

Neither separate nor equal : women, race, and class in the South /
    edited by Barbara Ellen Smith.
        p.   cm. — (Women in the political economy)
    Includes bibliographical references and index.
    ISBN 1-56639-679-4 (alk. paper).—ISBN 1-56639-680-8 (pbk. : alk. paper)
        1. Women—Southern States—Social conditions.   2. Minority women—
Southern States—Social conditions.   3. Women—Social networks—
Southern States.   4. Sex role—Southern States.   5. Southern
States—Race relations.   6. Southern States—Social conditions.
7. Southern States—Economic conditions.   I. Smith, Barbara E.   II. Series
HQ1438.S63N45   1999
305.42' 0975—DC21   98-40814

For my mother,

Winnifred Watson Smith,

feminist,

internationalist,

and

Southern

Contents

Acknowledgments

Creating a coherent volume out of essays by diverse authors is always a conceptual and stylistic challenge. I appreciate the valuable suggestions of Michael Ames, Kenneth W. Goings, Martha Schmidt, and Lynet Uttal.

Any edited book also involves labor-intensive logistics. I could not have kept up with the details without extensive assistance from graduate students Andreana Clay and Emily Haire. Thank you. Although readers who have undertaken similar projects may doubt my credibility, I am also grateful to all the contributors for their flexibility, good humor, and timeliness.

Introduction

Barbara Ellen Smith

There is much to learn from the American South. Many of the essential trends and dilemmas of the contemporary United States have a long history here. The weak labor movement, large disparity between rich and poor, and low level of social provision that once distinguished the region from the remainder of the country now put it in the vanguard of national trends.[1] Protestant fundamentalism, with its tradition-bound doctrines on gender and sexuality, has long been widely popular and deeply influential in the South; now it is spreading outward from this regional base to create Bible Belts across the United States. In the political arena, the past three decades of presidential elections and congressional actions are incomprehensible without reference to the power of Southern politicians, the shifting allegiances of Southern voters, and the profound impact of the civil rights movement in breaking up the solid South. Above all, a regional consciousness and political economy saturated with race—once considered so anomalous to the enlightened elsewhere—now make the South's history of racial violence and contention a portent.[2]

Despite the significance, perhaps even dominance, of the contemporary South, popular knowledge about the region tends to be shallow. Hackneyed images of Southern women as Scarletts, Mammies, and Daisy Maes epitomize this problem. At best, studies of the region—certainly of Southern women—may evoke puzzlement. As my non-Southern friends asked of my plans to put together a book about Southern women: "Why

1

work on a book about women in the South? Nobody writes books about women in the Midwest."

The question is important. In an era of intensified globalization, when populations, cultures, and capital move across the boundaries of nation-states in multiple forms and directions, the concept of a subnational region seems parochial and out of date. But it is precisely because of the historical construction of the secessionist South as an embattled region, where many of the present trends and icons of "America" may be viewed in sharp relief, that Southerners' experiences in the throes of globalization are so instructive. It is precisely in this time of profound economic insecurity and sociocultural change, when all manner of social problems tend to be blamed on poor women and children and those whose skin is anything but white, that the experiences of racially diverse women in a region legendary for both white supremacy and male supremacy are important to explore.

Even though region continues to matter in the South, context matters everywhere. Even though some white Southerners in particular tend to construct and interpret their context in regional terms, especially to out-siders, people everywhere invest meaning in the places they inhabit and create. This may well be another important lesson from the South, ever more pertinent in an age of mobility and dislocation: place matters, whether people construct that meaningful place as a street, neighbor-hood, hollow, city, or region, whether it is the place people currently re-side or a mythic home to which they hope to return. Those who study hu-man diversity in all its forms might do well to take thoughtfully and literally the question that Southerners, especially rural Southerners, ask of strangers all the time: "Where're you from?"

Despite the lessons to be learned from and about the South, scholarly examinations of its contemporary social trends are rare.[3] Nonfiction books about women in the contemporary South may be counted on one hand.[4] This neglect is peculiar to the social sciences, particularly sociol-ogy. Southern history, including Southern women's history, is a sprawl-ing academic subfield, and Southern fiction by women as well as men enjoys a prominent and esteemed position within the pantheon of Amer-ican literature. By contrast, studies of the contemporary South by social scientists occupy a tiny corner of any library. (The exception is Ap-palachian studies, which developed during the 1960s as an interdiscipli-nary movement across the humanities and social sciences and flourishes to this day.)

If it is true that the hot topics of academic scholarship follow social trends, however obliquely and belatedly, then we are due for a renaissance in contemporary Southern studies. If that develops, it will not simply take up where the dons of an earlier era, such as Howard Odum and Rupert Vance, left off, although hopefully it will be informed by their insights. Such a renaissance will also be able to benefit from studies of transnational migration, which is reconfiguring Southern culture and demographics; from analyses of global restructuring, which is transforming the region's economy; and perhaps above all from the searching questions posed by the multiracial wing of feminism, which challenge the stubborn preoccupation with men and race in the deep South and with men and class in the Appalachian South. A model of such feminist scholarship is already evident in the pathbreaking work of a new generation of Southern historians, who are examining the role of gender in everything from the military campaigns of the Civil War to the social activism of black women in the late nineteenth century (see Chapter 1). They are exploring women, men, and gender relations in terms of their often sexualized interplay with race, class, and other dimensions of inequality, asking new, complex questions about the region's past. Analogous questions about the present await only the scholars willing to pose and pursue them.

What is happening today among women in the South is both vital to developments in the United States as a whole and intriguing, complex, and contradictory in its own right. It also remains largely unexamined. One aim of this book is to give potential scholars a nudge in the direction of that unexplored territory.

Dilemmas of Regionalism

A series of dilemmas attend any analysis of the contemporary South. First and foremost, the region cannot be understood apart from its history, but that history is so complex and extensively analyzed that any summary is inevitably inadequate. Because of this contradiction, the three historical essays in Section I were selected more to be provocative than introductory. My own essay, for example, although hopefully it acquaints readers with the major themes of the book, certainly does not do the same for Southern history as a whole. It provides a highly truncated summary of a single historical period, drawing heavily on the work of Southern women's historians to contrast the structural configuration of race, class, and gender in the late nineteenth century with that of the South today.

The essays in the remainder of the book, although they focus on the present, also tend to be historically informed. They implicitly suggest that, if the South retains any meaningful regional distinctiveness, it does not lie so much in the person of essentialized Southerners as in the long shadows of history cast over all who live there. Historical contextualization allows the authors to analyze continuity and disruption among key groups of Southern women—such as rural black women in the Mississippi Delta, or female textile workers in the piedmont—who have been increasingly studied for their history but rarely for their experiences in the late twentieth century. As a group, the essays depict women whose experiences cannot be understood apart from a distinctive regional context, yet whose lives are so dramatically affected by global forces that regional distinctiveness is an insufficient explanatory framework.

Additional dilemmas attending works on the South are definitional. There is no standard geographic boundary to the region; the states included within its borders, especially along the perimeter, tend to vary somewhat arbitrarily from one analysis to another. Similarly, who counts as a Southerner? Daughters of the Confederacy who can trace their ancestry to the antebellum era? Yankees whose corporate employers relocated them yesterday to Atlanta? The uncertainty of these definitions underscores the constructed, dynamic character of the South and the questionable nature of any fixed criteria for regional authenticity, but it does not resolve the matter of what and who to include in a book on Southern women.

My approach is pragmatic and inclusive, not definitive or rigid. This collection incorporates case studies from as far north as West Virginia and as far west as the Mississippi Delta. Whether one limits the South to the eleven states of the Confederacy or expands it to include certain border areas, the region encompasses great social and geographic diversity: it ranges from portions of the Appalachian Mountains, east to the piedmont and coastal plain, and south through the Black Belt and the Mississippi Delta. The social and economic arrangements associated with each subregion vary widely, from the largely white working-class coalfields to the predominantly black, historically agricultural Delta. This collection seeks to reflect that diversity without making any pretense to comprehensiveness.

Proceeding from the conviction that it is precisely the momentous transformations within the South that make it such a compelling subject of study, the emphasis in most of the chapters is on change, disruption, and reconfiguration in the lives and actions of women. The impacts of global restructuring figure prominently. In Chapter 5 Cynthia D. Anderson and Michael D. Schulman, for example, analyze the gradual disappearance of the company town from the landscape of the piedmont, and the changing community life and work relations of women textile workers affected by corporate reorganization, technological innovation, and global markets. Ann M. Oberhauser and Anne-Marie Turnage explore the participation of rural women in West Virginia in the informal economy in Chapter 6. Technological standardization and corporate distribution of their apparel products reflect so-called post-Fordist production arrangements, yet their gendered, home-based survival strategies also harken back to the nineteenth century.

Even as global forces disrupt and reorganize workplaces and communities across the South, countervailing actions by women create and sustain enduring relationships among people in local communities. These efforts are examined in the case studies collected in section three. The essay by Cynthia M. Duncan, Margaret M. Walsh, and Gemma Beckley (Chapter 8) documents the community-building activities of black professional women, and argues for the political significance of this newly emergent, relatively independent middle class in the historically bipolar social context of the rural Delta. In Chapter 9 Carol Stack analyzes similar activities among women who are return migrants to the rural piedmont, but reaches more pessimistic conclusions about the extent of their insulation from the hostile power of local elites. In Chapter 10 Monica Appleby describes the intentional work of women whose prior invisibility in written histories of social change in Appalachia is testimony in part to their deep insertion into local communities: Catholic women religious who left the Glenmary order decades ago to live and work directly among people in the mountains.

The challenge posed by globalization to all of these efforts is not only to sustain the economic viability of local communities, but also to create an ethos of community solidarity that is not exclusionary. As essays by Loida C. Velázquez, Sally Ward Maggard, and Fran Ansley and Susan Williams relate, the global economy is arriving in neighborhoods across the South in the form of new racial-ethnic groups. Whereas in Chapter 7 Velázquez documents the often painful efforts of Latinas to build new ethnic identities and communities, in Chapter 12 Ansley and Williams focus on the attitudes and actions of more "native" Southern women toward their new neighbors. They follow a group of local labor activists who have struggled against concessionary bargaining and plant closings, as they visit their former employers' new plants in Mexico and simultaneously grapple with the arrival of Mexican workers in their own communities and workplaces. In Chapter 11 Maggard emphasizes how sexism fractured potential solidarity among workers in the prolabor coalfields of eastern Kentucky; a unionization drive among predominantly female hospital workers was ultimately defeated when, in a move that surely foreshadows the future, the employer imported foreign workers as strikebreakers and local, longtime supporters of the largely male United Mine Workers did little to support the women on strike.

The wide range of these case studies notwithstanding, there are important omissions from this book. Readers may be surprised or disappointed to find little emphasis on "traditionally Southern" women, that is, the typically white women who presumably function as bearers of a distinctive regional culture and way of life. Such women do exist, and, although this collection avoids investing Southern authenticity exclusively in certain groups, their role in regional culture and myth-making about, for example, the Lost Cause is important.[5] Unfortunately, I could find no new studies of such women. Similarly, I could locate no appropriate case studies of women in such urban centers as Atlanta, New Orleans, and Miami. Also, young women are missing from this collection, as are women from the coastal South. I can only hope that studies of the contemporary South, and especially of Southern women, will so flourish that in the future the editor of a similar volume will not face such a void.

Themes and Perspectives

Anyone who writes a social analysis of women today must deal with the question of diversity: how far to extend it, which forms to foreground, and what conceptual framework to use to explain it. For reasons of theoretical affinity and regional history, this collection features primarily race, gender, class, and, to a lesser extent, sexual identity. Although other forms of social differentiation among women are significant in certain contexts, these parameters are foundational, omnirelevant, determinant.

Unlike many other approaches, the essays in this collection treat race and other forms of difference neither as ascribed characteristics that inhere in individuals nor exclusively as forms of identity that individuals create. Rather, the emphasis is on race, gender, class, and sexuality as social relationships—dynamic, contested, and re-created daily by human action, but ultimately not voluntary or individual. Unlike poststructuralist perspectives, the essays tend to invoke dimensions of the social structure as the most cogent explanation for the intransigent dynamic of power that characterizes all of these relationships. (See Chapter 1 for a more thorough explanation of this approach.)

When I asked potential contributors to analyze differences among Southern women within a relational framework, I did not anticipate that their rich array of interpretations would so far exceed my original conceptualization. Some of these essays emphasize economic exchange, involving interdependence as well as potential exploitation among women of different class and spatial locations. Oberhauser and Turnage, for example, explore the ways in which the home-based, informal economic activities of relatively isolated rural women place them in market relationships with more class-privileged, urban women who buy their products.

Others interpret "relationality" as the intentional interpersonal interactions, involving direct negotiations of meaning, power, privilege, and

connection among diverse women. See, for example, Chapter 4 by Mahnaz Kousha, who analyzes the emotional dimensions of the complex relationships between African American domestics and their white employers.
Appleby documents a very different form of direct interaction: the work
of Catholic women religious, outsiders to Appalachia, who sank deep
roots in local communities and built relationships from the ground up.
Others explore the contentious difficulties involved in creating relationships of political solidarity across differences of nationality (Ansley and
Williams), race and sexual identity (Mab Segrest), and gender (Maggard).

Additional dimensions of social relations emerge in the chapter by Anderson and Schulman, who analyze the global forces shaping intraclass
dynamics and the potential for solidarity among women textile workers
in North Carolina. Similarly, Stack and Duncan, Walsh, and Beckley document intraracial relationships among African American women, whose
community-building work often extends across class lines. The contribution by Velázquez assesses the efforts of Hispanic women, recently arrived
in the South, to construct new identities and relationships of ethnicity.
Although all of these essays focus on the internal dynamics of race- and
class-defined groups of women, they also situate these women's activities
within a larger context of power relations with corporate CEOs, local political leaders, and white landowners.

The historical essays in Section I set the tone for the entire volume:
like Segrest's essay, they treat race as a compass, a relationship so central
in Southern history that women in diverse circumstances and political
struggles tend to orient themselves in terms of it. At the same time, the
historical chapters by Darlene Wilson and Patricia Beaver and by Patricia
B. Lerch contest conventional perceptions of the racial composition of
the South. In Chapter 2 Wilson and Beaver expose the political and economic processes whereby Appalachia became constructed as white, while
in Chapter 3 Lerch's focus on the Waccamaw Indians implicitly challenges the bipolar construction of race in other parts of the South. Both
constructions—of Appalachia as white and of the remainder of the South
as black and white—have lent an exaggerated simplicity and coherence
to the region. In both locales, whiteness has been conflated with regional
identity: the only culturally authentic Appalachians or Southerners are
white. Although the associated scholarship on white ethnicity has been
plentiful, insightful, and even trenchant in its findings, these authors suggest it is time to abjure such an exclusionary definition of the region's inhabitants. This may be especially important at a time when, at the national level, whiteness is conflated with "Americanness," thus erasing
from historical memory immigrant diversity and the processes whereby
"whites" were constituted as a fixed, coherent, and privileged race in the

first place. Racial amnesia in turn feeds demagogic responses to the worldwide migrations of the new millennium.

Unraveling the gendered aspects of these racial-regional constructions takes these authors into the tangled knot of race and sex in the South. Wilson and Beaver explore the historical agency of Native American women and their mixed-race offspring, which has been largely omitted from the historiography of Appalachia. Recovering this history, they argue, deprives contemporary Southern women of their apparently self-evident racial identities, but restores to them a legacy of independent foremothers who sought to circumvent constrictive racial and sexual norms. Lerch examines in part the same theme: Waccamaw Indian women in certain eras found their sexual freedom circumscribed, and their dependence on one another reinforced, by the changing position of their tribe within the black-white paradigm of race in the South. Lerch also documents the gendered dynamics of community life among the Waccamaw and the ongoing efforts of tribal members, now led by a woman, to create a respected, recognized ethnic niche.

In sum, this collection explores the relational construction of difference within and among diverse groups of Southern women. The authors explore multiple levels of relationality—structural, interpersonal, political, emotional. The social bonds that emerge from these chapters are exploitative, collaborative, contentious, and—in the final, moving essay by Segrest—spiritual. Taken as a whole, the essays suggest that, although the direct personal experience of "difference" may be separation and disconnection, the differences that divide us are also social relationships from which no one escapes.

Notes

1. The exception to this generalization is Appalachia, where a strong labor movement, particularly in the coalfields, was able to influence some states' policies.

2. Observers of the South have been debating convergence between the region and the rest of the United States for many years. See John Egerton, *The Americanization of Dixie; The Southernization of America* (New York: Harper's Magazine Press, 1974); Dewey Grantham, *The South in Modern America: A Region at Odds* (New York: Harper Perennial, 1994); Larry Griffin and Don Doyle, eds., *The South as an American Problem* (Athens: University of Georgia Press, 1995); John Shelton Reed, *The Enduring South: Subcultural Persistence in Mass Society* (Chapel Hill: University of North Carolina Press, 1974); Peter Applebome, *Dixie Rising: How the South Is Shaping American Values, Politics, and Culture* (New York: Harcourt Brace and Company, 1997); John Hennen, *The Americanization of West Virginia* (Lexington: University Press of Kentucky, 1996); Mary Beth Pudup, Dwight Billings, and

Altina Waller, eds., *Appalachia in the Making: The Mountain South in the Nineteenth Century* (Chapel Hill: University of North Carolina Press, 1995).

3. Although this is not to disparage or neglect the important social science works that do exist, the contrast with the proliferation of books and articles in Southern history and literature is still dramatic. See Reed, *The Enduring South, Southern Folk Plain and Fancy: Native White Social Types* (Athens: University of Georgia Press, 1986), *My Tears Spoiled My Aim and Other Reflections on Southern Culture* (Columbia: University of Missouri Press, 1993), and *Whistling Dixie: Dispatches from the South* (Columbia: University of Missouri Press, 1990); Earl Black and Merle Black, *The Vital South: How Presidents Are Elected* (Cambridge, MA: Harvard University Press, 1992); Griffin and Doyle, eds., *The South as an American Problem;* John Gaventa, Barbara Ellen Smith, and Alex Willingham, eds., *Communities in Economic Crisis: Appalachia and the South* (Philadelphia: Temple University Press, 1990); William W. Falk and Thomas A. Lyson, eds., *High Tech, Low Tech, No Tech: Recent Industrial and Occupational Change in the South* (Albany: State University of New York Press, 1988); and the series of papers by members of the Southern Anthropological Society, published as edited volumes by the University of Georgia Press.

4. Holly F. Mathews, ed., *Women in the South: An Anthropological Perspective* (Athens: University of Georgia Press, 1989); Caroline Matheny Dillman, ed., *Southern Women* (New York: Hemisphere Publishing Corporation, 1988); Patricia Stringer and Irene Thompson, eds., *Stepping Off the Pedestal: Academic Women in the South* (New York: Modern Language Association of America, 1982); Virginia Rinaldo Seitz, *Women, Development, and Communities for Empowerment in Appalachia* (Albany: SUNY Press, 1995); Carol A. B. Giesen, *Coal Miners' Wives: Portraits of Endurance* (Lexington: University Press of Kentucky, 1995).

5. For a different perspective on the question of regional authenticity, see Dillman, ed., *Southern Women;* and Carole Hill, "Anthropological Studies in the American South: Review and Directions," *Current Anthropology* 18 (1977): 309–33. See also Reed, *The Enduring South.* Hill's changed perspective is articulated in "Contemporary Issues in Anthropological Studies of the American South," in Carole Hill and Patricia Beaver, eds., *Cultural Diversity in the U.S. South: Anthropological Contributions to a Region in Transition* (Athens: University of Georgia Press, 1998), pp. 12–33. For an earlier piece on elite women, see Nancy Press, "Public Faces, Private Lives: The Women of the Downtown Group of Charleston, South Carolina," in Mathews, ed., *Women in the South,* pp. 95–109.

ENGENDERING HISTORY

1

The Social Relations
of Southern Women

Barbara Ellen Smith

"We need to recognize not only differences [among women]
but also the relational nature of those differences. Middle-
class white women's lives are not just different from
working-class white, Black, and Latina women's lives. . . .
Middle-class women live the lives they do precisely because
working-class women live the lives they do. . . . White women
live the lives they do in large part because women of color
live the ones they do."

—Elsa Barkley Brown

S
outhern women of different races and classes live in complex
relationship to one another. Young white women in Mississippi
who fashion themselves as Southern belles unknowingly rest
their delicacy on the contrasting cultural representations of
their African American peers. Working-class women in eastern
Kentucky, once dependent on the wages of their coal miner
husbands, now support their families by charging twenty-five
dollars a day to take care of others' children, thus making it feasible for middle-class mothers to pursue their careers. Women
who are midlevel bankers and stockbrokers in Atlanta, frustrated by the acts of sexism and the glass ceiling that they encounter each day, nonetheless enjoy the accoutrements of

privilege made possible by, among many others, the Cambodian women who dust and vacuum their offices at night. This web of relationships stretches wide, far beyond the South: women workers in a Philips electronics factory in Tennessee are unemployed because their employer just moved the plant to the U.S.–Mexican border, where he hires Latinas for the same reason—low wages—that he once hired Southern women.

Defining the race and class differences among Southern women as social relationships flies in the face of other perspectives, both academic and popular, that gained increasing influence during the 1980s and early 1990s. Poststructuralist approaches, for all of their manifold insights, have tended to reduce gender, race, sexual identity, and other social differentiations to discursive performances, artifacts of culture and language.[1] Extreme variants of poststructuralism neglect the material mechanisms, from job discrimination to rape, wherein race, class, and gender are continuously enacted and reinforced as forms of oppression. Similarly, popular approaches that seek to celebrate cultural differences tend to level all forms of inequality: in the pop variant of multiculturalism, for example, race and gender are thrown into a vat of social distinctions that may also include dress, religion, political affiliation, and the like—all presumably equivalent ingredients in the stew of diversity.[2] Not surprisingly, class, an altogether too material difference that resists reduction to cultural "taste," tends to be ignored.

During the same period, many feminist researchers have been working hard to disaggregate the unitary category "woman" through highly specific empirical studies. The rich proliferation of research that documents the divergent experiences and interests of distinct groups of women has tended to reinforce the political conclusion that women are indeed separated from one another by wide gulfs of difference. I do not bemoan this exploration or this conclusion, which seem necessary precursors and accompaniments to more adequate feminist theory and effective practice. What seems problematic, however, is a common tendency within these multiple approaches—poststructuralist, multicultural, feminist—to define "difference" as a collection of bounded categories, a taxonomy of social life. Implicitly, society is conceptualized as a grid of boxes (differences) into which individual members fit; the challenge for the feminist (or any enlightened, multicultural person) is to extend out of these boxes, to make the effort to learn about those of others, and—the greatest challenge of all—to establish political solidarity (or respectful relationships) with those who are different.

The analysis presented in this and other chapters of this book suggests that such a map of the social landscape is fundamentally inaccurate. As social beings, we have no choice about being in relationship with those who are different; difference *is* a relationship. We are only "different" in relationship to others whose social position contrasts with our own. More importantly, there is an internal relationship between those who are hierarchically defined as "different": whiteness, for example, a privileged racial position that conceals itself as the "normal American" experience in the United States, has no social meaning apart from blackness. It is not possible to comprehend the social privileges and historical experiences of people defined as white in this country without analyzing the social indignities and historical experiences of those defined as black. As Toni Morrison put it, "whiteness, alone, is . . . pointless."[3] Race, in other words, is not just a matter of difference, but a social relationship of power, privilege, and contestation.

In the South, the historical construction of race, class, and gender as extreme social polarities has rendered the interdependent, relational nature of these differences among women exceptionally vivid. The explicit codification of white supremacy in the contexts of first Native American genocide, then slavery, and later Jim Crow, fused a rich multiplicity of colors, ethnicities, and nationalities into a single deadly opposition, black and white. During the late nineteenth century, the concentrated ownership of land and capital, whether in the coal camps of Appalachia, the mill towns of the piedmont, or the vast farms of the Mississippi Delta, generated a similarly bipolar class structure in many rural locations.[4] Relations between men and women have varied greatly by historical era and by race and class; however, the logic of racial domination and resistance has tended to foster analogous extremes of gender. Within the chivalric code of white Southern culture, for example, white women depended on/were subordinated to the authority of white men to defend them, with physical terror and violence, from the archetypal "beast," black men.[5] Concomitantly, the social, symbolic, and literal emasculation of black men meant that their power as men was exercised primarily in relation to black women and children; it also lent a masculinist character to their counterassertions of power and integrity. ("I am a Man," proclaimed the placards of the striking sanitation workers in Memphis to whom Martin Luther King paid a fatal visit in 1968.)

As these last examples suggest, the historical construction of race, class, and gender in the South has rendered these differences not only polarized, with their relational character exceptionally evident, but also deeply intertwined. This acknowledgment immediately requires the addition of another dimension, sexuality, to the triad of race, class, and gender, for sexuality has often been the medium and the metaphor for links among these relations of power. In the antebellum era, the "explosive intimacy" of the plantation household was fueled by white planters' sexual access to and forced breeding of black slave women.[6] By contrast, elite white women's claims to privilege—and, in a later era, middle-class black women's demands for status and respect—rested heavily on piety and sexual repression.[7] By the early twentieth century, white working-class women began fashioning themselves in a new, freer mode: in sexualized class rebellions, they taunted the impotence of male scabs, managers, and police officers whom they encountered on picket lines and in court-rooms, in some cases adopting mannerisms that we would identify today as "butch."[8] These examples point to the provocative role of sexuality as a central symbolic and material force circulating through and among re-lationships of race, class, and gender.

The next section illustrates this overall approach by sketching the structural relationships among diverse groups of Southern women in the tumultuous social context of the late nineteenth century. White su-premacy, codified in the form of Jim Crow, involved overt, personalistic mechanisms of social control that allow us to see quite clearly the rela-tionships among race, gender, sexuality, and class, and thereby the struc-tural linkages among women themselves. The consciousness of race that imbued both black and white women's politics, and the associated im-plications for the intraracial politics of class and gender, are also evident. The analysis in this section is dependent on the exciting new scholarship of Southern women's historians, several of whom have recently focused their efforts on this period.[9]

Today, however, in the post–civil rights movement, post–Jim Crow, postmodern South, the social relations of Southern women are quite dif-ferent—multivalent rather than bipolar, global rather than regional. Moreover, the "technologies of oppression," the mechanisms whereby in-equality is continuously enforced, are far more covert and indirect. The conclusion briefly outlines the shifting, emergent contours of race, class, gender, and sexual identity in the global South, and identifies some im-plications for the relational understanding of women's differences today.

The Hegemony of Race in the Jim Crow South

Historian Ulrich Bonnell Phillips once summed up the central theme of Southern history in two words: white supremacy. Contemporary trends in historiography suggest a related but less static and unilateral formula-tion: race is the central theme of Southern political history, with contes-tations over its meaning and implications the main plot in diverse his-torical eras. Although white supremacy may be the "master" narrative, it developed in dialogical relationship with the "power of blackness," which Southerners of all races acted in various ways to construct and contain.[10]

This interpretation of race as a relationship of contestation helps to clarify the tumult and contradiction that characterized the last third of the nineteenth century in the South.[11] A time when lynching and extralegal terrorism against blacks reached record proportions, this period also saw the emergence of an ambitious and successful black middle class in the urban South. Economic boosterism and capitalist industrialization, associated with the emergence of the New South, coincided with the development of feudal-like restrictions, particularly on black sharecroppers, that replaced the slave system in Southern agriculture. Women, both black and white, became civic activists and skilled organizers as they worked through evangelical churches to promote education, sanitation, and social well-being; however, white women also worked to restore a mythic patriarchal authority to Southern white men through, among many other actions, the cultural construction of the "Lost Cause" of the Confederacy.[12]

The foremost structural development in the social relations of race, which emerged with a vengeance during the last decade of the century, was the institutionalization of Jim Crow. By the second decade of the twentieth century, virtually every legislature in the South had passed laws that required social segregation of the races and compromised the citizenship rights of black men.[13] Under the elaborate proscriptions of Jim Crow, Southerners enacted race in physical space. The races resided in separate neighborhoods, attended separate schools, worshiped in separate churches—in short, lived separate lives to an extent that is not so different from the racial segregation that exists in most U.S. cities today.

However, Jim Crow was more than social separation, for it encompassed customs of racial deference designed to ritualize whites' privileged claim to public space—whether the front of streetcars, the larger portion of sidewalks, the entire area of parks and beaches, even the visual panorama claimed by the eyes. (Racial etiquette required African Americans to avert their gaze from whites.)[14] The racialization of public space was intended to keep black bodies from apparent contact with white bodies, in some cases even from contact with the same objects—drinking cups, door handles, courtroom Bibles—that white mouths or hands would touch.[15] From the perspective of the white South, this elaborate physical separation encoded race as extreme biological difference, blackness as contamination. All this was going on while white Southerners, also as part of the routine of daily life, ate food prepared by black hands, nursed their white babies at black breasts, and allowed their most private physical needs to be taken care of by black domestics, who were overwhelmingly women. Such intimacies between blacks and whites were a long-standing component of the Southern racial hierarchy (and are one of many important contrasts between black-white relations in the North and South). It was the anonymous, less easily regulated space of the growing cities, where strangers thronged together in public life, that Jim Crow was designed in part to govern.

Although the codification of white supremacy was the manifest purpose of Jim Crow, racial segregation evolved from numerous sources and carried contradictory meanings; from the perspective of many black Southerners, segregation per se did not necessarily signify oppression. Indeed, African Americans in some cases established segregated organizations (such as churches) and lobbied for separate facilities (such as public parks) in order to secure control over their own social institutions and community life. Similarly, other people of color, such as the Waccamaw Indians of North Carolina, sought segregated schools in order to defend their autonomy and preserve their racial-ethnic heritage (see Chapter 3). Black Southerners contested Jim Crow to the extent that it involved the unequal allocation of rights and resources; they did so not only through formal organizations, but also in individual confrontations over public space, particularly on streetcars. The aim of this manifold resistance was not necessarily social integration, as many whites presupposed, but ranged from respectful treatment and access to public resources to equal rights.[16]

Southern historians have engaged in a long and fierce debate over the timing and origins of Jim Crow. What explains the delay in its legal codification (some twenty years after the defeat of Reconstruction and over thirty years after the end of the Civil War)? What social groups were the architects of this new racial regime? What is the relative significance of race versus class in its emergence? Without engaging this debate, it is clear from the voluminous scholarship accompanying it that the new racial code had antecedents in the slave system, the cornerstone of the antebellum political economy. In the more immediate term, it emerged in part from the dislocations of the Civil War, whose battles were fought primarily on Southern soil, with devastating consequences for the region's economy and social order. Military defeat (from the perspective of Confederate loyalists) brought federal troops of occupation and Reconstruction-era struggles over the economic, political, and social status of emancipated and, for men, enfranchised African Americans. Seeking to protect the historic privileges of their skin on this new, uncertain terrain, whites of all classes found common cause in enforcing a mixture of new and old forms of subordination on African Americans.[17]

Even as they reconstructed race with tools borrowed from the antebellum era, Southerners also rebuilt the region's postwar economy with structural arrangements that resembled the plantation system. Industrial capitalism grew vigorously in the late nineteenth-century South; however, the emergent class of white entrepreneurs and industrialists did not function as an agent of liberal individualism and democracy, racial or otherwise, as many modernization theorists would predict. Industrialization was largely a rural phenomenon, orchestrated by white investors, who established labor-intensive, low-wage industries such as textiles, and hired only poor whites, women and men, as mill hands. This truncated form of industrial capitalism did not encourage the development of major cities or a large middle class (black or white). Thus the race-class structure in many locations, whether agricultural or industrial, remained persistently bipolar; in rural areas with a large African American population, such as the Black Belt, class tended to coincide and elide with race.[18]

Moreover, for all their rhetoric of progress and innovation, the promoters of industrialization in the late nineteenth century—journalists, bankers, merchants, and other business and professional people—developed the New South in an economically dependent relationship with the Old. The premier New South industry, textiles, developed as an outgrowth of cotton production; indeed, many of the same planter families who controlled that agricultural crop invested in the mills. Thus the region's white capitalist and professional classes exerted little countervailing economic or political influence over the traditional planter elite. Economic and social alliance, including the powerful bond of whiteness, characterized relations between planters and these potential upstarts, and set the South on a distinctly conservative route to modernization.[19] (See Chapter 8.)

Among many other implications, this meant that the full, unmitigated power of the state could be mobilized in most eras and locations to defeat those who sought to contest the power of elites. For example, lower-class blacks and whites who, in the face of declining crop prices and elite control of credit and agricultural markets, joined the interracial populist movement of the late nineteenth century, soon found their democratic aspirations thwarted by a determined counterinsurgency. With lurid and sensationalistic appeals to racism, Democratic politicians and their affluent backers trampled this fragile interracialism and reunited whites across class lines in the name of racial supremacy.[20] In the elections of 1898 and most subsequent years, politicians pledged to white supremacist platforms triumphed and proceeded to pass Jim Crow laws throughout the Southern states. Brutal vigilantism made examples of those who contested the new racial arrangements. Similarly, over the following four decades, coal miners, timber workers, sharecroppers, mill hands, and others sought to unionize, in some cases across racial lines; they too faced the armed might of a relatively unified white elite.[21] With the exception of coal miners' successful organization of the United Mine Workers of

America, most of these labor initiatives ended in violent defeat.[22] The race-class configuration of the Jim Crow South thus helps to account not only for the contradictory character of the late nineteenth century, but also for certain distinguishing features of the region, such as its rurality, low rates of unionization, and poverty, to this day.

As should be clear from this brief synopsis, race and, to a lesser extent, class have not only dominated the political history of the South but its historiography as well. Only in the past two decades have feminist social historians managed to broaden this exclusionary emphasis to encompass women's lives and considerations of gender. The best of the new scholarship has investigated Southern women as people who experienced and contested the constraints of their gender in the context of race- and class-defined social groups. Thus this feminist approach neither neglects nor contests the salience of race, but demonstrates the racialized character of women's lives and the gendered content of racial domination and resistance. (Class has been less consistently addressed.)[23] Indeed, even as they explore the history of women in the South, feminist researchers have tended to affirm the significance of race: in probing the politics of gender, for example, they have uncovered the ubiquitous power of white supremacy to undermine both white and black women's aspirations for freedom.

Of special relevance to this chapter are those feminist historians who have focused on the Civil War and its aftermath; their research is transforming the historiography of the late nineteenth century, recasting the origins of Jim Crow and the role of women in the politics of the era. Drew Gilpin Faust, Lee Ann Whites, and others have concluded that the Civil War brought on a "crisis in gender," a time when white women of necessity assumed responsibility for Southern agricultural production, including, for elite women, the management of increasingly rebellious slaves. The exhaustion and, at times, impossibility of fulfilling both masculine and feminine duties rendered this new authority and independence largely unwelcome for white women, although the experience forever altered gender relations in the South. After the war, white women of all classes entered the wage labor force to support themselves and their families; many, however, viewed this change as lamentable, a measure of their loss and want. White men returned to their homes—when they returned at all—exhausted from combat, disillusioned by defeat, embittered by the wreckage of their land and other property. The postwar politics of white supremacy was thus in part a complex "gendered project," an effort to restore the patriarchal authority of white males in the face of military defeat, black emancipation, and disrupted patterns of gender relations.[24]

The significance of this new historiography does not lie so much in its revelation of white women's active role in the construction of both white supremacy and male supremacy; this is important but not surprising, given a historical context in which both black emancipation and the prospect of their own separation from male protection/provision represented frightening material loss and social breakdown to white women of all classes. More significantly, especially in their relevance to contemporary politics and social analysis, are the deep structural linkages between institutionalized racism and patriarchy, between white supremacy and male supremacy, which this new feminist historiography lays bare. In this it echoes an older legacy of black feminist politics, which pointed a century ago to the linkages between racial and gender oppression in the South.[25]

White women in the last third of the nineteenth century enlarged their rights to political activism and social independence.[26] They did so, however, within the constraints of their time and place, which offered little ideological or material support for white women's equality with or independence from white men. Within the political economy of the predominantly rural South, characterized by a mixture of labor-intensive agriculture and low-wage industry that persisted well into the twentieth century, white women of most classes had few possibilities to make a secure life for themselves apart from men. Widows might of necessity farm on their own, but such an arrangement was rare; similarly, single or widowed white women might obtain jobs in the textile mills, but the "family wage" system made their sole earnings scarcely sufficient to survive.[27] Moreover, the omnipresent logic of racial domination tended to draw a tight, patriarchal circle around white women, limiting their social freedom. Within the racist ideology of the white South, the black male who raped white females came to symbolize the horrors of emancipation and Reconstruction. Sexual violence also signified the fearsome consequences of independence for white women, legitimating their dependence on the physical, social, and economic protection of white husbands, fathers, brothers, and, if all else failed, the masculine state.

The cultural politics of white women, particularly elite women, thus reflected the constraints of their situation: they deployed white femininity as virtuous domesticity, a stratagem (conscious or not) that simultaneously reinforced their claims to racial superiority, to influence in politics and social affairs, and to protection/provision from white men. Lower-class white women, whose sacrifices and hardships during and after the Civil War tended to be especially severe, became symbols of Southern dignity in the face of loss, part of the cultural project of white supremacy. More privileged white women in some cases recognized that the new economic and social roles required of lower-class women, although deplorable in their origins, facilitated their own expanded place in the labor force and in other arenas, such as politics. They deployed imagery of the hard-working white widow to legitimate both racial supremacy and their own demands for greater freedom and influence as women.[28] Their valorization of femininity simultaneously secured white women's traditional role within the fundamental productive and reproductive unit of the heterosexual family, and enforced on white men their economic responsibilities to women and children. Hence the apparently contradictory politics and images of elite white women—feminist (suffragist) yet supportive of patriarchy, influential yet demure, strong yet dependent, the steel magnolia.[29]

If the Southern economy afforded white women few chances at economic independence, it offered black women even fewer. At the same time, systematic race discrimination compromised black men's capacity to function as patriarchs and providers, and required black women to work outside their homes. (More prosperous black women's withdrawal from the labor force after emancipation generated a storm of reaction from whites, who condemned them for "putting on airs" and seeking to claim the status of "lady.")[30] Although some middle-class black women engaged in professional occupations that served their segregated communities, particularly teaching, the great majority of working-class black women were employed in the lowest wage occupation in the United States, domestic service. This pattern of occupational segregation persisted until well after World War II.[31]

Among black women, the assertion of essentialized feminine virtue was, as with white women, a central feature of their cultural politics; above all a racial strategy, it arose nonetheless from their gendered position.[32] Endowing themselves with positive feminine traits—piety, moral virtue, concern for social well-being in such areas as education, health, and hygiene—black women of all classes both repudiated the racist ideology that legitimated their injurious treatment and claimed a significant role for themselves in the racial politics of the era. Among club women and other elites, the emphasis on "lifting as we climb" sometimes carried a distinct class judgment, the suggestion that the immoral and slovenly habits of the lower classes were the real burden pushing down the race.[33] Nonetheless, Southern black women of all classes emerged as important voices for social reform during the Jim Crow era, sometimes termed the "nadir" in race relations, when outspokenness on the part of black men could result in death.[34]

The parallels between their politics notwithstanding, black and white women were defined as polar opposites, locked together in mutually defining contrasts within the social context of the Jim Crow South. As the most prized possession of white men, white women were the emblem of racial supremacy, indeed, of the (white) South "herself"—ever threatened by Yankee aggression and black male lust. Whereas elite white women in particular were constructed as chaste and pious, the symbol of virtue and civilization, black women, within the oppositional logic of these race-gender contrasts, became depravity incarnate: unclean, promiscuous, savage. These interrelated, sexualized polarities of race and gender informed both black and white women's politics, but in ways that white women tended to exploit and black women to contest. Analogous polarities also differentiated men: whereas white men were refined, courageous, and intelligent, black men were stupid beasts, endowed with unnatural physical abilities in every respect. Thus the social ideology of white supremacy tended to construct two races but four genders. It endorsed not only racial superiority but also women's subordination and heterosexism as natural elements of the social order. Whoever crossed these sexualized boundaries in the wrong direction (i.e., interracially, homosexually, or both)—whoever, that is, except white men—committed cultural treason and received the commensurate punishment.[35]

Nowhere is this more evident than in the horrific violence of lynching, which rose to record highs in the Jim Crow South.[36] In this time and place, lynching was overwhelmingly an act of racial domination, typically justified by graphic rumors of a white woman's rape. Lynching enforced with terrifying materiality the trio of cultural icons described above: the ravished white female virgin, emblem of the embattled, civilized South; the beastial black male rapist, whose presumed actions signified racial equality and social regression; and the white male savior, emblem of Southern manhood and courageous defender of civilization. The absence of black women enhanced the symbolic power of the black male as a terrifying racial signifier, whose menace rested both on blackness and on masculinity; conversely, the white woman stood alone in her "pure" claim to femininity. In reality, black women were by far the most frequent victims of interracial sexual violence; their "absent presence" exposes the hypocrisy of this racist patriarchal scenario. Their absence may also attest to the "culture of dissemblance" and invisibility with which black women sought to protect themselves from violence and degradation.[37] That black women were later raped by white men, excited by the blood lust of lynching, may well be the untold finale to this atrocity.[38]

Although investigations at the time, most notably those by black journalist and newspaper publisher Ida B. Wells, suggested that the motives for lynching most frequently involved economic competition between black and white men, the eroticized link between sex, violence, and race persisted in the "folk pornography of the Bible Belt" (to borrow Jacquelyn Dowd Hall's evocative phrase).[39] Technically an act of extralegal vigilantism resulting in death, lynching was in fact far more: through torture and sexual mutilation, white men inscribed their gendered racial power on the very bodies of black men, removing them from the ranks of manhood; through ritualized murder, they cast black men from the ranks of humanity.

This highly schematic summary of race, class, and gender in the Jim Crow South obviously does not do justice to the variations and complexities of social relations in this vast and diverse region. Its purpose is to illuminate overall patterns in the construction of this matrix of inequality and to demonstrate the relational nature of women's differences during an era when the benign term "difference" obviously does not capture the connotations or consequences of these inequalities. For reasons that are specific to this time and place, the bipolar construction of race permeated much of the region, exerting an overweening influence in all social relationships. Race demarcated the boundaries of social life in family, neighborhood, workplace, politics, and the street. It functioned as a trump card, in most cases overriding other forms of solidarity. White supremacy was pervasively articulated and enforced at a structural and institutional level—through the courts, schools, legislatures, and so on—but it also resided in the personal racial authority of virtually all adult whites over blacks.

For over a century, African American women and men contested this system of racial domination. On rare occasions, white women broke their racialized bonds of gender and also lent their support to racial equality. (Significantly, several of these women, such as Jessie Daniel Ames, Katherine duPre Lumpkin, and Lillian Smith, had a long-term relationship with another woman that some today would consider lesbian.)[40] The post–World War II civil rights movement finally dismantled the explicit codification of white supremacy in the South. In challenging race-based hierarchy, the movement intrinsically challenged the historically specific configuration of social inequality in which white supremacy loomed so large and thereby inaugurated a new era of social relationships among Southern women. Whites throughout the region condemned these momentous changes as threats to the "Southern way of life"—a perspective that civil rights supporters tended to scorn as sentimental racist hyperbole. Developments today, however, suggest that those white resisters may have been right: the defeat of Jim Crow, along with other far-reaching political and economic changes in the late twentieth century, has indeed transformed the structure of race and other social inequalities in the U.S. South; increasingly, the "Southern way of life" is no more.

Conclusion: Women, Race, and Class in the Global South

More boundaries than those between nations are being crossed in the global South. The defeat of Jim Crow weakened not only the vigilantly patrolled boundaries between black and white, but also the racialized oppositions of gender; no longer formally segregated, black and white women, especially those of the same class, may now pursue common goals in workplaces, schools, community organizations, and other institutions. By expanding the opportunities of the black middle class, the civil rights movement also diversified the Southern class structure, especially in locations where race and class had tended to conflate. Other social movements have been influential as well: the second-wave women's movement, although not strong in the region, nonetheless legitimated the aspirations of women who sought freedom from abusive spouses, equal pay for equal work, and remedies for other gender injustices. During the 1970s and 1980s, a cultural movement of sexual minorities, visible primarily but not exclusively in the South's urban centers, began to contest the presumed biological polarity of masculine and feminine and the heterosexism on which it rests.[41]

Other border crossings have been less the product of collective social movements and more the result of global economic forces. Long a destination for labor-intensive domestic employers seeking a low-wage labor force, the South is now a point of departure for those employers who are moving production facilities out of the country.[42] Even as capital ebbs out of the South, however, it also flows in—at rates exceeding those of other regions of the United States. Corporations headquartered in Japan, Europe, and elsewhere find in the U.S. South an ideal location: First World amenities without First World costs. In the past ten years, steel mills have begun to loom over the cotton fields of the Mississippi Delta; I-85 from Atlanta to Richmond has become an international corridor of economic activity. Although traditional elites work to preserve the "good business climate" of the South, the influx of capital and corporations from other nations (as well as other parts of the United States) portends change in the relatively monolithic power structure that has dominated many Southern cities and towns.[43] Urbanization, economic growth, and the expansion of professional and technical jobs in the service sector also offer new opportunities and economic independence to educated women of all races.

This global political economy carries profound implications for race in the South. Especially in the wake of recent free trade agreements, global markets draw not only capital but also labor across national boundaries. In areas of the South that have been at most biracial in the past, including even portions of the rural Black Belt, immigrants from Mexico, the Caribbean, and other countries in Central America now seek a more prosperous life. Their effort to create an ethnic niche that is neither black nor white implicitly contests the Southern construction of race as a bipolar opposition; at the same time, they, too, are subject to processes of racialization, wherein they are defined as "Latino" within the racial schema of the United States (see Chapter 7).[44]

As a result of these manifold trends, race, class, and gender are becoming multivalent relationships. The bipolar construction of race is weakening; white supremacy, enforced through violence and direct personal authority, does not overtly regulate the social world of the late twentieth-century South. The open acknowledgment of varied sexual practices and identities is increasing, racial identities are diversifying, professional and technical classes are expanding; as a result, the differentiations among Southern women also multiply. This does not mean, however, that racial oppression has lessened, or that class and gender are no longer relations of inequality. Rather, the mechanisms of authority and social control wherein race, class, sexual identity, and gender are generated and reinforced have taken new form. The structural relationships among these dimensions of inequality have also changed.

In some respects, the South has finally adopted, albeit belatedly, modern, bureaucratic mechanisms of social control that were institutionalized in an earlier era throughout the rest of the United States. The enforcement of white supremacy no longer resides in the direct and personal power of all adult whites over blacks. Today, a complex of social institutions perpetuates racial privilege and disadvantage through apparently impersonal mechanisms within the courts, the public schools, and the electoral process. The formally democratic processes of these institutions, which presumably lodge rights in individuals rather than groups (i.e., whites), matured historically with the development of capitalism; even as it freed individuals from the bonds of feudal monarchies, the codification of democracy also functioned to secure the property rights of the upper classes and regulate working-class resistance. In that sense, class-based forms of social control have finally displaced the personalistic, race-based mechanisms that once prevailed in the South.[45]

There is more to the story, however. The global South is becoming not just modern but postmodern. The structure of key institutions that once encouraged secure and continuous, if oppressive, social relationships is changing. Transformations in the nature and terms of employment are fundamental in this regard. Young working-class white women, entering the labor force for the first time, are less likely to stay in the company town where they were born or to work in the textile mills where their mother was employed. They commute to the blank offices of suburban industrial parks, the retail stores of shopping malls, or the fast food franchises of urban strips. Many have no single employer or continuous relationship to a particular workplace; they patch together multiple jobs to make a living or work through an agency as a temporary. For working-class African Americans, now pitted against other people of color at the bottom of the labor market, the economic change is even more momentous; the political economy of the South, which once depended so heavily on their racialized exploitation, no longer requires their labor at all. Unemployment, rather than racially segregated employment, is more and more their lot.[46] Even for highly educated professional and technical workers, the terms of employment have changed: increasingly, subcontracting, consultancies and part-time arrangements characterize their work. Common to all of these situations is the ephemeral status of both employee and employer; the class interaction between boss and worker is becoming more indirect, disembodied, and, in some cases (e.g., chronic unemployment), nonexistent.

Parallel changes are occurring in the most intimate aspects of social life—sexual and familial relationships. With relatively high divorce rates and a host of new family arrangements, the meaning of "father" and "mother" becomes more unstable, the relationship between parent and child less continuous and certain. Divorce, remarriage, nonmarital sexuality, same-gender couples, multiple partners, commuter marriages, and a host of other possibilities diversify the meaning of sexual relationships, in some cases rendering them more discontinuous. Among adult women in the South, as all over the United States, more spend longer periods of time without any sexual partner, male or female, at all.

It is no wonder, in this context of interpersonal discontinuity and global dislocation, that so many scholars emphasize difference, fragmentation, and separation as hallmarks of our time. The pervasive mood of powerlessness also becomes more understandable—not because apathy has increased but because the locus of power is more obscure, the levers of influence less clear or effective. It is also not surprising that social activists, as exemplified in the final chapters of this book, are constructing new types of organizations, intentionally pursuing new forms of community; it is no longer possible to rely on stable relationships, forged over time in common workplaces and/or neighborhoods, as the basis of political solidarity.

However, the social fragmentation that characterizes our time and place does not mean that we have, in a structural sense, become delinked from one another. Differentiation does not mean autonomy or separation. Diversification does not mean freedom. Rather, the multiplication of racial, sexual, and class differences among Southern women means that our structural and interpersonal relationships with one another—relationships wherein "difference" is created—have grown even more complex. The remaining chapters of this book examine these relationships among Southern women. They suggest that the central political and ethical question for Southern feminists today is not how to "be in relationship" with those who are different from ourselves. The central question is what to do about the relationships we are already in.

Notes

The epigraph is from Elsa Barkley Brown, "'What Has Happened Here': The Politics of Difference in Women's History and Feminist Politics," *Feminist Studies* 18(2) (Summer 1992): 295–312.

1. There is an extensive, ongoing debate between poststructuralist and materialist feminists (a dichotomy that simplifies the numerous positions and nuances at stake). See, for example, Judith Butler and Joan W. Scott, eds., *Feminists Theorize the Political* (New York: Routledge, 1992); Marianne Hirsch and Evelyn Fox Keller, eds., *Conflicts in Feminism* (New York: Routledge, 1990); Linda Nicholson, ed., *Feminism/Postmodernism* (New York: Routledge, 1990); Linda Alcoff and Elizabeth Potter, eds., *Feminist Epistemologies* (New York: Routledge, 1993); Rosemary Hennessy, *Materialist Feminism and the Politics of Discourse* (New York: Routledge, 1993); Teresa L. Ebert, *Ludic Feminism and After: Postmodernism, Desire, and Labor in Late Capitalism* (Ann Arbor: University of Michigan Press, 1996).

2. Maxine Baca Zinn and Bonnie Thornton Dill, "Theorizing Difference from Multiracial Feminism," *Feminist Studies* 22(2) (1996): 321–31.

3. Toni Morrison, *Playing in the Dark: Whiteness and the Literary Imagination* (New York: Vintage Books, 1993), p. 59.

4. On the absence of a middle class in much of the South, see James C. Cobb, *The Selling of the South: The Southern Crusade for Industrial Development, 1936–1980* (Baton Rouge: Louisiana State University Press, 1982); and Cobb, *Industrialization and Southern Society, 1877–1984* (Lexington: University Press of Kentucky, 1984). On the class structure of various subregions, the literature is vast. On the Appalachian region, see Wilma Dunaway, *The First American Frontier: Transition to Capitalism in Southern Appalachia, 1790–1860* (Chapel Hill: University of North Carolina Press, 1996); and Mary Beth Pudup, Dwight Billings, and Altina Waller, eds., *Appalachia in the Making: The Mountain South in the Nineteenth Century* (Chapel Hill: University of North Carolina Press, 1995). On the piedmont, see Dwight B. Billings, Jr., *Planters and the Making of a "New South": Class, Politics, and Development in North Carolina, 1865–1900* (Chapel Hill: University of North Carolina Press, 1979); and Jacquelyn Dowd Hall et al., *Like a Family: The Making of a Southern Cotton Mill World* (Chapel Hill: University of North Carolina Press, 1987). On the Delta, see Neil McMillen, *Dark Journey: Black Mississippians in the Age of Jim Crow* (Urbana: University of Illinois Press, 1989); and James C. Cobb, *The Most Southern Place on Earth: The Mississippi Delta and the Roots of Regional Identity* (New York:

Oxford University Press, 1992). For an overview, see Rupert Vance, *Human Geography of the South* (Chapel Hill: University of North Carolina Press, 1932).

5. See Jacquelyn Dowd Hall, "'The Mind That Burns in Each Body': Women, Rape, and Racial Violence," in Ann Snitow, Christine Stansell, and Sharon Thompson, eds., *Powers of Desire: The Politics of Sexuality* (New York: Monthly Review Press, 1983), pp. 328–49; Hall, *Revolt Against Chivalry: Jessie Daniel Ames and the Women's Campaign Against Lynching* (New York: Columbia University Press, 1974).

6. Angela Davis, *Women, Race, and Class* (New York: Vintage Books, 1981); Elizabeth Fox Genovese, *Within the Plantation Household: Black and White Women of the Old South* (Chapel Hill: University of North Carolina Press, 1988); Dorothy Sterling, ed., *We Are Your Sisters: Black Women in the Nineteenth Century* (New York: W. W. Norton and Company, 1984); Catherine Clinton, "Caught in the Web of the Big House: Women and Slavery," in Walter J. Fraser, Jr., R. Frank Saunders, Jr., and Jon L. Wakelyn, eds., *The Web of Southern Social Relations: Women, Family, and Education* (Athens: University of Georgia Press, 1985), pp. 19–34; Clinton, "'Southern Dishonor': Flesh, Blood, Race, and Bondage," in Carol Bleser, ed., *In Joy and in Sorrow: Women, Family, and Marriage in the Victorian South* (New York: Oxford University Press, 1991), pp. 52–68.

7. Genovese, *Within the Plantation Household;* Clinton, "Caught in the Web" and *The Web of Southern Social Relations;* Evelyn Brooks Higginbotham, *Righteous Discontent: The Women's Movement in the Black Baptist Church, 1880–1920* (Cambridge, MA: Harvard University Press, 1993), esp. Chapter 7 on "The Politics of Respectability." As Elsa Barkley Brown remarked, "while white elite women's sexual history has included the long effort to break down Victorian assumptions of sexuality and respectability in order to gain control of their sexual selves, Black women's sexual history has required the struggle to be accepted as respectable in order to gain control of their sexual selves." See Brown, "'What Has Happened Here,'" p. 306.

8. See Jacquelyn Dowd Hall, "Disorderly Women: Gender and Labor Militancy in the Appalachian South," *Journal of American History* 73 (1986): 354–82. Sally Ward Maggard pursues the same theme in a different era and strike in "Gender Contested: Women's Participation in the Brookside Coal Strike," in Guida West and Rhoda Blumberg, eds., *Women and Social Protest* (New York: Oxford University Press, 1990), pp. 75–99.

9. Lee Ann Whites, *The Civil War as a Crisis in Gender: Augusta, Georgia, 1860–1890* (Athens: University of Georgia Press, 1995); Glenda Elizabeth Gilmore, *Gender and Jim Crow: Women and the Politics of White Supremacy in North Carolina, 1896–1920* (Chapel Hill: University of North Carolina Press, 1996); Ann Firor Scott, *The Southern Lady: From Pedestal to Politics, 1830–1930* (Chicago: University of Chicago Press, 1970). See the summary overview by Jacquelyn Dowd Hall, "Partial Truths: Writing Southern Women's History," in Virginia Bernhard et al., eds., *Southern Women: History and Identities* (Columbia: University of Missouri Press, 1992), pp. 11–29.

10. The phrase, the "power of blackness," is Herman Melville's; the appropriation of it was inspired by Toni Morrison's *Playing in the Dark;* see pp. 37–39.

11. There is much historical literature and debate on this era. See, for starters, W.E.B. Du Bois, *Black Reconstruction in America, 1860–1880* (New York: World Publishing Company, 1935); Joel Williamson, *The Crucible of Race: Black-White Relations in the American South Since Emancipation* (New York: Oxford University Press, 1984); C. Vann Woodward, *Origins of the New South, 1877–1913* (Baton Rouge: Louisiana State University Press, 1951); Woodward, *The Strange Career of Jim Crow* (New York: Oxford University Press, 1955); Cobb, *Industrialization and Southern Society.*

12. See Whites, *The Civil War as a Crisis in Gender;* Charles Reagan Wilson, *Baptized in Blood: The Religion of the Lost Cause, 1865–1920* (Athens: University of Georgia Press, 1980).

13. See Williamson, *The Crucible of Race;* and Woodward, *The Strange Career of Jim Crow.* The timing and precise codification of segregation and disfranchisement varied among Southern states. If one expands the definition of the South beyond the eleven states of the Confederacy, these variations increase. In West Virginia, for example, the state constitution required segregated schools but black men retained the franchise. See Joe Trotter, Jr., *Coal, Class, and Color: Blacks in Southern West Virginia, 1915–1932* (Urbana: University of Illinois Press, 1990).

14. See the writings of Richard Wright, particularly *Black Boy.*

15. Woodward, *The Strange Career of Jim Crow.*

16. See Kenneth W. Goings and Raymond A. Mohl, eds., *The New African American Urban History* (Thousand Oaks, CA: Sage Publications, 1996); Earl Lewis, *In Their Own Interests: Race, Class, and Power in Twentieth-Century Norfolk, Virginia* (Berkeley: University of California Press, 1991); Robin D. G. Kelley, "'We Are Not What We Seem': Rethinking Black Working-Class Opposition in the Jim Crow South," *Journal of American History* 80 (1993): 75–112; Kelley, *Race Rebels: Culture, Politics, and the Black Working Class* (New York: Free Press, 1994).

17. These few sentences reduce an extensive historical debate into a necessary but regrettable oversimplification. Some scholars, C. Vann Woodward in particular, have argued that Jim Crow arose late in the nineteenth century, the product of elite response to the threat of populism. See Woodward, *The Strange Career of Jim Crow.* For a different perspective see Joel Williamson, *After Slavery: The Negro in South Carolina During Reconstruction, 1861–1877* (Chapel Hill: University of North Carolina Press, 1965); and the summary of the debate by John W. Cell, *The Highest Stage of White Supremacy: The Origins of Segregation in South Africa and the American South* (New York: Cambridge University Press, 1982), esp. Chapters 4–7.

18. This was and to some extent still is true in the Mississippi Delta. See Cobb, *The Most Southern Place on Earth;* McMillen, *Dark Journey;* Hortense Powdermaker, *After Freedom: A Cultural Study in the Deep South* (New York: Atheneum, 1968 [1939]).

19. Billings, *Planters and the Making of a "New South";* Cobb, *Industrialization and Southern Society;* and for the original theoretical statement, Barrington Moore, Jr., *Social Origins of Dictatorship and Democracy: Lord and Peasant in the Making of the Modern World* (Boston: Beacon Press, 1966).

20. This is the thesis associated with Woodward. See *The Strange Career of Jim Crow.* On the populist movement, see Lawrence Goodwyn, *Democratic Promise: The Populist Movement in America* (New York: Oxford University Press, 1976).

21. Marc S. Miller, ed., *Working Lives:* The Southern Exposure *History of Labor in the South* (New York: Pantheon Books, 1980); David Alan Corbin, *Life, Work, and Rebellion in the Coal Fields: The Southern West Virginia Miners, 1880–1932* (Urbana: University of Illinois Press, 1981); Trotter, *Coal, Class, and Color;* Michael K. Honey, *Southern Labor and Black Civil Rights: Organizing Memphis Workers* (Urbana: University of Illinois Press, 1993).

22. On the great textile strike and its aftermath, see the moving video *The Uprising of '34.* See also Melton Alonza McLaurin, *Paternalism and Protest; Southern Cotton Mill Workers and Organized Labor, 1875–1905* (Westport, CT: Greenwood Publishing Corp., 1971); Hall et al., *Like a Family;* Liston Pope, *Millhands and Preachers: A Study of Gastonia* (New Haven: Yale University Press, 1942); Honey, *Southern Labor and Black Civil Rights;* and Miller, ed., *Working Lives,* especially the chapters by Leah Wise and Sue Thrasher, "The Southern Tenant Farmers' Union," pp. 120–42 and Jim Green, "The Brotherhood," pp. 22–39.

23. See, for example, Gilmore's prize-winning *Gender and Jim Crow.* Gilmore has, in my view, been rightly taken to task for her failure to analyze the implications of the class position of the women she investigates. See Hampton D. Carey, "Separate, Unequal, Female, and Active," *Race & Reason* 1997–98, pp. 53–55.

24. See George Rable, *Civil Wars: Women and the Crisis of Southern Nationalism* (Urbana: University of Illinois Press, 1989); Drew Gilpin Faust, *Mothers of Invention: Women of the Slaveholding South in the American Civil War* (Chapel Hill: University of North Carolina Press, 1996); Whites, *The Civil War as a Crisis in Gender;* Catherine Clinton and Nina Silber, eds., *Divided Houses: Gender and the Civil War* (New York: Oxford, 1992); Laura F. Edwards, *Gendered Strife and Confusion: The Political Culture of Reconstruction* (Urbana: University of Illinois Press, 1997); and the book review by Stephanie McCurry, "Steel Magnolias," *Women's Review of Books* 14 (6) (March 1997): 13–14.

25. Alfreda Duster, ed., *Crusade for Justice: The Autobiography of Ida B. Wells* (Chicago: University of Chicago Press, 1970); Miriam DeCosta Willis, ed., *The Memphis Diary of Ida B. Wells* (Boston: Beacon Press, 1995); Hazel Carby, *Reconstructing Womanhood: The Emergence of the Afro-American Woman Novelist* (New York: Oxford University Press, 1987). Hall's comments in "Partial Truths" alerted me to this relationship between the new historiography and this earlier legacy.

26. There is conflict over the extent to which white women became independent of patriarchal authority during this period. For an early, important analysis emphasizing women's new independence, see Scott, *The Southern Lady.* For alternative views, note the tensions underlying the varied positions in Bleser, ed., *In Joy and in Sorrow.* Racial violence also required black women to seek protection of and from men.

27. Single women, of whatever marital history, often depended on the advice and direction of males when they farmed on their own. See the description of her mother's widowhood and her brother's new authoritative role on their farm in Katherine DuPre Lumpkin, *The Making of a Southerner* (New York: Alfred A. Knopf, 1947); and the accounts in Faust, *Mothers of Invention.*

28. See the fascinating discussion in Lee Ann Whites, "The De Graffenried

Controversy: Class, Race, and Gender in the New South," *Journal of Southern History* 54 (3) (1988): 449–78.

29. See the collection by Bernhard et al., eds., *Southern Women,* especially the chapters by Mary Martha Thomas, "The Ideology of The Alabama Woman Suffrage Movement, 1890–1920," pp. 109–128; and Elizabeth Hayes Turner "'White-gloved Ladies' and 'New Women' in the Texas Woman Suffrage Movement," pp. 129–156; Marjorie Spruill Wheeler, ed., *Votes for Women! The Woman Suffrage Movement in Tennessee, the South, and the Nation* (Knoxville: University of Tennessee Press, 1995); Mary Martha Thomas, *The New Woman in Alabama: Social Reforms and Suffrage, 1890–1920* (Tuscaloosa: The University of Alabama Press, 1992); Whites, "The De Graffenried Controversy;" McCurry, "Steel Magnolias." The analysis here emphasizes elite white women only because research on poor white women's cultural politics is rare. See Edwards, *Gendered Strife and Confusion;* Stephanie McCurry, *Masters of Small Worlds: Yeoman Households, Gender Relations, and the Political Culture of the Antebellum South Carolina Low Country* (New York: Oxford University Press, 1995); Victoria Bynum, *Unruly Women: The Politics of Social and Sexual Control in the Old South* (Chapel Hill: University of North Carolina Press, 1992).

30. Jacqueline Jones, *Labor of Love, Labor of Sorrow: Black Women, Work, and the Family from Slavery to the Present* (New York: Basic Books, 1985).

31. See ibid.; Susan Tucker, *Telling Memories Among Southern Women: Domestic Workers and Their Employers in the Segregated South* (Baton Rouge: Louisiana State University Press, 1988).

32. Higginbotham, *Righteous Discontent;* Kathleen C. Berkley, "'Colored Ladies Also Contributed': Black Women's Activities from Benevolence to Social Welfare, 1866–1896," in Fraser, Saunders, and Wakelyn, eds., *The Web of Southern Social Relations,* pp. 181–203; Stephanie Shaw, *What a Woman Ought to Be and Do: Black Professional Women Workers During the Jim Crow Era* (Chicago: University of Chicago Press, 1996); Gilmore, *Gender and Jim Crow.*

33. See the careful treatment of this theme in Higginbotham's *Righteous Discontent* and Shaw's *What a Woman Ought to Be and Do.*

34. See Gilmore, *Gender and Jim Crow,* for a discussion of the gendered implications of the racial politics of this era.

35. The Southern record on the treatment of homosexual liaisons is blurry and contradictory. See, for example, the essays in John Howard, ed., *Carryin' on in the Lesbian and Gay South* (New York: New York University Press, 1997), especially the chapters by Martin Duberman "'Writing Bedfellows' in Antebellum South Carolina: Historical Interpretation and the Politics of Evidence," pp. 15–33; and William Armstrong Percy III, "William Alexander Percy (1885–1942): His Homosexuality and Why It Matters," pp. 75–92. Some authors argue that homosexuality on the part of white males, including interracial relationships, was permissible and even authorized in the South by a racial system that essentially allowed white men sexual access to all other people. Other scholars find a strict taboo against such relationships, perhaps especially among white males whose virility depended on heterosexuality.

36. For the classic sociological treatment, see Arthur F. Raper, *The Tragedy of Lynching* (New York: Dover, 1970 [1933]). For a more recent historical interpretation, see Hall's, *Revolt Against Chivalry* and "'The Mind That Burns in Each Body.'"

37. Darlene Clark Hine, "Rape and the Inner Lives of Southern Black Women: Thoughts on the Culture of Dissemblance," in Bernhard et al., eds., *Southern Women*, pp. 177–190.

38. For a discussion of the relationship between the rape of black women and the lynching of black men, see Hall, "'The Mind That Burns in Each Body.'"

39. Ibid., p. 335.

40. See Hall, *Revolt Against Chivalry;* Lumpkin, *The Making of a Southerner;* Lillian Smith, *Killers of the Dream* (New York: W. W. Norton and Co., 1961).

41. There is little on the "second-wave" women's movement in the South, indeed little from a gender perspective on the contemporary South at all. An important exception is Sara Evans, *Personal Politics: The Roots of Women's Liberation in the Civil Rights Movement and the New Left* (New York: Vintage Books, 1980). See also Barbara Ellen Smith, "Crossing the Great Divides: Race, Class, and Gender in Southern Women's Organizing, 1979–1991," *Gender & Society* 9(6) (1995): 680–96. On the lesbian and gay South, see Mab Segrest, *My Mama's Dead Squirrel: Lesbian Essays on Southern Culture* (Ithaca, NY: Firebrand, 1985); the literary magazine *Feminary;* James T. Sears, *Lonely Hunters: An Oral History of Lesbian and Gay Southern Life, 1948–1968* (Boulder, CO: Westview Press, 1997); Howard, ed., *Carryin' on.*

42. See John Gaventa, Barbara Ellen Smith, and Alex Willingham, eds., *Communities in Economic Crisis: Appalachia and the South* (Philadelphia: Temple University Press, 1990); John Gaventa and Barbara Ellen Smith, "The Deindustrialization of the Textile South: A Case Study," in Jeffrey Leiter, Michael Schulman, and Rhonda Zingraff, eds., *Hanging by a Thread: Social Change in Southern Textiles* (Ithaca, NY: ILR Press, 1991), pp. 181 96; Paul DeLeon, ed., *Appalachia's Changing Economy: A Reader* (New Market, TN: Highlander Research and Education Center, 1986).

43. See Barbara Ellen Smith, "The Postmodern South: Racial Transformations and the Global Economy," in Carole Hill and Patricia Beaver, eds., *Cultural Diversity in the U.S. South: Anthropological Contributions to a Region in Transition* (Athens: University of Georgia Press, 1998), pp. 164–78. See also "The Boom Belt," *Business Week,* September 27, 1993, for an example of local chamber of commerce efforts to keep higher wage corporations out of the South.

44. Smith, "The Postmodern South."

45. Hall makes this point in "'The Mind That Burns in Each Body.'"

46. Smith, "The Postmodern South."

2

Transgressions in Race and Place

The Ubiquitous Native Grandmother in America's Cultural Memory

Darlene Wilson and Patricia D. Beaver

n the early nineteenth century, Anglo-Americans in Appalachia took extreme measures, both legal and extralegal, to disenfranchise or otherwise disempower people who were classified as "nonwhite." The non-white category included Native Americans, former Africans, and people of mixed ancestry designated "FPCs," or free persons of color. Many residents with multiethnic ancestry in the mountainous sections of Tennessee, Virginia, Kentucky, and the Carolinas either self-identified or were redesignated by census-takers as "Melungeons"; others called them "mountain niggers."[1]

In this chapter, we explore the "hidden transcripts" by which Appalachians have claimed links, primarily through kinship to Native American or mixed-ancestry "grandmothers," to this complex racial past.[2] Regional scholarship generally focuses on the European ancestry of Appalachian people and the historical agency of presumably "white" males. Women's activities and the possibility of progeny from relationships between native women and early male European inmigrants are underexplored.[3] Yet this cross-cultural embrace occurred and clearly advantaged early male settlers with enhanced opportunities to subsist, persist, and even prosper and multiply in the southern upcountry of Appalachia.

By the nineteenth century, however, ancestral links to native grand-mothers undermined the claims to whiteness of those who sought racial privilege; they also implicitly challenged the emerging concept of race as a fixed biological reality. Their existence therefore tended to be hidden from public scrutiny by genealogical lies and evasions as well as by legal and social constrictions. Today, it is possible to find traces of the "native granny" in both oral tradition and documentary sources. Her silenced story contests the myth of Appalachia's lily whiteness and offers an opportunity for both recoloring and engendering Appalachian history.

The history of mixed-ancestry Appalachians, especially women, includes multiple episodes of repression and cultural erasure that persist to this day. In the twentieth century, descendants of these ethnically mixed mountain residents have been marginalized by labels such as "triracial isolates," "mestizos," "mulattoes," "mixed bloods," "racial isolates," "racially mixed people," and "little races."[4] A graduate-school professor of history has interpreted the Melungeons as "Indian-wannabees" who became "irrelevant" to the history of the indigenous people of the southeastern United States when they mixed with other groups and abandoned their traditional Indian cultures.[5] Similarly, according to inhabitants interviewed in the late 1870s, all the "real Indians" disappeared from the mountainous area along the boundary of Virginia and Kentucky "around 1840" (a date that too closely parallels the westward removal of eastern tribes in 1838 to be coincidental), although many so-called halfbreeds remained.[6]

Whatever their labeling, they and their descendants remain an American other, outside the current "ethnoracial pentagon" that defines/assigns race according to five categories: "Euro-American (usually white); Asian American; African American; Hispanic (or sometimes Latino); and Indigenous Peoples (or sometimes Native American)."[7] The apparent fixity of this schematic obscures the historical process by which these categories emerged. During the colonial period, political leaders in the increasingly plantation-oriented South cooperated to create new racial categories, including those of "white" and "black," thus affirming for the next two centuries the fiction of races as real biological entities. A radical departure from the European systems for social differentiation, which were national, ethnic, and class-based, these new categories for labor and social control were encoded into the young nation's law and culture.[8]

By 1800, mixed-ancestry Appalachians had themselves begun to deny their ancestry in order to work around restrictive legal mechanisms; throughout the following century, they engaged in a process of whitening in order to survive, achieve citizenship, attain legal rights and protection, and retain access to property. For some families, an outright denial of mixed, or African, or Native American heritage was impossible; others could more easily obscure their ancestry in order to enjoy the armor of whiteness. Many simply "went West," but this option was less viable for females who often bore the responsibility of caring for elderly and younger relatives. By welcoming the embrace of "new blood," especially in the form of light(er)-skinned, blue-eyed male in-migrants, Appalachian mixed-ancestry women helped to diffuse remnant markings of "otherness"; by acquiring Anglo-sounding surnames, they facilitated their family's or clan's entry into public records as "white," and thereby secured title to ancestral lands.[9]

With the conquest of Western and Plains native groups at the end of the nineteenth century came a groundswell of sentimentalism toward Native Americans.[10] Some ethnically colorful Southerners more readily claimed some degree of native ancestry, commonly Cherokee (widely considered the most "civilized," according to whiter perspectives, of the so-called five civilized southeastern tribes), through vague references to an unnamed but ubiquitous grandmother or great-grandmother. As he had in earlier novels and nonfiction writings, John Fox, Jr., drew from real models in 1914 to capture this sea-change in attitudes when he fictionalized an exemplary Appalachian woman. His character, "Alliphair," is dark, mysterious, and sensuous, and displays an unusually strong will and talented command of manly skills, especially if gunplay and/or political debate are involved. She claims her gender peculiarities to be the result of having had, somewhere back in her lineage, at least one Cherokee grandmother "of whom she is *no longer ashamed*" (emphasis added).[11]

Despite credible physical, documentary, and oral evidence, some scholars still tend to dismiss ethnically "white" Americans' claims to Indian heritage as part of the American post-Removal fantasy. In "The Tribe Called Wannabee," Rayna Green suggests that the quest is a two- or three-century-old "illness" with a "deadly purpose": "Indians are in effect, loved to death through playing Indian, while despised if they want to act out their real traditional roles on the American landscape."[12] Still, unaware of this critique of those who would appropriate Indian identity, year after year students from the South have readily claimed an Indian (many great-s) grandmother about whom little else could be said. More recently, as validation of multiculturalism sparked new inquiry into the diversity of nationalities represented in U.S. frontier and colonial history, some willingly affirmed that older family residents took their genealogical mysteries to their graves: "it" was shameful, they had refused to talk about "it," but "it" somehow involved mixed ancestry. Appalachian descendants, drawn by the possibility of their own ethnic diversity, must dig for evidence long buried by ancestors who feared the prying eyes of neighbors, gossip, discrimination, scorn, and legal reprisals from Jim Crow-ed regimes.

Despite an easing of anti-Indian sentiment, antiblack racism persisted as the twentieth century progressed. Not all mountain "whites" were equally white or even equally "mixed" race; when their ancestry was allegedly African, they were subject to campaigns of racial investigation that approximated witch hunts. In the early 1920s, Walter A. Plecker, Virginia's top official for vital statistics, warned school administrators in Lee County (on the state's western border with Kentucky and Tennessee) to be on alert for descendants of FPCs, especially Melungeons; he believed they had already attempted to pass as white in order to enroll their children in white-only schools. Plecker included a list of representative surnames to be distributed to school registrars, who could then act immediately to purge their rolls of these children of color. The author of Virginia's infamous Racial Integrity Act of 1924 and the architect of elaborate schemes to rid the South of "mongrel races" (schemes that were admired by the Nazis and other proponents of eugenics and racial purity), Plecker determined to mark all Melungeons (and other mixed-ancestry population groups) as not-white; to that end, he secured legislation that sought to control the mobility of mixed-ancestry women, provided for their involuntary sterilization, and demanded that all old and new documents of vital statistics (birth, death, and marriage) be forwarded to Richmond so that a certificate attesting to the "true"color of the registrants could be attached.[13] His reach and influence were widespread, as his reputation and handiwork can be traced both nationally and internationally: Plecker-related documents regarding Melungeons and other mixed-ancestry groups with ties to Virginia have been located in England, Germany, Denmark, and the states of Missouri, Minnesota, Texas, Louisiana, Oregon, California, and Washington. Closer to home, in August of 1942, he pursued his purge across the state line, writing to the Tennessee secretary of state: "We have in some of the counties of southwestern Virginia a number of so-called Melungeons who came into that section from Newman Ridge, Hancock County, Tennessee, and who are classified by us as of negro origin though they make various claims, such as Portuguese, Indians, etc. The law of Virginia says that any one with any ascertainable degree of negro blood is to be classified as colored and we are endeavoring to so classify those who apply for birth, death, and marriage registrations."

In response to Plecker's inquiry, Mrs. John Trotwood Moore, Tennessee state librarian and archivist, quoted from the account of Captain L. M. Jarvis, "an old citizen of Sneedville," who wrote in his eighty-second year that Melungeon origins were to be found in the Cherokee and white mixtures that occurred following settlement of that region in 1790: "They (Melungeon people) were reliable, truthful, and faithful to anything they promised. In the Civil War most of the Melungeons went into the Union army and made good soldiers. Their Indian blood has about run out. They are growing white."

Plecker responded to Mrs. Moore by insisting that, on the contrary, Melungeons originated in the "descendants of slaves freed by their master before the War between the States," all of whom "have the same desire . . . to become friends of Indians and to be classed as Indians." As for their claim to Portuguese ancestry, Plecker asserted that such origins would still link them to Africans, since "at one time there were many African slaves in Portugal. . . . Today there are no true Negroes there but their blood shows in the color and racial characteristics of a large part of the Portuguese population of the present day. That mixture, even if it could be shown, would be far from constituting these people white."

Plecker continued by asserting that Melungeon origins "reaching back in some cases to or near to the Revolutionary War, show them to be descendants of freed Negroes" and thus fix their race as "colored." All legal weight had to be mustered against these people, "who are now causing trouble in Virginia by their claims of Indian descent, with the privilege of inter-marrying into the white race, permissible when a person can show his racial composition to be one-sixteenth or less Indian, the remainder white with no negro intermixture." According to Plecker, "none of our Virginia people now claiming to be Indian are free from negro admixture, and they are, therefore, according to our law classified as colored. In that class, we include the Melungeons of Tennessee." He apparently convinced Moore, who, in subsequent correspondence, gratefully accepted Plecker's clarification of her own state's history and congratulated him and his staff for their honorable endeavors.[14]

An inversely skewed caste system operated in many Southern black communities, both pre- and postemancipation, where opportunities for social, political, and economic advancement opened more readily to those who appeared to have mixed ancestry—the lighter the skin tone, the more avenues into social prominence and economic prosperity. Blacks with discernible Indian or white ancestry could situate themselves as an other(ed)-group, separated by their allegedly superior genetic infusion from the mass of lower-class, darker-skinned blacks. However, as others have shown, their caste position also reflected their nonaffiliated state, which was already contested: they were less-or-more-than-real Indians, more-or-less-than-real blacks, but never really white enough.[15] So it has been for the Melungeons, disparaged by the white majority for having a dark(er) genetic heritage, by the black community for trying so hard to "pass" for white, and by Native Americans for escaping Removal and abandoning their indigenous ethnicity. Melungeon women were doubly cursed for they bore, both literally and figuratively, the markers of miscegenation.

Indian Grandmothers and Male Offshore Others

A word portrait of the Melungeon or mountain "native granny" may be gleaned from legends surrounding the Melungeons and documents attesting to their existence. We define "Melungeon" as a label given to the first true American cultural fusion and diffusion, the result of native women's embrace of different "male offshore others," be they Ottomans, Englishmen, Portuguese, Spanish, fleeing African laborers, shipwrecked gold-seekers, or willing castaways. Pocahontas's rescue of John Smith is the popularized, romanticized, now Disneyfied version of the relationship. However, historians and anthropologists have indeed confirmed that, in many native groups in the Southeast, women had primary responsibility for community-keeping, food production, and resource allocation; thus, they enjoyed considerable autonomy throughout the colonial period in deciding whether these male offshore others would be allowed to live, remain as "visitors," or become a permanent part of their community.[16] By aligning themselves in formal and informal relationships with these men, the native women became critical partners, hardly passive, in mediating the rapid changes that followed "Contact."

The wealth of resources available to those who could negotiate in the Appalachian backcountry sparked intense competition among European powers eager to gain a foothold in the American Southeast. While the Spanish brought new forms of warfare and disease to the native populations, they also established mines, colonial outposts, and forts in the region. French and English officials and frontiersmen struggled for control, but their success often depended on the cooperation and guidance of native peoples. Along with trade connections, these first-contact Europeans left behind mixed-ancestry offspring who were conceived through sexual relations, in some cases in the context of formal marriages, with native women.

As scholars and native lore have demonstrated, for the first century or so after Contact, Native Americans did not differentiate between "pale-skinned" and darker-skinned newcomers; in effect, they had to learn about Eurocentric racism over the next century through firsthand experiences. Plantations and other new commercial endeavors in the Southeast initially depended upon Indian enslavement, an unsatisfactory arrangement that was replaced by the use of imported Africans, predominantly younger males. They were put to work and live alongside native women slaves; together, they produced new laboring-class offspring who, unlike their European counterparts who received their status patrilineally, would be forever enslaved by virtue of their mothers' status. In addition, ethnic mixtures occurred in and around the Appalachians when male Europeans—traders, squatters, adventurers, soldiers serving various European crowns—as well as escaping African slaves encountered Native American women and contributed to the gene pool of the upcountry South.

Beginning in the mid-seventeenth century, English-speaking travelers in the southern Appalachian region encountered communities of ethnically mixed peoples who defied easy categorization.[17] When later waves of European migrant families flowed into the area and came to dominate the cultural landscape, their very survival in outlying places sometimes depended upon the hospitality of these more-native-than-not women and their mixed-ancestry offspring who retained local, on-the-ground power via kinship and clan-oriented networks. Throughout the colonial period, social and genetic intermingling was not uncommon. Indeed, various imperial authorities sought to encourage European-Indian intermarriage. In the seventeenth century, the French in Canada endorsed intermarriage with Indians for speedier religious conversion. Likewise, the British in Nova Scotia and in Virginia sought to create social ties and mutual obligations of self-interest with Indians by offering any white person who married an Indian a bounty of fifty acres and ten pounds sterling, or fifty acres and a cow. Such colonial policies continued to be favored after the Revolution. In 1784, Patrick Henry introduced a bill in the Virginia House of Delegates to offer tax relief, free education, and ten pound bonuses to whites and Indians who intermarried. In 1816, U.S. Secretary of War William Crawford, concerned about conflict with Indians in the South and West, recommended that marriage with Indians be encouraged if all other efforts to establish harmony failed.[18]

Such efforts notwithstanding, at the same time Southern politicians sought to control the captive African labor force and to rid themselves of such Indian nuisances as the "wasting" of their communal lands, especially those lands that contained valuable mineral resources. They also aimed to assist their Northern counterparts in subduing threats of working-class rebellion.[19] Legislation encoded the cultural construction of new race categories: the amalgamation categories "white," "black" or "Negro," and "mulatto" served to privilege whites, to disenfranchise and enslave blacks and the offspring of slave women of mixed ancestry, and to marginalize and otherwise control mulattoes and free persons of color. The severe social, economic, and legal consequences of such racial categorization tended to blur the distinction between class, or economic position, and race. Working-class whites sought to classify themselves as "free labor" in order to disaffiliate from other workers who, because of race, labored under more restricted terms. This "enracing" of class functioned to divide and control the laborers of both North and South, whatever their circumstances.

The clarity of the new racial categories was of course more apparent than real. They failed to encompass the complexity of ethnic interaction and mixing, of which the emergence of Melungeons is but one example. The first written record of the term "Melungeon," by John Sevier (first governor of Tennessee and one of the state's principal organizers), was made circa 1782–84 but actually recounts a decade or more of contact with "a Colony of dark-skinned, reddish-brown complexioned people, supposedly of Moorish descent, who called themselves Malungeons [sic], and claimed to be Portuguese. They live to themselves exclusively . . . in the high ridges . . . and are looked upon neither as negroes or Indians. . . . [They have] fine European features, straight black hair and dark blue eyes."[20]

For this community to self-identify as Melungeon and claim a Portuguese affiliation during the eighteenth century, one could argue, might simply translate as, "Don't kill me! I'm not Spanish or English or French." However, this interpretation denies credibility to their self-identification and may underestimate their wisdom in negotiating with hostile incoming whites. The group's assertion of their Melungeon identity during the colonial period may also be interpreted as their refusal to cooperate with emergent racial/national classification schemes. Melungeon identity perhaps proved useful at times in allowing individuals to claim selective genealogical connections to safe ethnicities, that is, to whomever was not at war with their neighbors or other protagonists.

By the Revolutionary period, the term "Melungeon" had become common, especially in new Appalachian communities where early records reveal efforts to establish local institutions such as churches. After 1783, victorious white men in valleys adjacent to the Appalachian chain in Virginia demanded that everyone who looked like (or self-identified as) an Indian had to wear some type of badge or carry a pass when traveling from one place to another. Melungeons and other mixed-ancestry people resisted these sanctions and sought to participate fully in community life. Thus, as early as 1801, the minutes of the Stoney Creek Primitive Baptist Church (near Fort Blackmore in Washington County, Virginia, now Scott County) included regular references to the Melungeons as a distinct population group. Genealogist Jack Harold Goins of Rogersville, Tennessee, researched these records and in November 1993 offered this interesting assessment:

The minutes reveal that the congregation was composed of whites, Melungeons, free Negroes and slaves. From 1801 to 1805 88 new members were added: 33 of these were persons bearing familiar Melungeon names: Gibson, Collins, Moore, Bolin, Bolling, Sexton, Osborne, Maner and Minor.

The congregation made an effort to overcome the prejudice against dark-skinned people prevalent in that period, but reading between the lines, it was apparent that the whites were greatly relieved when the Melungeons began an exodus to [Claiborne County,] Tennessee. According to the minutes, by 1807, most of the Melungeons were gone: eight had received letters of dismission, and five others had been excommunicated for various unrepented sins.

The Melungeons occasionally came back to visit and stayed in the homes of the church members. The problem that had been solved by the removal of the Melungeons then rose again. The minutes of September 26, 1813 reveal: "Church sat in love. Bro. Killgore, Moderator. Then came forward Sis. Kitchen and Complained to the Church against Sis. Susanna 'Sookie' Stallard for saying she harbored them Melungins."[21]

For several decades, a half-century perhaps, being Melungeon or of mixed-ancestry had been considered more desirable in certain contexts than being Indian, black, Virginian, or even white—until the onset of more institutionalized repression and racism. Being Melungeon did not become downright dangerous until the 1830s, after the Nat Turner revolt led to a backlash against all free persons of color and freed slaves. Legislatures in Virginia, North Carolina, and Tennessee quickly disenfranchised landholders and many mountain inhabitants who were renamed "FPC" against their will. Virginia's legislature ordered all FPCs to leave the state or obtain written permission from their resident county's political leaders to remain. The records of county courts in western Virginia prior to the Civil War contain the texts of petitions filed by white(r) men on behalf of mulatto women, who were often referred to as possessing "good moral character" and being "willing and eager" to obey the new regime. For others and their offspring, being in close proximity to borderlands such as Kentucky, which lay adjacent to increasingly hostile states, took on new significance.

Evidence suggests that during this period, contrary to some of the later legends and recent analyses, Melungeons did not go into hiding but continued to participate in larger regional economies and even promoted their communities for tourism. In the earliest published description of Melungeons known to the authors, the March 1849 issue of *Littell's Living Age* (No. 254-31) reprinted an account that had first appeared in a Knoxville newspaper. Although tinted by the cultural lens of its unknown writer, the variety of topics touched upon mandate extensive quotation:

We give to-day another amusing and characteristic sketch from a letter of our intelligent and sprightly correspondent, sojourning at present in one of the seldom-visited nooks hid away in our mountains. . . . Now this gorge and the tops and sides of the adjoining mountains are inhabited by a singular species of the human animal called MELUNGENS [*sic*].

The legend of their history, which they carefully preserve, is this. A great many years ago, these mountains were settled by a society of Portuguese Adventurers, men and women—who came from the long-shore parts of Virginia, that they might be freed from the restraints and drawbacks imposed on them by any form of government. These people made themselves friendly with the Indians and, freed as they were from every kind of social government, they uprooted all conventional forms of society and lived in a delightful Utopia of their own creation, trampling on the marriage relation, despising all forms of religion, and subsisting upon corn (the only possible product of the soil) and wild game of the woods. These intermixed with the Indians, and subsequently their descendants (after the advances of the whites into this part of the state) with the negros and the whites, thus forming the present race of Melungens. They are tall, straight, well-formed people, of a dark copper color, with Circassian features, but wooly heads and other similar appendages of our negro. They are privileged voters in the state in which they live and thus you will perceive, are accredited citizens of the commonwealth. They are brave, but quarrelsome; and are hospitable and generous to strangers. They have no preachers among them and are almost without any knowledge of a Supreme Being. They are married by the established forms but husband and wife separate at pleasure, without meeting any reproach or disgrace from their friends. They are remarkably unchaste, and want of chastity on the part of females is no bar to their marrying. They have but little association with their neighbors, carefully preserving their race, or class, or whatever you may call it: and are in every respect, save they are under the state government, a separate and distinct people. Now this is no traveller's story. They are really what I tell you, without abating or setting down aught in malice. They are behind their neighbors in the arts. They use oxen instead of horses in their agricultural attempts, and their implements of husbandry are chiefly made by themselves of wood. They are, without exception, poor and ignorant, but apparently happy.

Having thus given you a correct geographical and scientific history of the people, I will proceed with my own adventures.

. . . .We stopped at "Old Vardy's:" the hostelrie of the vicinage . . . in time for supper, and thus despatched, we went to the spring, where were assembled several rude log huts and a small sprinkling of the natives, together with a fiddle and other preparations for a dance. Shoes, stockings, and coats were unknown luxuries among them—at least we saw them not.

The dance was engaged in with right hearty good will, and would have put to the blush the tame steppings of our beaux. Among the participants was a very tall, raw-boned damsel with her two garments fluttering readily in the amorous night breeze, whose black eyes were lit up with an unusual fire, either from nature or the repeated visits to the nearest hut, behind the door of which was placed an open-mouthed stone jar of new-made corn whiskey, and in which was a gourd, with a "deuce a bit" of sugar at all, and no water nearer than the spring. Nearest here on the right was a lank lantern-jawed, high cheekbone, long-legged fellow who seemed similarly elevated. Now these two, Jord Bilson (that was he) and Syl Varmin (that was she), were destined to afford the amusement of the evening: for Jord, in cutting the pigeon-wing, chanced to light from one of his aerial flights right upon the ponderous pedal appendage of Syl, a compliment which this amiable lady seemed in no way to accept kindly.

"Jord Bilson," said the tender Syl, "I'll thank you to keep your darned hoofs off my feet."

"Oh, Jord's feet are so tarnel big he can't manage 'em all by hisself." Suggested some pasificator near by.

"He'll have to keep 'em off me," suggested Syl, "or I'll shorten 'em for him."

"Now look ye here, Syl Varmin," answered Jord, somewhat nettled at both remarks, "I didn't go to tread on your feet but I don't want you to be cutting up my rustles about. You're nothing but a cross-grained critter, any-how."

"And you're a darned Melungen."

"Well, if I am, I ain't nigger-Melungen, anyhow—I'm Indian-Melungen, and that's more 'an you is."

"See here, Jord," said Syl now highly nettled, "I'll give you a dollar ef you'll go out on the grass and fight it out."

Jord smiled faintly and demurred, adding—"Go home Syl, and look un-der your puncheons and see if you can't fill a bed outen the hair of them hogs you stole from Vardy."

"And you go to Sow's cave, Jord Bilson, ef it comes to that, and see how many shucks you got offen that corn you took from Pete Joemen. Will you take the dollar?"

Jord now seemed about to consent, and Syl reduced the premium by one half and finally came down to a quarter, and then Jord began to offer a quarter, a half and finally a dollar: but Syl's prudence equalled his, and seeing that neither was likely to accept, we returned to our hotel, and were informed by old Vardy that the sight we had witnessed was no "onusual one. The boys and gals was jist having a little fun."

This account, although lavishly embellished in accordance with the dominant style and perceptions of the time, extends our interpretation of Melungeon identity as a form of racial resistance. It suggests that Melungeons transgressed not only the boundaries of race but also those of patriarchy—a possibility that we explore further in the last section of this chapter. It also suggests, in Syl's debate with Jord, Melungeon cognizance of racial stigma and differentiation. Although willing to dance and drink with Syl, when push came to shove, so to speak, Jord was quick to label Syl as a "nigger-Melungen" and thus inferior to his own status as an "Indian-Melungen."

Whereas Syl and Jord used the vernacular of their place, more academic terms prevailed in elite circles. The new racial categories received the blessing and support of science, as nineteenth-century craniometry lent "quantifiable evidence" for a racial hierarchy in which whites ranked superior to Indians who, in turn, ranked higher than blacks.[22] Melungeons and other mixed-ancestry people caught between or encompassing the categories strove in some cases to become "whiter" or, at the least, sought recognition as an acceptable white-Indian admixture. The remote "hollers" of Appalachia—such as Blackwater Springs and Newman's Ridge along the border of Virginia and Tennessee, the area described in the 1849 account quoted above—provided sanctuary for those who needed more time to get "white enough" and/or to acquire the social status or "markers" of patriarchal respectability. In this way, traditional native or mixed-ancestry women's sexual and social freedom was trapped between two emerging paradigms: just as racial categorization depended upon racial integrity, so Anglo-American patriarchy relied upon strict control of women's sexuality.

Even as Appalachia whitened and assumed the Anglo-American mantle of patriarchy, women of color defined, modified, and contextualized the other, less scrutinized aspects of regional rural life. Accounts of the 1870s are echoed by contemporary informants recalling their own childhoods of circa 1930, when mountain women "learned to stay put and keep their skin covered" to avoid the tanning rays of the sun.[23] In 1882, John Fox, Jr., declared that almost every cabin he encountered in his summer travels around Cumberland Gap (where the states of Tennessee, Virginia, and Kentucky converge) harbored a similar shadowy presence: the ubiquitous, cronelike "granny" who tried to keep her face averted, even hidden, by a deep-brimmed bonnet, but who, if confronted squarely, proved to have "skin like deeply-tanned leather" or "mature tobacco" as well as black eyes. Their granddaughters, Fox thought, tended to assume a skills-based equality with men, were quick-tongued and even "sassy," and, he warned his brothers, were clearly a "dark and prolific race."[24]

Race, Class, Gender, and Miscegenation

The sources of Melungeon ethnicity and the geographical origins—whether French, English, Spanish, Portuguese, Ottoman, Moor, or African—of the male offshore others who contributed to the eastern U.S. and, specifically, to the Appalachian gene pool, continue to be debated.

N. Brent Kennedy's ongoing search for the roots of Melungeon ethnicity has led him to Spain, Portugal (for evidence of Iberian settlers), and more recently Turkey, where he has compiled an abundance of controversial linguistic evidence for the presence of Ottoman (Turkish and other Muslim) sailors on the east coast of the United States in the late sixteenth century.[25]

Kennedy is struggling against the backdrop of a century of race-drenched speculation on the origins of Melungeon ethnicity, beginning with the 1891 writings of Will Allen Dromgoole, who penned several published accounts of their ongoing disenfranchisement. She vividly reveals the extent to which Melungeon miscegenation came to be seen as a despicable evil and gendered crime against nature. Regarding Melungeon origins, Dromgoole relates that "the Malungeons believe themselves to be of Cherokee and Portuguese extraction . . . a remnant of those tribes, or that tribe, still inhabiting the mountains of North Carolina, which refused to follow the tribes to the Reservation set aside for them."[26] Dromgoole herself is writing within a climate of repression and revulsion against voluntary race mixing between black and white. While much of the white-black miscegenation within plantation society was perpetuated by white male coercion of enslaved women, with mixed-race offspring often incorporated into the patriarchal household, voluntary race-mixing in the mountains was considered anomalous. Relying on the prevailing racial theory of the era, which likened the fourth-generation mulatto woman to a mule, Dromgoole carefully explains that Melungeons had to have substantial Indian admixture, since a "race of mulattoes cannot exist as these Malungeons [sic] have existed. . . . The [Negro] race goes from mulattoes to quadroons, from quadroons to octoroons, and there it stops." She further argues that since "octoroon women bear no children," and, by implication, Indians can bear children after three generations of racial mixing, Melungeons must be part Indian because "in every cabin of the Malungeons may be found mothers and grandmothers, and very often great-grandmothers."[27]

While documenting the mistreatment that Melungeons had experienced, Dromgoole also presents a scathing criticism of their appearance, social behaviors, and economic status that unintentionally reveals the arbitrariness of racial identity circa 1890. Visiting the very same neighborhood featured in the 1849 account quoted above, she names both crime and criminal, that is, light and dark women participating in miscegenation: "At this church I saw white women with negro babies at their breasts—Malungeon women with white or with black husbands and some, indeed, having the three separate races represented in their children, showing thereby the gross immorality that is practiced among them. I saw an old negro whose wife was a white woman, and who had been several times arrested, and released on his plea of 'portygee' blood, which he declared had colored his skin, and not African."[28]

Later cultural commentators such as Brewton Berry dismissed the Melungeons' claims of descent from outcast populations along with similar claims of other mixed-ancestry communities in the United States, including "the Arabs in New York State, the Moors in Delaware, the Cubans in North Carolina, the Turks and the Greeks in South Carolina."[29] Berry railed against the repetition of "monotonous themes of shipwrecked sailors," which he considered "no more than unimaginative attempts . . . to account for the swarthy skins of their neighbors who insisted they were not Negroes, but who were obviously not pure white."[30] During the same period, in researching *Roots,* Alex Haley could more easily have traced his Irish father's ancestry, but the blackness of his skin was understood to rule his white heritage "inconsequential."[31]

The official historical record is complicated by such prejudicial accounts as well as by courthouse burnings and other forms of trail-blurring; however, the *vernacular history*—the community-sanctioned version chosen for transmission round the hearth and circle of family—remains rich with underexplored evidence regarding the relationship between Melungeon racial classification and class power. A few examples suggest how closely political patterns of Melungeon disenfranchisement paralleled ground struggles over choice tracts of land. The folktale "Old Horny's Own," published in 1940 from recordings by staff members of the Tennessee Writers' Project, clearly illustrates the convergence of our themes of inquiry: here, although the Indian woman is a fixed component of Melungeon ethnicity, the decisive factor in her offsprings' racial classification is not ancestry but economic rivalry over land and other resources. This story first offers the outsiders' explanation of Melungeon origins: "The old grannies say one time Old Horny got mad at his old shrewwife and left hell and wandered all over the earth till he reached Tennessee [where] Old Horny found him an Injun gal and started in housekeeping." The tale continues with a more practical and local explanation of Melungeon origins, compatible with contemporary lines of inquiry, which situates Melungeon ethnicity in the union of mutinous Portuguese "sailormen" and Indian women. Yet the subtle addition of a third ethnicity, African, provides the spark that ignites the conflagration of economically based, race-driven repression as well as the legal mechanism to disenfranchise Melungeons and steal their land:

> So the white settlers commenced acoming in and noticed what good creek-bottom farms the Melungeons had. Them great grandpappies of ours just wanted them farms till they hurt. They was a breed that got what they

wanted. If the Melungeons had been plain Injuns, it wouldn't been no
trouble to kick them out. But here they was, a'speaking English, and on
top of that, they was Christians. Some of them had fought in the war
against the English. Well, the white settlers didn't want to do nothing that
wasn't right with the Lord and the Law. So they scrabbled around and
studied it from all sides and directions. They knowed the Melungeons, like
the Cherokees had let runaway slaves hide out amongst them. This with
their dark skin was enough to make our grandpappies see pretty plain that
the Melungeons was a niggerfied people. The more they looked at them
good Melungeon bottom lands, the plainer they saw that nigger blood. So
they passed a law. They fixed it so that nobody with nigger blood could
vote, hold office, or bear witness in court. Then they got busy and sued for
the bottom lands. Pretty soon the Melungeons lost all their holdings in law
suits. They couldn't testify for themselves on account of the new law, and
white settlers had the backing of that law and, if they needed it, the militia.
There just wasn't nothing left for the Melungeons to do but move into the
high ridges.[32]

The depopulation alluded to in this story occurred in 1830–50; a similar effort to rid the mountains of Melungeon communities occurred after the Civil War, when coal and timber interests saw that the steeper
lands contained the richer resources. One buyer of coal options was encouraged by his superiors to offer the Melungeon mountaineer a pen to
sign away his mineral rights after commenting on his swarthy appearance; the buyer reported having amazing results when he remarked idly,
"Funny, you (or your granny) don't look all white," or "You must have a
lot of Indian blood or something in you."[33] Read against this process of
industrialization and the Jim Crow backdrop of racial tensions in 1891,
Dromgoole's harshly worded conclusions reflect public opinion of the
day: Melungeons were like the Indians in "their fleetness of foot, cupid-
ity, cruelty . . . their love for the forest, their custom of living without
doors . . . and their taste for liquor and tobacco." Since racial mixtures
were "pathetic," resulting in "unclean" people, the sooner they disappeared, the better for all: "They are going, the little space of hills 'twixt
earth and heaven allotted them, will soon be free of the dusky tribe. . . .
The most that can be said of one of them is, 'He is a Malungeon,' a syn-
onym for all that is doubtful and mysterious—and unclean."[34]

Yet the Melungeons didn't disappear over the next century, and each
decade brings new scholars to ponder Melungeon ethnicity and its relevance to class relations. In 1951 Edward T. Price estimated there were between 5,000 and 10,000 Melungeons dispersed widely throughout the
mountains of North Carolina, Tennessee, Virginia, and elsewhere; in
each community where they appear, the Melungeons "form a recognized
class of peasants or laborers, a group dipped or believed to be dipped in

alien tint, and a closely in married clan."[35] Arguing that the Melungeons originated prior to 1800 in North Carolina and Virginia, Price discounts the theory that they were a mixture of "significant portions of the blood of dark-skinned peoples other than the readily available Negroes and Indians." He claims instead that the "Indian fraction is more important" than any rumored dark offshore male contribution and that "the Melungeons themselves may have started [the Portuguese rumor] to counter the hints of Negro blood."[36] Comparing the Melungeons with other "mixed bloods," specifically the Croatan Indians of Robeson County, North Carolina (later to be labeled "Lumbee"), Price concludes that the "Melungeons' ancestors should be regarded as emigrants from a general society of mixedbloods in Virginia and the Carolinas consisting of certain loci of concentration and a floating population that connected them." For him, the numerous mixed communities represent "a curious colored phase of the transplantation of Appalachian culture into the Middle West."[37]

Commentators from outside the region, and elites within the region who would offer testimony, have joined to condemn the miscegenation that, from their perspectives, accounted for the racial confusion the Melungeons represented. Race-mixing violated almost all vehicles of elite domination: class-based claims to land and other resources, patriarchal norms of female chastity, and white assertions of racial purity and superiority. Although the evidence is scanty, those who appear in some cases to have self-identified as Melungeon women viewed their own disputed origins and identity quite differently.

The Challenge to Patriarchy

A subtle theme of female will and independence, exemplified by Alliphair, Syl, and Dromgoole's "unclean" women, is woven through the vernacular history of the Melungeons. While this concept may stand as a morality tale condemning women's sexual independence and its racial consequences, it may also represent mountain women's resistance to that condemnation and their attempts to exercise free will. For example, an actual Melungeon woman, Mahala Mullins, born Mahala Collins in the 1830s, is embroidered in the Tennessee folktale "Six Hundred Honest Pounds."[38] In the tale, "Betsy" Mullins appears in the classic twin roles of trickster and heroine. The story reveals long-lived tensions within white(r) Southern culture about dark women, (white) femininity, miscegenation, and proper sexuality.

In this story, Betsy is exceedingly obese, and "her dark face, with high cheekbones and slanting eyes as black as swamp water," is evidence that "everybody knowed" she was a Melungeon. Defying every standard of womanly appearance, dress, and behavior, she outwrestles the strongest and meanest of the crowd of white men, winning by trickery the right to sell her illegal liquor in front of the very law itself at a public gathering. She whistles up her liquor, which is delivered by her "seven dark and barefoot" husbands, whom she is said to have married the year before, when she was just sixteen.

Adding more husbands and pounds year by year, Betsy continues to sell illegal liquor from her mountain fortress. She even defies Washington officials, who repeatedly try to see justice served, through her cleverness and ultimately through her knowledge of the law. Mythic Betsy Mullins defies rules of racial purity and white supremacy, patriarchy, civil law, and proper sexuality; her exaggerated multiple transgressions link racial rebellion with subversions of gender, and thereby point up the intimate relationship between race and gender oppression in the South.

The fate of historical Mahala Mullins's offspring was unfortunately less victorious. Mullins did live in an inaccessible cabin and make moonshine, and she was indeed never arrested, allegedly because of the impossibility of bringing her to jail.[39] Nonetheless she—and her clan of relatives and descendants—increasingly witnessed the "envelopment" of their native environment by the imperialist society, with a narrowing of choices and the gradual proletarianization of their families and communities. Simultaneously, their history and its interrelated themes of racial transgression and female independence were also enveloped—by the reconstruction of Appalachia as white and the redefinition of its historical actors as male.

And yet, the association of Melungeon ethnicity with independent women remains active even today. As recently as 1995, a Wise County, Virginia, male acquaintance related to one of this essay's authors the current state of affairs between his son and his son's ex-wife, who were fighting for custody of their one child. "See," he said, "she's a Melungeon— changed her name and [her son's] back to her original surname and [she] won't let Bob see the boy, even for visits." When he was asked what such behavior had to do with being Melungeon, he explained that her family were old-style Melungeons who believed that women had the "free will" to marry, divorce, or breed but that no man could "own" them, their property, or their children. He added, "They and their kind never got broke in properly, I guess."[40]

Whether "broke in" to Southern white patriarchy or not, mountain women find in stories of Indian grandmothers and Melungeons a "hidden transcript" of resistance to white patriarchy. The mythic transgressions of native grandmothers and their Melungeon descendants exemplify and inspire contemporary women's resistance to male domination and their desire for freedom. In her challenge to the white patriarchal construction of Appalachia, the native grandmother also explains and dignifies the suffering of subsequent generations of mothers and grandmothers—those who were forced into the shade.

Recent discussion of Melungeon history has resulted in an outpouring of interest—indeed passion—among mountain residents in Kentucky, North Carolina, Tennessee, West Virginia, and Virginia as well as in all the points of out-migration; these descendants are eager to hear and comprehend a multitude of family mysteries that were hushed, insults that were suffered, humiliation that was endured.[41] As Appalachians and Americans with bountiful genealogical possibilities, as descendants of "people of color" who were everything not "white" by late nineteenth- and early twentieth-century standards, our "native" grandmothers might have been Amerindian, African, and/or various combinations of native, African, and Euro-American.

Tracing the ancestry of our individual (great-great- . . .) grandmothers is, for most of us, not possible; in the broad landscape of history, it may not even be most important. What does matter is that we continue to search for the innumerable lost grandmothers—of whatever hue or inflection—whose existence exposes the fiction of our own racial, ethnic, intensely gendered identities.

Notes

1. The term "mountain nigger" appears in newspaper accounts, court records, and oral historiography. Examples of the term's ubiquity can be traced in the private correspondence and research materials produced by Kentucky journalist and novelist John Fox, Jr. (1862–1919). See his Correspondence Files, Notes for Lecture/Readings, 1880–1919, and Unpublished Notebook, 1910, in Fox Family Papers, Special Collections, Margaret I. King Library, University of Kentucky, Lexington; in the notebook, see the third "leaf" for the notation "Malungeons − mountain niggers."

2. The classic text on "hidden transcripts" is James Scott, *Domination and the Arts of Resistance: Hidden Transcripts* (New Haven: Yale University Press, 1990). Examples of such transcripts for Appalachian women include in-family religious training, folk tales, and folk wisdom.

3. See, e.g., Rodger Cunningham, *Apples on the Flood: The Southern Mountain Experience* (Knoxville: The University of Tennessee Press, 1987); J. Wayne Flynt, *Dixie's Forgotten People: The South's Poor Whites* (Bloomington: Indiana University Press, 1979); Kenneth W. Keller, "What About the Scotch-Irish?" in R. Mitchell, ed., *Appalachian Frontiers: Settlement, Society, and Development in the Preindustrial Era* (Lexington: University Press of Kentucky, 1991).

4. See Charles Hudson, *The Juan Pardo Expeditions: Explorations of the Carolinas and Tennessee—1568* (Washington, DC: Smithsonian Institution Press, 1990). Also

see Edgar Thompson, "The Little Races," *American Anthropologist* 74 (1972): 1295–1306; Brewton Berry, *Almost White* (New York: Macmillan, 1963); Edward T. Price, "A Geographical Analysis of White-Negro-Indian Racial Mixtures in Eastern United States," *Association of American Geographers Annals* 43 (June 1953): 138–55; Price, "The Melungeons: A Mixed-Blood Strain of the Southern Appalachians," *The Geographical Review* (1951): 256–71, Price, "Mixed-Blood Populations of Eastern United States as to Origins, Localizations, and Persistence" (Ph.D. diss., University of California, Berkeley, 1950); C. A. Weslager, "Trends in the Naming of Tri-Racial Mixed Blood Groups in the Eastern United States," *American Speech* 22 (1947): 81–87; Arthur H. Estabrook and Ivan E. McDougle, *Mongrel Virginians* (Baltimore: Williams and Wilkins, 1926). See also Jack D. Forbes, *Africans and Native Americans: The Language of Race and the Evolution of Red-Black Peoples* (Urbana: University of Illinois Press, 1993); Forbes, "The Manipulation of Race, Caste, and Identification: Classifying AfroAmericans, Native Americans, and Red-Black People," *The Journal of Ethnic Studies* 17(4) (1992): 1–51; Forbes, "Envelopment, Proletarianization, and Inferiorization: Aspects of Colonialism's Impact upon Native Americans and Other People of Color in Eastern North America," *Journal of Ethnic Studies* 18 (4) (1991): 95–122.

5. Interviews with Darlene Wilson, 1994.

6. See, e.g., D. Reedy, ed., *School and Community History of Dickenson (and Wise) County, Virginia* (Johnson City, TN: Mountain People and Places, 1992).

7. David A. Hollinger, *Postethnic America: Beyond Multiculturalism* (New York: Harper-Collins/Basic Books, 1995), pp. 23–24.

8. See Theodore Allen, *The Invention of the White Race,* Vol. 1, *Racial Oppression and Social Control* (New York: Verso, 1994); David Roediger, *The Wages of Whiteness* (London: Verso, 1991).

9. See N. Brent Kennedy with Robin Vaughan Kennedy, *The Melungeons: The Resurrection of a Proud People: An Untold Story of Ethnic Cleansing in America* (Macon, GA: Mercer University Press, 1994); Manuel Mira, *The Forgotten Portuguese: The Melungeons and Other Groups—The Portuguese Making of America* (Franklin, NC: PAHRF—Portuguese-American Historical Research Foundation, 1997); Eloy Gallegos, *The Melungeons: The Pioneers of the Interior Southeastern United States* (Knoxville, TN: Vallagra Press, 1997); Mattie Ruth Johnson, *My Melungeon Heritage: A Story of Life on Newman's Ridge* (Johnson City, TN: Overmountain Press, 1997); Melanie Lou Sovine, "The Mysterious Melungeons: A Critique of Mythical Image" (Ph.D. diss., University of Kentucky, Lexington, 1982); Saundra Keyes Ivey, "Oral, Printed, and Popular Culture Traditions Related to the Melungeons of Hancock County" (M.A. thesis, Indiana University, Bloomington, 1976); Ivey, "Aunt Mahala Mullins in Folklore, Fakelore, and Literature," *Tennessee Folklore Society Bulletin* 41(1) (March 1975), pp. 1–8; Donald B. Ball, "A Bibliography of Tennessee Anthropology: Including Cherokee, Chickasaw, and Melungeon Studies," *Miscellaneous Papers Number One* (Knoxville: Tennessee Anthropological Association, 1976); Lisa Alther, "The Melungeon Melting Pot," *New Society* 36 (706) (April 15, 1976); Jean Patterson Bible, *Melungeons Yesterday and Today* (Johnson City, TN: Overmountain Press, 1975); Bible, "A People with an Unknown Past," *Baltimore Sunday Sun Magazine,* June 13, 1971; Avery F.

Gaskins, "An Introduction of the Guineas: West Virginia's Melungeons," *Appalachian Journal* 1(3) (Autumn 1973): 234–37; Jacqueline Daniel Burks, "The Treatment of the Melungeon in General Literature and Belletristic Works" (M.A. thesis, Tennessee Technological University, Cookeville, 1972); Phyllis Cox Barr, "The Melungeons of Newman's Ridge" (M.A. thesis, East Tennessee State University, 1965).

An oft-cited "authority" with firsthand knowledge of early twentieth-century Melungeons is Bonnie Ball (Bonnie Sage), *The Melungeons (Their Origin and Kin)*, 7th ed. (Johnson City, TN: Overmountain Press, 1981). This is Ball's most comprehensive publication, and includes bibliographies on and analyses of Melungeons and their social conditions in Southern states, especially the Appalachian region; also see the following works by Ball: "The Melungeons," *Historical Sketches: Historical Society of Southwest Virginia* 2 (1966); "A Vanishing Race," *Mountain Life and Work* 36 (Summer 1960): 39–42; America's Mysterious Race," *Read* 16 (May 1944): 64–67; "Mystery Men of the Mountains," *Negro Digest* 3 (January 1945): 39–41; "Virginia's Mystery Race," *Virginia State Highway Bulletin* 2(6) (April 1945): 2–3; "Who Are the Melungeons?" *Southern Literary Messenger* 3(2) (June 1945): 5–7.

See also Louise Davis, "The Mystery of the Melungeons," *Nashville Tennessean Magazine*, September 7 and 29, 1963 reprinted in *Tennessee Valley Historical Review* 1 (1) (1972): 22–29; L. F. Addington, "Mountain Melungeons Let the World Go By," *Baltimore Sunday Sun*, July 29, 1945, p. A3; William L. Worden, "Sons of the Legend," *Saturday Evening Post*, October 18, 1947, pp. 28–29 ff.; James R. Aswell, Gaily Wellhead, Jeannette Edwards, E. E. Miller, and Lean B. Lipscomb of the Tennessee Writers' Project, *God Bless the Devil! Liars' Bench Tales* (Chapel Hill: University of North Carolina Press, 1940); James Aswell, "Lost Tribes of Tennessee's Mountains," *Nashville Banner*, August 22, 1937; Celestin Pierre Cambiare, *East Tennessee and Western Virginia Mountain Ballads* (London: Mitre Press, 1935); Paul D. Converse, "The Melungeons," *Southern Collegian*, December 1912, pp. 59–69; Will Allen Dromgoole, "The Malungeons," *The Arena* 46 (March 1891): 479; Dromgoole,, "The Malungeon Tree and Its Four Branches," *The Arena* 3 (June 1891), pp. 470–79; Swan M. Burnett, "A Note on the Melungeons," *American Anthropologist* 2 (October 1889): 347.

10. See, e.g., Robert F. Berkhofer, Jr., *The White Man's Indian* (New York: Alfred A. Knopf, 1978); Vine Deloria, Jr., *Custer Died for Your Sins* (New York: Macmillan, 1969).

11. John Fox, Jr., "The Courtship of Alliphair," in *In Happy Valley* (New York: Scribner's and Sons, 1917), pp. 34–70.

12. Rayna Green, "The Tribe Called Wannabee: Playing Indian in America and Europe," *Folklore* 99(1) (1988): 50. See also n. 9 above; S. Elizabeth Bird, ed., *Dressing in Feathers* (Boulder, CO: Westview, 1996).

13. An excellent discussion of Plecker's dubious "legacy" can be found in Helen Rountree, *Pocahontas's People: The Powhatan Indians of Virginia Through Four Centuries* (Norman: University of Oklahoma Press, 1990); for verified copies of all Plecker documents and correspondence cited here, see "A Melungeon Home Page" at: http://www.clinch.edu/appalachia/melungeon/. See also J. David

Smith, *The Eugenic Assault on America: Scenes in Red, White, and Black* (Fairfax, VA: George Mason University Press, 1993). Plecker was the author of various essays, tracts, and pamphlets that were published by "official" state sources in Virginia and by eugenics-related organizations and individuals. See, e.g., the brochure by Plecker, *Eugenics in Relation to the New Family and the Law on Racial Integrity* (Richmond: D. Bottom, Superintendent, Public Printing, 1924); this essay also appeared under the title *Virginia's Attempt to Adjust the Color Problem,* and can be viewed via the above website.

14. For the correspondence cited here, see the following files of correspondence with the Tennessee Archivist in the Tennessee State Archives, Nashville: Plecker to Moore, August 5, 1942; Moore to Plecker, August 12, 1942; Plecker to Moore, August 20, 1942; Moore to Plecker, September 10, 1942. Transcripts are available via the website cited in n. 13.

15. Peggy Pascoe, "Miscegenation Law, Court Cases, and Ideologies of 'Race' in Twentieth-Century America," *The Journal of American History* 83 (June 1996): 44–69; Fon Louise Gordon, *Caste and Class: The Black Experience in Arkansas, 1880–1920* (Athens: University of Georgia Press, 1995); Naomi Zack, *Race and Mixed Race* (Philadelphia: Temple University Press, 1993); Maria Root, *Racially Mixed People in America* (Newbury Park, CA: Sage Publications, 1992); Kathy Russell, *The Color Complex: The Politics of Skin Color Among African Americans* (New York: Harcourt Brace Jovanovich, 1992); Patricia Morton, *Disfigured Images: The Historical Assault on Afro-American Women* (Westport, CT: Greenwood Press, 1991); Peggy Pascoe, "Race, Gender, and Intercultural Relations: The Case of Interracial Marriage," *Frontiers* 12 (1991): 5–18; Williard B. Gatewood, *Aristocrats of Color: The Black Elite, 1880–1920* (Bloomington: Indiana University Press, 1990); Paul R. Spickard, *Mixed Blood: Intermarriage and Ethnic Identity in Twentieth-Century America* (Madison: University of Wisconsin Press, 1989); J. Owens Smith, *The Politics of Racial Inequality: A Systematic Comparative Macro-Analysis from the Colonial Period to 1970* (New York: Greenwood Press, 1987); Mamie Garvin Fields with Karen Fields, *Lemon Swamp and Other Places: A Carolina Memoir* (New York: Free Press, 1983). See also Jon Michael Spencer, *The New Colored People: The Mixed-Race Movement in America* (New York: New York University Press, 1997).

16. See, e.g., Alonso de Posada Report, *A Description of the Area of the Present Southeast United States in the Seventeenth Century* (1686), ed. and trans. Alfred Barnaby Thomas, (Pensacola, FL: Perdido Bay, 1982); John Clayton, *Transcript of the Journal of Robert Fallam: A Journal from Virginia, Beyond the Apallachian Mountains, in Sept 1671. Sent to the Royal Society by Mr. Clayton, and Read Aug. 1, 1688 Before the Said Society,* reprinted in Clarence W. Alvord and Lee Bidgood, eds., *The First Explorations of the Trans-Allegheny Region by the Virginians, 1650–1674* (Cleveland: Arthur H. Clark Co., 1912), pp. 183–95; Nicholas Cresswell, *The Journal of Nicholas Cresswell, 1774–1777* (New York: The Dial Press, 1924); Johann David Schoepf, *Travels in the Confederation (1783–1784),* trans. Alfred J. Morrison, 2 vols. (1911; reprint, New York: Bergman Publishers, 1968). For secondary analyses, see Richard Sattler, "Women's Status Among the Muskogee and Cherokee," in Laura S. Klein and Lillian A. Ackerman, eds., *Women and Power in Native North America* (Norman: University of Oklahoma Press, 1995), pp. 214–28; Daniel Maltz and JoAllyn Archambault,

"Gender and Power in Native North America," in ibid., pp. 230–50; Colin G. Calloway, *The American Revolution in Indian Country: Crisis and Diversity in Native American Communities* (Cambridge: Cambridge University Press, 1995); Tom Hatley, *The Dividing Paths: Cherokees and South Carolinians Through the Revolutionary Era* (New York: Oxford University Press, 1993); Andrea Cornwall and Nancy Lindisfarne, "Dislocating Masculinity: Gender, Power, and Anthropology," in A. Cornwall and N. Lindisfarne, eds., *Dislocating Masculinity: Comparative Ethnographies* (New York: Routledge, 1994); Teresa Valle, ed., *Gendered Anthropology* (London: Routledge, 1993); Carol Devens, "Separate Confrontations: Gender as a Factor in Indian Adaptation to European Colonization in New France," *American Quarterly* 38 (1986): 461–80; Laura E. Donaldson, *Decolonizing Feminisms: Race, Gender, and Empire-Building* (Chapel Hill: University of North Carolina Press, 1992); Julia V. Emberly, *Thresholds of Difference: Feminist Critique, Native Women's Writings, Postcolonial Theory* (Toronto: University of Toronto Press, 1993); Carol Groneman, "Nymphomania: The Historical Construction of Female Sexuality," in J. Terry and J. Urla, eds., *Deviant Bodies: Critical Perspectives on Difference in Science and Popular Culture* (Bloomington: Indiana University Press, 1995), pp. 219–49; Ann Laura Stoler, *Race and the Education of Desire: Foucault's History of Sexuality and the Colonial Order of Things* (Durham: Duke University Press, 1995); William Loren Katz, *Proudly Red and Black: Stories of African and Native Americans* (New York: Atheneum, 1993); Theda Purdue, "Nancy Ward," in G. J. Barker-Benfield and Catherine Clinton, eds., *Portraits of American Women: From Settlement to the Civil War* (New York: St. Martin's Press, 1991), pp. 83–100; Sidney Kaplan, "Historical Efforts to Encourage White-Indian Intermarriage in the United States and Canada," *International Social Science Review* 65(3) (1990): 126–32; Susan Hegeman, "Native American 'Texts' and the Problem of Authenticity," *American Quarterly* 41 (1989): 265–83; Arnold Krupat, "An Approach to Native American Texts," *Critical Inquiry* 9(2) (December 1982): 331; Mary C. Wright, "Economic Development and Native American Women in the Early Nineteenth Century," *American Quarterly* 33 (1981): 525–36; Theda Purdue, *Slavery and the Evolution of Cherokee Society, 1540–1866* (Knoxville: University of Tennessee Press, 1979); David T. Haberly, "Women and Indians: The Last of the Mohicans and the Captivity Tradition," *American Quarterly* 28 (1976): 431–43; Charles Hudson, *The Southeastern Indians* (Knoxville: University of Tennessee Press, 1976)

17. See, e.g., Clayton, *Transcript of the Journal of Robert Fallam*, pp. 183–95; for a comprehensive listing of the many references to mixed-ethnic communities, see Mira, *The Forgotten Portuguese*, pp. 28–58.

18. On relationships of co-dependency, see Durwood Dunn, *Cades Cove: The Life and Death of a Southern Appalachia Community, 1818–1937* (Knoxville: University of Tennessee Press, 1988), pp. 8–9. On cross-cultural marriage and colonial policy, see Sidney Kaplan, "Historical Efforts to Encourage White-Indian Intermarriage in the United States and Canada," *International Social Science Review* 65(3) (1990): 126–32.

19. See, e.g., Roediger, *The Wages of Whiteness;* also see Noel Ignatiev, *How the Irish Became White* (New York: Routledge Press, 1995); Allen, *The Invention of the White Race;* and Morton J. Horwitz, *The Transformation of American Law, 1780–1869* (New York: Oxford University Press, 1992).

20. Sevier to the governor of North Carolina, c. 1782–84, Tennessee State Archives; examined and cited by Louise Davies, "The Mystery of the Melungeons," *Nashville Tennessean,* September 29, 1963, p. 11; also cited in Samuel Cole Williams, *Early Travels in the Tennessee Country* (Johnson City, TN: Watauga Press, 1928), p. viii.

21. Jack Harold Goins, *Gowen Family Foundation Newsletter,* November 1993. Records of the Primitive Baptist Association are available from the Wise County Historical Society, Wise, Virginia; excerpts were published in Emory Hamilton's pamphlet *Primitive Baptist Association Minutes* (Johnson City, TN: Overmountain Press).

22. Stephen Jay Gould, *The Mismeasure of Man* (New York: W. W. Norton and Company, 1981).

23. See, e.g., Kennedy with Kennedy, *The Melungeons;* Johnson, *My Melungeon Heritage;* and Reedy, ed., *School and Community History.*

24. See John Fox, Jr., to his younger brothers Everett and Horace Fox, September 1882, Correspondence File, 1882, Fox Family Papers.

25. Kennedy with Kennedy, *The Melungeons.*

26. Dromgoole, "The Malungeons," p. 472.

27. Ibid.

28. Ibid., p. 475.

29. Berry, *Almost White.*

30. Ibid., p. 36.

31. See Hollinger, *Postethnic America.* Also see Zack, *Race and Mixed Race;* and Naomi Zack, ed., *American Mixed Race: The Culture of Microdiversity* (Lanham, MD: Rowan & Littlefield, 1995).

32. See Aswell et al., *God Bless the Devil!,* pp. 207–10.

33. John Fox, Jr., to his brother James, Correspondence Files, 1893, Fox Family Papers.

34. Dromgoole, "The Malungeons," p. 475.

35. Price, "The Melungeons," pp. 256–71.

36. Ibid., p. 271.

37. Ibid.

38. Aswell et al., *God Bless the Devil!,* pp. 226–43; this folktale is also available via the website http://www.clinch.edu/appalachia/melungeon/archive.htm.

39. See Kennedy with Kennedy, *The Melungeons.*

40. Darlene Wilson, interview with B. B. Tiller, Wise, Virginia, 1995.

41. See, e.g., Joan V. Schroeder, "The Melungeon Woodstock: A People Find Their Voice," *Blue Ridge Country* 10(6) (November–December 1997); John Shelton Reed, "Mixing in the Mountains," *Southern Cultures* 3(4) (Winter 1997–98): 25–36.

3

"A Good Ol' Woman"

Relations of Race and Gender in an Indian Community

Patricia B. Lerch

riscilla Jacobs, chief of the state-recognized Waccamaw Sioux of North Carolina, represents a new generation of Indian women leaders in the South. Like Wilma Mankiller, former chief of the Oklahoma Cherokee, Jacobs symbolizes the accomplishments of Indian women from her region. The public details of her people's story reveal how the relations of gender and race, both within the Waccamaw and between the Waccamaw and other groups, have shifted over time. In recent years, facilitated in part by the complex implications of the modern civil rights movement for Southern Indians, Jacobs and other contemporary Waccamaw have defined a new era for Indian women and their tribe. This chapter explores the historical processes whereby the Waccamaw, especially women, have sought to negotiate the meanings of race and gender among themselves and in relationship to other social groups in the South.

For over three hundred years, the lives of the Waccamaw Indians have been bound up with the history of European colonization and war, African enslavement and resistance—in short, with the history of the U.S. South as it was played out in the southeastern corner of North Carolina. As background and context for the contemporary identity claims of Waccamaw women, this chapter explores their strategies of survival—materially, within the local agricultural economy, and culturally, as a people—from the late nineteenth century to the present. It draws on data from personal interviews, historical research, and ethnographic observations conducted over the past fifteen years. How have time, place, gender, and race shaped the cultural and economic lives—and been shaped by the actions—of Waccamaw women? How have Indian women of the late twentieth century, such as Priscilla Jacobs, transformed the meaning of gender and race and yet remained connected to the Waccamaw past?

Susan Stanford Friedman's concept of relational reality, or "positionality," as she phrases it, provides a useful reference point from which to examine these questions about the history of Waccamaw women. As she argues, "within a relational framework, identities shift with a changing context, dependent always upon the point of reference. Not essences or absolutes, identities are fluid sites that can be understood differently depending on the vantage point of their formation and function."[1] From her perspective, what seems to be "difference" between the Waccamaw and their white neighbors is in fact a relational and fluid interaction. Along the boundaries defined by race and gender, there exists a dynamic interplay wherein the meaning of difference is created and defined by those players involved in the social drama of living together.

To adapt Friedman's example to the Waccamaw, from the white—and often the dominant—perspective, Jacobs's people have generally been perceived as "not-white," or "people of color." In some periods, whites have singularly defined the Waccamaw as "Indians"; at other times, the emphasis has been on their "mixed-race" status—partly white and partly other people of color. In relation to people of color, Waccamaw have been viewed as Native American. In relation to Native Americans, they are Waccamaw. The changing terms of these definitions reflect, as we shall see, the changing historical position of the Waccamaw in the complicated racial dynamics of the U.S. South. This chapter emphasizes how the Waccamaw, especially women, have continuously sought to define an identity and social location for themselves.

The Social Relations of Survival

Priscilla Jacobs's people live today in the territory and hunting grounds of the Eastern Siouans, a group of tribes sharing similar language and culture. Among this larger group, historic documents name the Waccamaw and Cape Fear Indians as tribes who roamed the Green Swamp, the shores of Lake Waccamaw, and the many streams and "branches" (creeks) of southeastern North Carolina and northeastern South Carolina.[2] This part of the Atlantic seaboard lies outside the large plantations and other slaveholding areas of the "Cotton South."[3] Indeed, some historians romantically characterized the region as a "paradise for poor people" because of the relative ease of making a subsistence living.[4] Tribes like the Waccamaw and Cape Fear hunted, foraged, and planted crops, especially corn, for survival.[5] Jacobs's tribe members say they are the "people of the falling star," referring to an Indian legend about how a star fell from the sky to form Lake Waccamaw. In 1715 there was a fairly large Waccamaw settlement around the lake.[6]

During the eighteenth century the Eastern Siouans, being few in number and lacking the power to prevent European encroachment on their lands, found themselves living in close proximity to the European colonies, with which they became connected through ties of aid, friendship, trade, and political alliance.[7] Over time, European settlement patterns, diseases, wars, and hostility brought many changes. First, the Waccamaw and Cape Fear, skilled traders both with other tribes and with Europeans, learned to use guns in their wars against each other and the English. They also used this technology to raid more sedentary and acculturated Indians for cattle. Second, they acquired European manufactured goods that equipped them, materially and psychologically, to survive along the margins of European settlement; here, they might occupy undesirable, swampy land but live in relative seclusion as they remade their communities under the exigencies of political and military defeat. Third, the Waccamaw economy shifted as Euroamerican farming techniques blended with Indian approaches. Some Indian communities sought to avoid these influences by moving away from the Europeans, but eventually war and defeat changed the lives of all the coastal tribes.[8]

In the nineteenth century securing a land base became an obvious key to community survival for the coastal tribes. We do not know exactly how the ancestors of the modern Waccamaw learned the importance of land titles and deeds, but it is clear that, by 1780, they were registering property with the county courthouses. Although most of these documents record the names and activities of men, daughters also inherited parcels of land, thus allowing a handful of Waccamaw women to accumulate property.

Throughout the nineteenth century, most Waccamaw remained agriculturalists and retained title to their own land. Indian households, as identified by genealogical research, are listed in the Agricultural Schedules of the federal manuscript census returns for 1880.[9] Nearly 90 percent of the Waccamaw households recorded in that census owned their farms, although they were small in comparison with the average local non-Indian farm. Indian farmers also owned an average of 253 acres of woodland, which were of great economic importance to many families; in fact, the value of forest products from this area exceeded that of farm products.[10]

The Waccamaw farms of 1880 reflected the crop diversification of the region's agriculture. Farmers raised Indian corn, cow peas, sweet potatoes, rice, milk cows, oxen, poultry, swine, and sheep, and produced eggs, milk, butter, and cheese. Indian households connected with their white and black neighbors through the sale of surplus crops within an increasingly complex regional market system that included stores, gristmills, riverboats, and, later, tobacco warehouses. The white neighbors of the Waccamaw owned and controlled all points of distribution and exchange within this system, where Waccamaw men, and sometimes women, provided labor and commodities. The capital necessary for successful farming was also controlled by white bankers and creditors. Control of key economic resources thus lay in the hands of the white society.

The land records of the late nineteenth century show clearly the vicissitudes of the system as Waccamaw lost, sold, and/or bought land. Cash income from "public" work (wage work done outside one's own home or farm) increasingly supplemented subsistence farming. Waccamaw men worked as farm laborers, day laborers, and tar and turpentine laborers. If cash demands for taxes and other needs were too great, some Waccamaw sold their farms and turned entirely to wage labor to support themselves.[11] This trend is evident in the declining proportion of farmers (from 48% to 42%) and the rising proportion of day laborers (from 22% to 42%) among Waccamaw men from 1870 to 1900.

The naval stores industry, which created a demand for tar and turpentine, provided important cash income to many Waccamaw households.[12] Waccamaw men collected crude turpentine from the pine trees growing in the vast tracts of forests surrounding their homes. As of 1910, the southern Atlantic states continued to lead the nation in the value of this forest product, with North Carolina ranking first in the region.[13] This extractive industry involved small groups of men who in the winter "boxed" pine trees by removing a portion of the bark and cutting incisions into the trunks to release resin, or crude turpentine, that was collected in the spring and summer. The men harvested the resin in containers attached to the trees and later transferred it into barrels. Special turpentine stills, owned and operated by the Indians' white neighbors, distilled the crude turpentine.[14] Distilling was also done by the Waccamaw using technologically less sophisticated kilns—simple, saucer-like excavations in the ground, in which they burned pine. These kilns could be built anywhere, in a farmer's field or in the center of the forest. Large kilns loaded with good wood might yield 160–80 barrels of tar.[15] Coopers, or barrel makers, and wheelwrights rarely appeared among occupations for Waccamaw men, listed in the census returns, but older informants remember fathers, uncles, and male relatives who engaged in these skilled trades.[16]

Waccamaw men also made money by cutting railroad ties and floating them out of the Green Swamp.[17] As important as such work was to individual households, it only supplemented subsistence farming, which remained the major source of support for families through the early twentieth century.

Waccamaw women's labor focused on the household economy: they supervised the household garden, which supplied their family with food; processed food crops for home consumption; sold surplus food crops to earn cash; made their family's clothing and quilts; and raised nonfood crops such as tobacco and cotton.[18] In official records kept by whites, married Waccamaw women were given credit for running a household more often than single women. For example, in the 1880 census, a husband was typically listed as being the "head" of the household and his wife as "keeping house." Later, in 1900, as the need for cash income increased, the census lists 85 percent of these women as "keeping house." During these same years, unmarried women living within Indian households sometimes worked outside the home, although not at the same rates as unmarried men. As one Waccamaw woman expressed it, "Ya, the girls mostly stay home. Stay do the cooking and housecleaning, work in the garden, work on the farm."[19] Age was more important than gender in assigning farm work to children; those considered too young to work as wage earners tended garden plots, weeding and keeping them clear of grass. Older boys and girls minded cows and hogs, which were driven daily to graze in the pine woods.

Like their African American neighbors, some Waccamaw women earned wages as domestic workers and as field hands. Indian women's wage work was chiefly day labor rather than live-in domestic service, which was more common among African American women.[20] At thirteen years of age, many Waccamaw girls started working in the homes of local white families, cleaning, ironing, scrubbing floors, and scalding the bed boards in order to rid them of any parasitic or insect infestation. Picked up in the morning and returned home in the early evening, wagon loads of young and adult women traveled to their employer's home or farm, which was sometimes simply down the road or across the field. Remembering her mother and aunts who had worked for white families during the summer and winter months, an elderly Waccamaw woman reflects on being left alone as the white employer came down to pick up female relatives: "In the winter time then in the summer time they'd [her mother and aunts] work with the hoe. They'd like chopping cotton, weeding corn. . . . Yea, and if anybody [white] got sick why they [the whites] came down here heap time, get 'em a mule and a wagon, horse and buggy, carry up there and let 'em [her mother and aunts] wait on 'em [the whites]."[21]

Crops planted in the spring demanded attention from all family members during the long summer growing season. Women's work paralleled men's: they walked between the rows of corn cutting the weeds, while the men followed behind "hilling" up the rows. Men and women shared many tasks but had slightly different work schedules. Waccamaw women rose before dawn to prepare the family breakfast, after which they, their partners/husbands, and the older children went out into the fields. The women then left the fields before the men at midday to prepare the meal for their families. Depending on the workload, both men and women returned to the fields in the afternoon and worked until the evening. Work and tools were often without gender definition; for example, hand-held hoes and the "Boy Dixie" plow and mule were used by both men and women. Although households formed autonomous economic units, Indian families cooperated with their Indian and occasionally white neighbors by forming groups to "swap" work. Their ties to their white neighbors thus included reciprocal labor exchanges as well as wage work. As the demands of home production eased during the summer, both men and women sought part-time, seasonal employment.

Fall signaled the approach of harvest time, the culmination of the agricultural year, when most crops were processed for winter storage and home consumption. Waccamaw men and women harvested by hand and took their corn to a gristmill typically owned by a white neighbor. Women dried vegetables and smoked hams. Men marketed cash crops, and women sold surplus eggs. In the 1890s, cotton was grown as a cash crop and sold through a local wholesaler. Tobacco replaced cotton as the major cash crop after 1910 and was sold to merchants who opened tobacco warehouses in communities surrounding the Waccamaw area. Older Waccamaw describe the labor-intensive process of raising, harvesting, and packaging tobacco for market. Again, women played an important role, working with men. One older farmer remembers the importance of tobacco as a source of cash: "Man had a twelve acre farm way back yonder, he was 'Mr. It.' He doing alright. [Question: Would that be enough to support a family?] Oh, four acres of tobacco and one mule, come out with some money. Anyway, you eat all day when you sold tobacco. Go to the market and eat all day."[22]

Race, Gender, and Community Life

Little is known of the historic Indian community's internal organization aside from observations made by white explorers, soldiers, traders, and government officials. Men are typically mentioned in leadership positions requiring interaction between Indians and whites. By the late nineteenth century, although men and women participated equally in the economy of the household, men continued to represent the community to the outside world; white commissioners appointed them to school committees and key local political posts, and even in local Indian churches, only men preached.

Articulating with the dominant system thus meant being subject to emergent Euro-American norms of race and gender. Precisely how such hierarchical practices may have affected the Waccamaws' self-definition as a people is unclear. In the first two federal censuses, of 1790 and 1800, the ancestors of the modern Waccamaw were placed racially in the category "All Other Free Persons" instead of one of the two other classifications, "Free White" and "Black Slave." The racial grouping "All Other Free Persons" included Indians, free blacks, and people of mixed descent. Similarly, it is unclear how the requirements of white recordkeepers may have (mis)construed gender relations within the Waccamaw community. We must not conclude from census records, which, between 1790 and 1840, trace only the names of household heads and define them primarily as men, that these households were routinely male-dominated. It is not until 1850 that the names of other family members appear in the census.

It is clear that the present-day Waccamaw include people with long lineages, such as Priscilla Jacobs, whose ancestors reach back to the first census of 1790. Waccamaw from these families married each other, forming a highly interrelated set of people central to the community. Occasionally, these "core" families extended their membership through marriage or partnerships with other, unrelated people. Many of the older people recall that there were always a few who married or cohabited with Indians from more distant communities within the state and also with non-Indians. Marrying or cohabiting with non-Indians involved Indian women more frequently than men. For a time in the eighteenth and early nineteenth centuries, the Waccamaw may have accepted this arrangement in part because of its obvious economic benefits for the Indian community as a whole; in addition, their flexible descent system allowed offspring to identify with kin of either the mother or the father, thereby preserving the right of incorporating children of such unions into the community as Indian. Kin ties to white families who owned and operated the businesses that controlled the distribution of farm products, tar, turpentine, lumber, barrels, gristmills, and river barges made good economic sense, since such links could lead to more favorable marketing or employment arrangements for the Waccamaw; for white businesspeople, they eased the flow of goods and labor in the regional marketing system.

However, these racialized and gendered relationships with local whites changed dramatically in the Jim Crow era that followed the Civil War. Conservative policies initiated after the defeat of Reconstruction centralized power and reversed reforms begun by Republicans.[23] The North Carolina General Assembly appointed local justices of the peace who, in turn, appointed the county commissioners. Thus, in the post-Civil War period, local people rarely directly controlled county government in North Carolina. Briefly in 1890, a populist government in Raleigh ushered in liberal reforms that gave more power to local residents, potentially nonwhite as well as white. These reforms were short-lived, however, as conservatives quickly organized to retake control of the legislature and the local governments in 1898. In the nearby city of Wilmington, there was a full-scale revolt over the legally constituted government, which forced a large number of African Americans to leave the city.[24] The disenfranchisement of blacks also affected Indians and all nonwhite people, because, in the biracial climate of the South, any suspicion of nonwhite heritage placed one in the second-class category of "colored."[25]

The Waccamaw reacted to these ominous trends by asserting their Indian identity and rearticulating their relationship with the dominant majority culture. Delineating more rigid racial boundaries around "Indian" served to distance them from the more stigmatized race of African American; at the same time, it legitimated their claim for separate schools for their children and legal recognition as an American Indian community. The Waccamaw organized internally through their council, known by 1910 as the Wide Awake Indian Council, to promote their goals as a people and to deal with the county, state, and federal governments.

The historic pattern of racial mixing involving Indian women and white men came under fire from both whites and Indians during this period, especially after 1898, when the institutionalization of Jim Crow required racial segregation in North Carolina. An older Waccamaw man recalls how those times were described to him circa 1915: "A lot of them whites was taking Indian women but they didn't want the Indian men to marry them."[26] From then on the Indian Council warned people to restrict "the mixing." The community also developed a reputation for violence that reportedly kept out non-Indians. Taken as a whole, local accounts suggest that this change in racial interaction was accomplished in part by the potentially threatening assertions of Indian men of their "right" to Indian women. However accomplished, the consequences fell more heavily on Indian women than men. Indian women had taken white partners in the past, and, from these unions, children of mixed descent were born. For the most part, these children were identified as nonwhite, Indian, or people of color. They did, however, inherit property from their white fathers, thus helping their mothers secure a land base in the area. After 1910, when the Indian Council publicly discouraged such "mixing," these unions became more difficult.

The isolation that the Wide Awake Indian Council advised was both self-imposed and externally forced upon the Waccamaw. Although it disadvantaged women and their mixed-race children by limiting their ties to white (and black) men, this isolation and the related emphasis on self-sufficiency also solidified women's central position in the Waccamaw agricultural economy and community life. Two of the most respected and essential functions carried out by women well into the twentieth century were midwifery and herbal healing. These skilled activities drew their practitioners into relationship with all the households in the community, and especially with other women.

In the 1980s, I interviewed women in their seventies and eighties who said they had never had any need to call a physician to attend them at childbirth. An elderly Waccamaw man fondly recalled his mother, who had served the community for many years as a midwife: "My mother never lost a patient. . . . She tended to many a woman. . . . And she had a disposition about her that . . . she was in control. . . . Ya, she was not only a mother, she was a doctor."[27]

Another older woman recalled her mother-midwife's advice, which mixed faith in the Lord with words of assurance and courage: "But my mama said that heap a time she'd come and tell me before I had da baby, she said, now . . . have faith in the Lord and he will heal and he'll deliver that baby. He put it der. He had it put there and he'll take care of you. And she, I believe, was a good ol' woman."[28]

Experienced midwives could tell when a woman was ready to deliver her baby. They came to the woman's home when she entered labor and sometimes stayed up to nine days while the mother rested. Mothers, sisters, and sisters-in-law helped the new mother in the month following her delivery, relieving her of her heaviest work. If there were any complications following birth, a physician would be sent for from the nearby white communities, but dirt roads and wagon travel could delay the doctor's arrival by many hours. Many infants died in the meantime.[29]

The responsibility of ministering to the medical needs of family and friends fell to women with knowledge of herbal teas and other remedies. A 1947 document details the kinds of problems that midwives and herbalists handled, showing that anxieties and fears concerning childbirth and infant care were common.[30] Additional problems included lice, itch, backache, weight loss, sore throat, colds, measles, toothache, and goiter. More serious ailments included heart disease, venereal disease, diphtheria, asthma, pneumonia, colitis, and "nerves." In most cases, midwives and herbalists prescribed teas made from local wild plants.

Such traditions persisted well into the period after World War II. Although it is still possible to find elderly Waccamaw women with knowledge of midwifery and herbal healing, and many more whose babies were delivered by such midwives, these practices are becoming less and less common. Brenda J. Moore, a Waccamaw Indian community developer employed by the North Carolina Commission of Indian Affairs, noted in 1992 that "tribal elders such as Bertha Patrick and Joe L. Patrick still practice medicine the old way, with natural cures. [But] few know how to 'talk the fire' out of a burn anymore like Vera Mitchell [did]."[31] Although the respected positions of Waccamaw women as healers and midwives have all but disappeared, Priscilla Jacobs and the members of her generation are encouraging the recognition and veneration of such traditions, embodied today in the tribe's elders, as part of the contemporary politics of race and gender.

A New Woman for a New Day

Priscilla Jacobs represents a new generation of Indian women in North Carolina and indeed in the South. In 1985, she became chief of the Waccamaw after the death of the previous chief, her father, Clifton Freeman, Sr. Priscilla's admiration for his inclusive concern for all in the community was evident in her comments, quoted in the local newspaper, at the time of his death: "My father was the type, he wanted you to have whether he had or not. . . . The biggest thing my father desired was to see that people had decent places to live."[32]

Traditionally, the role of chief among the Waccamaw passed to a male heir. But in 1985 all three of Clifton Freeman's sons declined to take the position; this left the decision of chiefly succession up to the Waccamaw Siouan Development Association (WSDA), organized and incorporated by Chief Freeman in 1974. The community, the WSDA, and Priscilla Jacobs herself reached the conclusion that she should become the next chief, thus breaking the tradition of male succession. Her qualifications included not only her lineage as a chief's daughter and member of a core family, but her seven years of work with the WSDA and her Christian ministry. In her words, she worked on "social needs" through the WSDA and "spiritual needs" through her ministry. The local paper noted at the time that "a female chief would not be unusual. Last Saturday, Wilma Mankiller became the first woman to lead a major American Indian tribe when she became principal chief of the Cherokee Nation of Oklahoma."[33]

Jacobs's approach to leadership of the Waccamaw drew on a long familial tradition established by her two great-uncles and her father, all of whom had been chiefs. They in turn followed the philosophy articulated by the Wide Awake Indian Council in 1910. Their efforts to promote and institutionalize a distinctive, legitimate identity as Indian people focused on control over their children's education, federal recognition as an Indian tribe, and economic self-sufficiency.

Generations of Indian women and men had fought for Indian schools. Clifton Freeman, his uncles W. J. Freeman (chief, 1924–48) and the Reverend R. T. Freeman (chief, 1949–64), and others won the right to establish Indian schools in 1934 and then went on to try for federal recognition of their tribe in 1948–50. Priscilla Jacobs accompanied her father in 1949 as part of a tribal delegation to Washington, D.C., where they petitioned Congress to pass a bill that would make the Waccamaw an official Indian tribe of the United States. Despite strong support on several fronts—the Association of American Indian Affairs of New York, lawyer and legal expert Felix Cohen, and anthropologists Alexander Lesser and D'Arcy McNickle—the Waccamaw bill failed to get out of committee. In the postwar era (1949–50), Congress was "terminating" tribes rather than granting federal status to unrecognized ones. In witnessing these events as a child, Priscilla learned to appreciate the leadership skills and political goals of her great-uncles and her father.[34]

The 1950s brought renewed local efforts to address issues of Waccamaw economic development. For example, Reverend Freeman and the Council of Wide Awake Indians of the Waccamaw Tribe of the Siouan Nation, as they now referred to themselves, pressed local authorities for improvements in roads, drainage, electrical services, and schools. By 1955, they succeeded in convincing the Columbus County School Board and the state to support the Waccamaw Indian High School in their community.

The civil rights movement of the 1960s brought both opportunities and setbacks for the Waccamaw. The traditional Indian goals of self-determination and self-sufficiency gained currency in Indian circles in part due to the nationalist philosophy and influence of some elements of the civil rights movement. Self-sufficiency was also promoted for very different reasons by agents of the federal Bureau of Indian Affairs (BIA), who pushed policies such as termination of federal trust status for American Indians. (Although trust status meant subjection to BIA authority in certain aspects of Indian life, it also brought material benefits.) Clifton Freeman became chief in 1964 and immediately organized the Waccamaw Indian Improvement Club, which sought outside investment and industry for the community. Working closely with his new council and club, Chief Freeman succeeded in attracting a small audio device company to open in the abandoned Waccamaw Indian High School. Under Chief Freeman, the club also improved employment opportunities for Indians by sending representatives to nearby county seats to lobby for their hiring.

The civil rights era also brought the closing of Indian schools. In 1964, the year that Clifton Freeman became chief, Congress passed the Civil Rights Act, and the state of North Carolina desegregated its public schools. On March 3, 1965, Waccamaw parents received a memo from the Columbus County School Board that read: "In compliance with the 'Civil Rights Act of 1964' every child in the Columbus County School System shall have the right to attend a school freely selected without regard to race or color, effective with the 1965–1966 school year."[35] This news was greeted by the Waccamaw with a mixture of dismay and fear. Many regretted the closing of the Indian schools, while others feared that integrated schools would mean their quick assimilation and extinction.[36]

Concerned about the cultural vacuum that would be created by the loss of such a key community institution, Chief Freeman and his daughter sought a remedy. They had experienced the power of unity with other Indian people to achieve political, social, and cultural objectives through their activism in such regional and national organizations as the Coalition of Eastern Native Americans and the National Congress of American Indians (NCAI). For example, the NCAI, founded in 1944 as a pan-Indian political organization, represented Indians before the U.S. government, acting as a lobby for Indian rights. By the 1960s, it played a part in educating non-Indians about Indian culture, preserving treaty rights, and generally promoting the welfare of aboriginal Americans. Powwows and pan-Indian meetings were common events of this era.

During the late 1960s, Priscilla Jacobs and her father made plans to introduce the pan-Indian powwow as a way to "revive the culture" and replace the school as a unifying symbol of their community. Thirty years later she recalled those early powwows:

> [The purpose was]. . . to revive our Indian culture. This was a way of doing it—letting other people see. Mostly we had always had a problem with recognition as Indians anyway. Most people [non-Indians] didn't know anything about Indians—[just] a group of people out here in the woods that nobody knows much about, never even thought about too much. It was our intention to bring [Indian] people together for fellowship, to see what each other was doing, to share our arts and crafts with one another, [to share] the progress. At that time, all the Indian tribes were doing the same thing. We were all getting started in it at the same time, trying to revive our culture. That was the purpose of the powwow at that time.[37]

Priscilla remembers those first powwows with a touch of nostalgia, as she regrets the commodification of Indian culture that has transformed the contemporary version: "Back then [1970–76], we didn't have to worry about paying someone to come do drums or do dancing—it was mostly a sharing thing then, we were sharing with each other, and it was real good. The purpose somewhere down the line got from the culture and tradition to a money-making festival. That's the way I see it."[38]

Although its meaning has changed, Priscilla and her father acomplished a great deal by introducing the powwow. Today it is a major regional tourist event and provides the modern Waccamaw with the most important public celebration of their culture and history.[39]

Chiefs Freeman and Jacobs also sought to institutionalize their Indian identity through organization on the state level. In 1970 they worked effectively with Indian leaders across the state to organize the first Commission of Indian Affairs, which offered the opportunity to formalize existing ties among the Indian communities. As an organization within the state government formed to serve the interests of Indian people throughout North Carolina, one of its primary responsibilities is to provide a procedure for state recognition of Indian groups. The commission is also the primary agency responsible for representing the needs of Indians to the governor.

Chief Priscilla Jacobs is a modern woman. She is a wife, a mother, a grandmother, a working woman, a minister, a political leader, and a role model for Waccamaw girls and boys. Her public achievements and political leadership, although unusual for a Waccamaw woman, do not rest on a repudiation of Indian tradition, but on the simultaneous celebration and transformation of tradition. Chief Jacobs is as nurturing and supportive as the women of her grandmother's generation. For example, she runs the children's dance team. Yet she is strong and assertive, unafraid to speak publicly about Indian affairs around the state. She has a deep spiritual life, and, unlike the women of an earlier generation, whom the Baptist church did not allow to become ministers, she is the most well-known woman preacher from her tribe. Perhaps the women's movement of the 1960s and 1970s influenced her decision to accept the position of chief when her brothers showed no interest. More likely, however, she grew up with a strong political sense, nurtured and strengthened through her close association with her father.

Chief Jacobs's public leadership and promotion of Indian cultural practices have opened the way for recognition of the very different accomplishments of older women. For example, in 1996 Elizabeth Lee Graham Jacobs, an eighty-five-year-old Waccamaw woman, earned praise for her lifelong craft of quilting when she received the North Carolina Folk Heritage Award from the state government. Ms. Lee, as she is called, is a leader of a previous generation of women who worked behind the scenes supporting their families, churches, and community. The accomplishments of Priscilla Jacobs and other women of the current generation rest on the efforts of these earlier healers, midwives, agriculturalists, and craftspeople, who in very different circumstances also negotiated for recognition and respect as Waccamaw and as women. At the 1996 annual powwow, tribal council chairman Michael A. Lewis acknowledged the entire community's debt to them: "To our elders, we thank you for your foresight, guidance and encouragement. The stories you tell us, about the struggles and advancement of our ancestors, give direction to the path we must follow today . . . [and] tomorrow."[40]

Notes

1. Susan Stanford Friedman, "Beyond White and Other: Relationality and Narratives of Race in Feminist Discourse," *Signs* 21(1) (Autumn 1995): 16.

2. Most scholars classify the southeastern tribes as "Eastern Siouans." See James Mooney, *The Siouan Tribes of the East,* Smithsonian Institution Bureau of American Ethnology, Bulletin 22 (Washington, DC: U.S. Government Printing Office, 1894), pp. 65–76; John R. Swanton, "Probable Identity of the 'Croatan' Indians," *Senate Report No. 204,* 73rd Congress, vol. 1, 1934, pp. 3–6; A. L. Kroeber, *Cultural and Natural Areas of Native North America,* University of California Publications in American Archaeology and Ethnology, vol. 38 (Berkeley: University of California Press, 1932), pp. 92–95; Chapman J. Milling, *Red Carolinians* (Columbia: University of South Carolina Press, 1969), p. 203.

3. Roger L. Ransom and Richard Sutch, *One Kind of Freedom: The Economic Consequences of Emancipation* (Cambridge: Cambridge University Press, 1977).

4. A. Roger Ekirch, *Poor Carolina: Politics and Society in Colonial North Carolina, 1729–1776* (Chapel Hill: University of North Carolina Press, 1981).

5. Lewis H. Larson, *Aboriginal Subsistence Technology on the Southeastern Coastal Plain During the Late Prehistoric Period* (Gainesville: University Presses of Florida, 1980).

6. John R. Swanton, *The Indians of the Southeastern United States,* Smithsonian Institution Bureau of American Ethnology, Bulletin 137 (Washington, DC: U.S. Government Printing Office, 1946), p. 203. This village was the southern boundary of their territory. See E. Lawrence Lee, *The Lower Cape Fear in Colonial Days* (Chapel Hill: University of North Carolina Press, 1965), pp. 80–81.

7. Mooney, *The Siouan Tribes,* pp. 65, 76.

8. For example, the Waccamaw and the Cape Fear got involved in the Tuscarora War of 1711–12 and the Yamasee War of 1715. See Lee, *The Lower Cape Fear,* pp. 67, 76, 80–81. These wars permanently altered Indian-white relations in the region. The Cape Fear, greatly weakened by these wars, became less important to the European settlers (see ibid., pp. 80–81; and Milling, *Red Carolinians,* p. 226). The Waccamaw fared a little better and still received attention from European officials who sought alliances and trade with them. By December 16, 1716, a Mr. Waties, a trading factor, was told by the Commissioners of the Indian Trade, located in Charles Town (now Charleston, SC), to slow down the sale of guns and ammunition to the Waccamaw because they were using them to raid neighboring tribes for cattle. The commissioners of the Indian trade directed traders to

exchange ammunition, liquor, and other goods for Indian slaves with tribes, like the Waccamaw, who were "in Amity with this Government." See W. L. McDowell, *Colonial Records of South Carolina: Journals of the Commissioners of the Indian Trade, September 20, 1710–August 29, 1718* (Columbia: South Carolina Archives Department, 1955) pp. 95, 137. Eventually hostilities relations broke out, involving the Waccamaw in another war in 1720. See John R. Swanton, *The Indian Tribes of North Carolina*, Smithsonian Institution Bureau of American Ethnology, Bulletin 145 (Washington, DC: U.S. Government Printing Office, 1952), p. 101; Milling, *Red Carolinians*, pp. 226–27. After 1720, there was so much frontier turmoil that the authorities had a hard time locating either the Waccamaw or the Cape Fear. Some Waccamaw were raided and captured by the Seneca in 1725. See N. D. Mereness, ed., *Travels in the American Colonies* (1916; reprint, New York: Antiquarian Press, 1961), p. 18. Others were joined by the Cape Fear in settlements near the Catawba of South Carolina. See Swanton, *The Indians of the Southeastern United States.* p. 203. Some Cape Fear were reported to have settled around the parishes of Saint Stephen and Saint John, South Carolina, near the Pee Dee Indians under a chief called "King Johnny." See Swanton, *The Indian Tribes*, p. 103. John Herbert's map located a small settlement on the upper limits of the Lumber and the Pee Dee rivers. See Stanley A. South, "Tribes of the Carolina Lowlands: Peedee-Sewee-Winyaw-Waccamaw–Cape Fear–Congaree-Wateree-Santee" (manuscript, Institute of Archaeology and Anthropology, University of South Carolina, Columbia, n.d.), p. 34. Still others placed the Cape Fear and the Waccamaw back in their old territory near Lake Waccamaw perhaps as late as 1734. See James Sprunt, *Chronicles of the Cape Fear River, 1660–1916*, 2nd ed. (Raleigh: Edwards and Broughton, 1916), p. 40. This suggests that one or both of these groups remained in the vicinity of Lake Waccamaw until and after that date, and that their presence and Indian identity were known to travelers. This area must have been fairly remote from most of the white settlements, however, because their precise whereabouts were still of some concern to the British as late as 1755. In a letter to King Haigler of the Catawba, Governor James Glenn of South Carolina reminded Haigler that he (the governor) had persuaded the Waccamaw and the Cheraw to settle near the Catawba. See Glenn's speech to Haigler, n.d., encl. no. 3 in Glenn to the Lords Commissioners of Trade and Plantations, May 19, 1755, *British Public Records Office Relating to South Carolina 1663–1782*, vol. 26, pp. 184, 194, 203–11, microfilm reel no. 3292 (Columbia: South Carolina Archives Department, 1955). It is unclear from this correspondence, however, whether the Governor was successful. The Cheraw may have ended up in a settlement along the border of South and North Carolina and become the modern-day Lumbee. The remnants of the Waccamaw and the Cape Fear removed themselves further into their old territory, eventually to reside in the vicinity of the modern Waccamaw community.

9. U.S. Bureau of the Census, Manuscript Schedules, Bladen County, North Carolina, 1880. In Carver's Creek Township, for example, of 153 farms listed, 121 were owned, 28 sharecropped, and 4 rented.

10. U.S. Bureau of the Census, Manuscript Schedules 3, Columbus and Bladen Counties, North Carolina, 1880.

11. Phillip J. Wood, *Southern Capitalism: The Political Economy of North Carolina, 1880–1980* (Durham: Duke University Press, 1986).

12. Annual wages in North Carolina's tar and turpentine industry ($192.74) ranked higher than those in its flour mills ($133.16) and textile mills ($125.91). Tar and turpentine hired primarily men, whereas textile mills hired primarily women, according to the 1870 census. See U.S. Bureau of the Census, *A Compendium of the Ninth Census (June 1, 1870).* (Washington, DC: U.S. Government Printing Office, 1872), p. 865.

13. U.S. Bureau of the Census, *Thirteenth Census of the United States: Abstract of the Census* (Washington, DC: U.S. Government Printing Office, 1913), p. 419.

14. A.C.W. Little, *Columbus County, North Carolina: Records and Recollections* (Whiteville: Columbus County Commissioners, 1980), p. 348.

15. Lee, *The Lower Cape Fear,* pp. 150–51.

16. Ms. Carolina, interview with the author, 1982. The names of all interviewees herein are fictitious.

17. Ibid.

18. Jill Henning, "The Craft of Identity: Quilting Traditions in the Waccamaw Sioux Tribe" (M.A. thesis, Department of Folklore, University of North Carolina, Chapel Hill, 1995).

19. Ms. Jossie, interview with the author, 1983.

20. Dolores Janiewski, "Sisters Under Their Skins: Southern Working Women 1880–1950," in Joanne V. Hawks and Sheila L. Skemp, eds., *Sex, Race, and the Role of Women in the South* (Jackson: University Press of Mississippi, 1983), pp 13–35.

21. Ms. Carolina, interview with the author, 1982.

22. Mr. Bill, interview with the author, 1983.

23. Wood, *Southern Capitalism,* pp. 104–5.

24. Ibid., p. 116.

25. Ransom and Sutch, *One Kind of Freedom,* p. 197; Wood, *Southern Capitalism,* pp. 118–19.

26. Mr. Joe, interview with the author, 1983.

27. Ibid., 1984.

28. Ms. Carolina, interview with the author, 1983.

29. Information on infant deaths is drawn from the U.S. Bureau of the Census, Manuscript Schedules, Columbus and Bladen Counties, North Carolina, 1900.

30. Records of the Bureau of Indian Affairs, Record Group 75, Waccamaw File, 1949–50, National Archives, Washington, DC.

31. Quoted in Jeanne Farris, "A Community Reaches Back to Its Ancestors," *Coastwatch,* September–October 1992, p. 19.

32. *Wilmington Morning Star,* December 19, 1985, p. 11A.

33. Ibid.

34. Patricia B. Lerch, "State-Recognized Indians of North Carolina, Including a History of the Waccamaw Sioux," in J. Anthony Paredes, ed., *Indians of the Southeastern United States in the Late Twentieth Century* (Tuscaloosa: University of Alabama Press, 1992), pp. 62–64.

35. Minute Book IV, March 3, 1965, Columbus County Board of Education, Whiteville, NC.

36. Patricia B. Lerch, "Powwows, Parades, and Social Drama Among the Waccamaw Sioux," in Pamela R. Frese, ed., *Celebrations of Identity* (Westport, CT: Bergin & Garvey, 1993), p. 78.

37. Quoted in Patricia B. Lerch, "Pageantry, Parade, and Indian Dancing: The Staging of Identity Among the Waccamaw Sioux," *Museum Anthropology* 16(2) (1992): 27–34.

38. Quoted in Lerch, "Powwows," p. 80.

39. Patricia B. Lerch and Susan Bullers, "Powwows as Identity Markers: Traditional or Pan-Indian?" *Human Organization* 55(4) (1996): 390.

40. Michael A. Lewis, "Welcome," in *Waccamaw Siouan 26th Annual Powwow, North Carolina Indian Heritage Month Kick-Off, October 18–19, 1996* (Bolton, NC: WSDA, 1996), p. 3.

MAKING
A LIVING

4

Race, Class, and Intimacy in Southern Households

Relationships Between Black Domestic Workers and White Employers

Mahnaz Kousha

omestic household service typically brings together women of contrasting social positions for work that is distinctive in its site and tasks. Elite women, most commonly white and middle or upper class, employ less privileged women, often of a subordinated racial and/or ethnic group, to carry out the gendered household duties for which all women in the United States tend to be responsible.[1] In short, some women pay other, less privileged women to do stigmatized "women's work." Whether cleaning toilets, cooking dinner, ironing shirts, or pushing a baby carriage, domestic workers take care of many basic personal needs of members of the household where they are employed.

In the South, the interpersonal dynamics between black domestics and their white employers have been different from those in other parts of the United States.[2] The history of explicit, codified subordination of African Americans paradoxically has permitted greater closeness—emotional, psychological, physical—between blacks and whites in Southern households. Unlike their Northern counterparts, the Southern white women who employ black domestics have not needed to engage in rituals of social distance or persistently assert their authority in order to establish their superiority;

until very recently, white supremacy was so pervasively required and enforced throughout the South as to be taken for granted. Further, the racialized political economy of the South historically meant that white employers of black domestics included not only elite but also working-class women whose financial status was not so different from that of the black domestics. Finally, shared aspects of Southern culture, from food to religion to elaborate racial etiquette, also drew together black domestics and their white employers. Thus, being "closer in class and culture, operating within a clearly defined system of social and racial inequality . . . Southern black and white women developed a kind of mistress/servant relationship that was psychologically satisfying, to some degree, to both groups of women."[3]

Gender conventions, like so much else in the South, have been highly racialized in ways that also figure in the domestic-employer relationship. Elite white women traditionally have rested their delicacy—both symbolically and materially—on the more sturdy image and hard labor of black women who took care of their households. Rigid gender constraints that persisted well after World War II, combined with race and class privilege, meant that many elite white Southern women spent a substantial portion of their married lives confined in their homes. In wealthier households, one of the few adults with whom they had frequent, regular contact on a daily basis was their black domestic worker. In some cases, elite white women became emotionally dependent on their domestics, making them into personal confidantes who were exposed to the most intimate details of their employers' lives.

As a result, domestic service in the South has not been limited to cleaning, cooking, or child care but has included a hidden "emotional labor" wherein workers were compelled to respond to their employers' emotional needs. Arlie R. Hochschild's research is relevant in this regard. She sees women as a subordinate social stratum involved in emotional work that enhances the status and well-being of others.[4] Such work "requires one to include or suppress feelings in order to sustain the outward countenance that produces the proper state of mind in others."[5] Although this unseen emotional labor is crucial to performing many tasks, it is not recognized as "real labor." As Hochschild asserts, "low-status people—women, people of color, children—lack a status shield to protect them against the poor treatment of their feelings. They become the complaint department, the ones to whom dissatisfaction is fearlessly expressed. Their own feelings tend to be treated as less important."[6]

Representing a subordinate social stratum, African American household workers in the South were involved in enhancing the status and psychological well-being of their white employers while suppressing their own feelings of fear, anger, and dislike. They indeed functioned as "complaint departments," listening to mistresses, children, and the elderly in the family. Because their race and occupational status did not grant them any power to intervene or right the wrongs committed by those more powerful, they witnessed abusive family relationships and unhappy marriages while keeping their thoughts to themselves.

This chapter explores the different strategies that private household workers chose to use to handle this emotionally intimate yet socially distant relationship with their employers. My research on twenty-four domestics and employers suggests that, while some domestics chose to maintain their distance and stay emotionally detached, others became close to their employers and willingly acted as consolers, doctors, and confidantes. In other words, from the domestics' perspective, their emotional relationships with their white women employers ranged from strong attachment to detachment. Their choice of how to define this relationship depended on the individual characteristics of both women and the dynamics of the white family. These emotional strategies were not mutually exclusive: in one family the worker may have maintained a detached attitude toward the employer, but may have become attached to the children or the elderly. In another family, she may have established close ties to the white woman.

Although at each extreme apparently opposite, these emotional strategies represented attempts to maintain personal integrity and assert a measure of power in a relationship of domination. For the detached group, claiming to avoid emotional closeness with the employer and her family functioned as a statement of independence and integrity. These domestics were available for their employers, but they defined their job as a means to an end. It must be noted, however, that maintaining distance required hard work from these women, especially when they had been with their employer for many years. The second group claimed not only to love their employers but also to share all their life stories and hardships with them. They testified to a loving and mutual relationship, thereby asserting the significance of their own role and work.

White female employers, for their part—however much they acknowledged emotional ties to black domestic workers—never described the relationship in mutual or egalitarian terms. The intimacy of their revelations and conversations as women took place, for them, within the rigid hierarchies of race and class. Any suggestion that this emotional relationship constituted a "friendship" trespassed on their race and class privilege and evoked counterassertions of social and emotional distance. How African American domestic workers responded to the demand for their emotional labor, and how they and their white employers retrospectively defined the emotional component of their work relationship in Southern households, is the topic of this chapter.

Methodology

This study is based on twenty-four oral interviews with two groups of Southern women in Kentucky: twelve African American female household workers and twelve white female employers. The women ranged in age from sixty-two to eighty-two years old. The white women were from the middle and upper-middle classes, whereas their employees were working class. In order to locate potential subjects, I contacted women involved in community work and in oral history programs in addition to the managers of several retirement and nursing homes. All interviews were conducted during 1988–89.

All of the black women began work in the 1930s, when they were young and still in secondary school. Some began to work as domestics when they were as young as twelve. The majority remained in private household work throughout their years of paid employment. When the job options available to black women began to expand in the postwar era, three of the black respondents quit domestic service and secured clerical jobs in the public sector. At the time of the interviews, three of the black women continued to work part-time as household workers and two held full-time government jobs; the others had retired.

The white women I interviewed lived in three retirement homes. The majority of this group were widows, except for one woman who lived with her husband in the retirement home and one who had never married. Of the twelve white women, ten were full-time homemakers. The single woman had held a full-time university position; one other informant had started her own business while maintaining her family. Four of the white women indicated that they had held part-time jobs before their marriage, but matrimony had brought an end to their careers. The other six women did not indicate any employment outside of the home.

Strategies of Detachment: "I Will Leave If the Grass Is Greener on the Other Side of the Street"

Private household workers inevitably learn personal information—in some cases, innermost family secrets—in the course of their employment in other people's homes.[7] Witnessing interpersonal dynamics, love affairs, frictions, and abuses (both physical and emotional) literally comes with the territory. The physical structure of the house (for example, sleeping arrangements) communicates information about the family's habits and interactions. The household worker may not be interested in knowing the intimate details of her employer's life, but they are nonetheless revealed when she enters her employer's private domain. She cannot close her eyes to what she cleans; she cannot shut her ears to what she hears. Further, many employers consider private household workers to be harmless; they may even treat such workers as "invisible" and make little effort to conceal from them potentially embarrassing information about their home lives.[8]

An example comes from Toni Jones, sixty-seven years old at the time of our interview, who eventually quit domestic service to work in a hospital. While employed as a domestic, she recognized that one of her employers had a drug problem simply by cleaning her bedroom. Jones recalled the incident:

> She had days she would be in bed sick, shut off in her room. She'd be sick a couple days and I'm finding this very strange. What's wrong, you know, we don't see her? She doesn't have to come out if she doesn't want to, but this is a young woman, this woman is only thirty-eight. I didn't know whether she was living or what. So I'd go and knock on the door, 'cause it would scare me, and see if I could do anything. But then when I was cleaning her purses, [in] almost every one of them I found a bag of pills. And, of course, what can I do? And I thought, this is what it is.

In addition to identifying her employer's drug addiction, Jones also concluded that the husband encouraged his wife's drug dependency. Although she claimed to maintain a detached attitude toward her employer, Jones was nonetheless disturbed by the unequal gender relationships in this particular family, commenting that "she's the good wife behind her husband. She is the good woman that is in the background and that rubbed me wrong because . . . that's a second-class position."

Some white women employers add to the information that domestics inevitably acquire by discussing intimate aspects of their personal lives and feelings. The employer's willingness to disclose private information is not only a function of the domestic's familiarity but also her inferior social position. Allowing friends, neighbors, or relatives access to information about family dynamics or personal feelings could be harmful to one's ego and self-esteem, or even dangerous to one's social position, but sharing it with a domestic is not considered a threat. Domestics are not part of the family or the employer's race- and class-defined social circle; moreover, they may be fired. If a domestic's comments about her employer were made known, they could be easily refuted because of the domestic's lack of power in her employer's social circles. Not therefore perceived as a threat, a domestic worker is a person to listen, share, and talk with, but not necessarily someone to listen to or consult on a problem. Thus, a domestic is a perfect "complaint department" for an employer.

Sometimes the mere presence of a domestic, the fact that she is coming to work, can be a pleasant part of the employer's day. Particularly for those Southern white women who were isolated in their homes, domestic workers were important links with the outside world, with other human beings. The arrival of the household worker broke the monotony and silence of the "big house." Maggie Billings, a sixty-eight-year-old part-time household worker, described her morning routine with one employer:

> In the mornings, when I'd go there, she was the nicest thing, she would say, "Come on in, come in, I'm waiting for you. I got the coffeepot on and I made us some little cheese bits" or whatever, you know, little cakes. She'd have set out places on the table and I would sit there and she would talk and tell me the scoop. . . . Honey, you hear a lot of stories. They tell you everything. I would look at my watch sometimes and it would be twelve o'clock. And I hadn't even started to work. And then sometimes, she would sit there and talk to me until one o'clock and then say, "You can just clean up the kitchen and then go." And pay me.

This self-disclosure is not necessarily reciprocal. The white employer has no comparable access to direct information about the black domestic's family life or personal feelings, although she may seek to gain it. Other studies have depicted the strong tendency of employers to feel free to inquire about their domestic's private life.[9] Because of their privileged race and class standing, employers may see it as their right to ask about such details while the same right—that of questioning their employers— is denied to the domestics. Domestics often tend to preserve their privacy by trying to change the topic of conversation, leaving the room, not telling the truth, or simply confronting the employer. Thus, whatever knowledge the employer may gain through questions and conversations is both limited and conditional. It is limited because it is the kind of information that the employer is interested in having. It is conditional because securing the information depends upon the domestic's willingness to share her private life.

Martha Poole, a seventy-year-old woman who was still working part-time at the time of our interview, described herself as a household worker who tried to maintain her own privacy and emotional distance from her employers. Nonetheless, she had stayed with the same family for thirty years because they treated her fairly. During summers and at Christmas, when the white family was in New England, Poole was paid so she did not have to look for a new job. She knew many intimate details of her employer's life. Some of this information was gathered by simply being in the household for a long period of time; other knowledge came from conversations with her employer. When asked if she in turn opened up to her employer and talked about her family, Poole said, "No, I never did; it wasn't their business. They volunteered to do that [talk with me] on their own; I didn't ask them for it."

These domestic workers described numerous examples of abusive marriages among their employers; their stories suggest that many of the elite white women for whom they worked experienced isolation and unhappiness in their families and turned to their female domestic workers for solace. Poole, for example, recalled many such stories about her multiple employers. One was about a mistress who "was very nice." In Poole's words:

> They had money. But he gave her five dollars a week to spend. She told me about it. She said, "He only gives me five dollars a week." The husband was in a car business and he'd bring her a new car every year. And then at the end of the year if anything happened, if she didn't do something that he thought she should do, he'd send and get the car and make her walk all over the town. And she would just cry. She couldn't leave him because, "Well, he told me that if I left him he would pay people to testify that I wasn't a fit mother and take the children away from me."

Poole added, "Which he could have because he was rather mean. I have seen him sit down and eat his food at the table and not say a word to her. It was a very unhappy couple."

Poole knew not only everyday details of this family's life but also many of its private aspects. The house was divided into two sections: three bedrooms on one side were occupied by the wife and children, and the two bedrooms on the other side were for the husband's winter and summer use. Poole continued: "If he came home and something was wrong or out of place on his end of the house, he would raise holy hell. Everything had to be just right for him, but for her and the children, anything would do."

Poole also recounted stories of two other employers who had unhappy marriages. One employer expressed her happiness after her husband's death. Poole recalled:

> When she got a little too much to drink, she told you all different things. She told me that she was glad when that son of a bitch died. She said, "When he was sick I had to sit by his bed the whole time and I made that damn rug and I'm just as sick of it as I can be." She also said, "I couldn't come out and say good morning to none of my help, he'd get jealous." Her meals had to be served up there in the room with him.

Another employer thought of her husband as "the meanest man that God ever made. He held a gun on me one night all night long and dared me to move."

Maggie Billings also related tales of unhappy marriages. One employer explained that she refused to travel with her husband because he wanted her to remain in the hotel room. Billings recalled that the woman told her:

> "I used to travel with my husband and I got tired of staying in the hotel room. I would go down to the lobby and sit there and read and watch people." She said one time she went down there and sat in the lobby and her husband came in and he pitched a fit about her being in the lobby. He didn't want her down there where other men could see her. She said, "Maggie, I didn't do a thing, but I went upstairs and I packed my trunk and I came home and I haven't been to no place with him [since]."

After a few moments of silence Billings added, "She was real nice, a real lovely person, just as nice as she could be."

Private household workers like Maggie Billings, Martha Poole, and Toni Jones became listeners and observers in a one-way relationship with their employers. They played the role of "best friends" and confidantes while not benefiting from the status and equality associated with these positions. They were treated as insiders but expected to act as outsiders. They were talked to, but were not expected to initiate a conversation or offer their opinions.

Their response to this demand for their emotional labor was complex. Their narratives often emphasized their employers' unhappiness and emotional neediness, and thereby magnified the significance of their own role; at the same time, their refusal to reciprocate with personal self-disclosure reinforced their self-depiction as strong and emotionally self-contained. They did not share their life stories or experiences in part because they knew their status did not provide them with relationships based on equality and mutual respect; not sharing information was a means of demonstrating their insight and power. They remained mysterious and unknown, and could, as a consequence, feel intact. "Sticking to a work basis" enabled some of these women to perceive their time in white homes as merely a job and thereby sustain their personal integrity. This emotional strategy was based in part on the collective consciousness among African American household workers about how to survive in asymmetrical relationships with white employers.[10]

Even with a detached stance, however, the intimate setting carried a strong potential for attachment that the worker had to resist. She could get attached to children who were mistreated. She could come to feel sorry for the elderly who were taken for granted. She could become concerned about women employers who remained in abusive relationships.[11] It can take extraordinary effort to remain detached when one has intimate knowledge of a family. Indeed, "detached attachment" may better describe the strategy of many domestics who claimed detachment. This term was developed to describe the emotional stance of family daycare providers who must respond emotionally yet not become overly attached to the children they are paid to take care of.[12] Mildred Charlton, seventy years old at the time of our interview, expressed the ambivalence of "detached attachment" in the following passage: "It's hard to deal with the separation. That's one of the things that I found very difficult—the separation. I never built any kind of a strong relationship. I just did my work and handled it that way and didn't get myself emotionally involved in anything."

As Bonnie Thornton Dill has shown, although many African American women stayed in household service all their lives, they were capable of redefining their jobs, restructuring salient features, and maintaining their sense of self-worth and personal dignity.[13] Since most domestic workers needed a job, they often used indirect strategies to preserve it. Women such as Maggie Billings and Toni Jones responded as necessary to their employers' demands for emotional labor, but they also minimized the extent of that labor by pursuing a strategy of emotional detachment. They remained with their employer if they were treated fairly, but they left if new opportunities developed. Even Billings said, "I will leave if the grass is greener on the other side of the street."

Strategies of Attachment: "We Are the Best of Friends"

Not all private household workers claimed to stay detached. Some became loving lifetime companions to their employers. Unlike the first group, they did not merely listen to their employer's problems and feelings, they also shared their life stories. Creating a dialogue with their employers enabled this group of domestic workers to take pride in their mutual sharing and understanding.

However, mutual sharing and expressions of love did not bring genuine equality or a balance of power to this relationship. Expressions of love and caring, although admirable, still moved within the constraints of socially unequal positions—white women and black women, employers and workers. Thus, these intense interpersonal interactions did not ultimately challenge racial and class barriers. Interviews indicated that the women, especially employers, had little comprehension that their relationships rested on acceptance of the unequal power relations of class and race.

I met Mary Fine, a seventy-six-year-old retired household worker, through her former employer, Janet Rorty, whom I also interviewed. At the time of our interview, Fine was living alone in a government housing project. Very attached to her employer of fifty years, she maintained that she and Rorty were still the "best of friends." Fine described the relationship:

> When Mr. Rorty died, she [Janet Rorty] was so lonely, then we really got to be companions. Most of the day, we'd go out, we'd talk. She'd go to the office. I'd just sit at the office and read books, just being company with her. And she was lonesome and so lonely. Then when the evening comes, and I would get off of work, she would bring me home, and she would sit in the car and would talk. I wanted to get in the house, 'cause my husband was at work, and I had to have dinner ready for him. And most of the time, when he would come home, I'd still be sitting in the car . . . [laughing] . . . talking to her.

Fine perceived her former employer's marriage as abusive and wondered why Rorty missed her husband so much after his death. The children, for example, were a constant source of conflict and jealousy. Fine believed that Robert Rorty did not want his wife to love her sons more than she loved him. Fine recalled: "The boys were very fearful of their father . . . Well, I don't know, maybe because they were boys, . . . he thought that she shouldn't be so close to them, so loving to them." To Fine, the husband was jealous not only of his sons but also of his wife's friends. "She had a lot of friends when she married. But he was a person that wanted her for himself. She gave up all those friends for him, and that's why she was so lonely." Fine added that a "lot of times she [Janet Rorty] would have to really put her foot down. And sometimes take abuse 'cause he was, sometimes, he would be abusive."

For more than fifty years, Mary Fine and Janet Rorty shared many of their life experiences; each was a widow at the time of her interview. After Robert Rorty's death, Janet was left alone without the friends she had given up for him, and Fine was her chief confidante. At the time of the interview, neither could drive, so they were unable to visit each other, but they kept in touch through telephone. Fine found a young white woman to take care of Rorty's needs at the retirement home. Fine asserted, "Always I was their family. We had a wonderful relationship. . . . All these years that I worked with her, we still, we are the best of friends."

The case of Mary Fine and Janet Rorty comes close to representing a relationship based on mutual understanding and friendship. Fine expressed her love not only for Rorty but also for her sons. Rorty, for her part, said, "I loved her [Fine] very much and still do. And we talk all the time. She still knows all about me." Both women were proud of their mutual sharing and understanding.

However, while Fine believed that she was part of the family and that she and Rorty were the best of friends, Rorty saw the relationship differently. Rorty did express her love and admit that they always shared everything. Nevertheless, she was unable to repudiate her own privilege and superior race and class standing in order to claim Fine as an equal.

> Well, I don't know. It's just like somebody that comes and scrubs, and washes the dishes and everything, but we were just a little bit closer, a little bit different. She used to say that she felt like we were sisters. And I never particularly cared for her making that remark. But, she used to always tell people that she feels like she was my sister instead of my servant. I think it made her feel good.

Paradoxically, it was the race and class distance that enabled this white employer to become so intimate with her black domestic; yet, in the end, after more than fifty years together, it was also race and class that prevented her from identifying Mary Fine as a "sister" or "friend."

Like Janet Rorty, Leslie White felt great sorrow when her husband died. Betty Davidson, her household worker of many years, however, was there to help. White described the time: "After my husband died, she'd [Davidson] make an old-fashioned for me every evening before dinner. And I'd have it in the library while I watched the news. She spoiled me to death. She was very good to me."

Toni Jones, who was detached in most of her employee/employer relationships, did have one employer, Roberta Harding, to whom she became attached. Her comments about this relationship sound very much like Mary Fine's description of her friendship with Rorty. Jones recalled that Harding "was probably the closest friend I've ever had. And rarely do you meet people that, especially if you are of a different race, you can talk about anything and feel comfortable with. She was that kind of person. I felt like she was more like a sister. She appreciated me."

Jones and Harding talked about politics, school integration, the relationship between whites and blacks, their children, and men. They advised each other. However, when Jones had a job offer with better opportunities for advancement, she left her position with Harding. After working for her for twenty years, quitting was not easy. Jones recalled: "I had been there so long. I remember when I told her and it hurt so bad. I thought about it a long time before I got to tell her that I was going to be leaving." Until Harding died four years later, Jones called and maintained their contact.

Mildred Charlton, despite her claims to "detached attachment," believed that she met some of her best and most lasting friends when she worked as a domestic. She worked for one family for four years, long enough to save money and go to college. She kept in touch with them and believed that her employer was probably the best friend she ever made in her life; however, she realized the limitations of this relationship and knew that, while she would use the word "friend" to describe her employer, the employer would not reciprocate. She was quick to explain that her former employer's family saw friends as those in their own social circle: "They might talk about how much they love me or that sort of thing, but I don't think, I can't think of an instance where the word 'friend' has been used."

These domestic workers experienced the demand for emotional labor from their employers, but they chose to respond quite differently from the first group. Rather than claiming emotional distance and detachment, they reciprocated their employer's self-disclosure with revelations and intimate information of their own. Although in one sense opposite from a strategy of detachment, reciprocity endeared them to their employers, giving them a different but very important source of emotional power in this otherwise unequal relationship. A strategy of attachment allowed them to redefine emotional labor as friendship, and thereby assert equality with their white, class-privileged employer.

This definition of the employer-domestic relationship as a friendship was not advanced by any of the employers, however, even those who acknowledged strong attachment, even love, for their domestics. The lopsided nature of the relationship was evident even after employment had ended in the pattern whereby the women maintained contact. Among these twenty-four women it was usually the domestic who took the initiative and kept in touch with the employer. In other words, the person with less social power made the telephone calls. The unequal nature of race/class relations seemed to place the favorite household worker in an everlasting state of emotional labor, while it entitled the white employer to enjoy regular phone calls from her former employee, being reminded that she is still loved. Former employers only called when the favorite domestic had missed a few calls.

Through revelations of personal feelings and problems, the vulnerability of their white female employers became known to these black domestic workers. This sharing, however, did not bring a balance of power between the two women. White women characterized their household workers as "my right hand," "the best domestic," "the ideal help," and "my jewel." They did not call them "sister" or "friend." Race and class boundaries, enforced in these cases by white employers, counteracted the potential for interpersonal egalitarianism, or friendship, that some of the black domestic workers sought to assert.

Conclusion

Cooking dinners, scrubbing floors, washing dishes, and performing other physical tasks are not the only demands of domestic service. In Southern households, domestic workers have also been called upon to perform extensive emotional labor. Although other research has focused on the emotional relationship of black domestics to white children, this study examined the interaction between adult women—white employers and black domestics.[14] The findings suggest that, in response to their employers' demands for emotional labor, these domestics engaged in emotional strategies ranging from detachment to attachment; regardless of where it was located on this continuum, each strategy functioned as a claim to emotional integrity and social power in a relationship of inequality.

Elite white Southern households, dependent for their very existence on the hierarchies of race, class, and gender, were the all-important context for these interactions between black domestic workers and their white employers. The paradoxical nature of these subordinations both defined these women in relationship with each other and at the same time drove them apart. Although some of the domestics sought to transcend structural inequalities through individual claims to friendship, none of the employers was able to reciprocate. Elite white women's race and class privilege prevented them from claiming black domestics as equals, but did not obviate their own gendered subordination; indeed, insofar as many were dependent, financially and otherwise, on abusive husbands, their enjoyment of privilege rested on acceptance of their own subordination. Their function within the microcosmic setting of their own households was thereby contradictory: on one level victims, they were also beneficiaries and enforcers of the larger system of social inequality in the South.

Notes

1. See David Katzman, *Seven Days a Week* (New York: Oxford University Press, 1979); Judith Rollins, *Between Women: Domestics and Their Employers* (Philadelphia: Temple University Press, 1985); Susan Tucker, *Telling Memories Among Southern Women: Domestic Workers and Their Employers in the Segregated South* (Baton Rouge: Louisiana State University Press, 1988).

2. See Katzman, *Seven Days;* and Rollins, *Between Women.*

3. Rollins, *Between Women,* p. 220.

4. Arlic R. Hochschild, *The Managed Heart: Commercialization of Human Feelings* (Berkeley: University of California Press, 1983).

5. Ibid., p. 7.

6. Ibid., p. 181.

7. See Tucker, *Telling Memories;* Elizabeth Fox-Genovese, *Within the Plantation Household: Black and White Women of the Old South* (Chapel Hill: University of North Carolina Press, 1988).

8. See Rollins, *Between Women,* for a revealing discussion of domestics' "invisibility" to their employers.

9. See Katzman, *Seven Days;* Bonnie Thornton Dill, "Making Your Job Good Yourself: Domestic Service and the Construction of Personal Dignity," in Ann Bookman and Sandra Morgan, eds., *Women and the Politics of Empowerment,* (Philadelphia: Temple University Press, 1988), p. 50; Dill, "'The Means to Put My Child Through': Child-Rearing Goals and Strategies Among Black Female Domestic Servants," in La Frances Rogers Rose, ed., *The Black Woman,* (Beverly Hills: Sage Publications, 1980), p. 118.

10. See Dill, "The Means"; Victoria Byerly, *Hard Times, Cotton Mill Girls: Personal Histories of Womanhood and Poverty in the South* (Ithaca, NY: ILR Press, 1986); and Tucker, *Telling Memories.*

11. See Dill, "Making Your Job Good"; Mahnaz Kousha, "African American Private Household Workers, White Employers, and Their Children," *International Journal of the Sociology of the Family* 25(2) (Autumn 1995): 67–89.

12. Cynthia K. Nelson, "Mothering Others' Children: The Experiences of Family Day-Care Providers," *Signs* 15(3) (1990): 586–605.

13. Dill, "Making Your Job Good."

14. Ibid.; Kousha, "African American Private Household Workers."

5

Women, Restructuring, and Textiles

The Increasing Complexity of Subordination and Struggle in a Southern Community

Cynthia D. Anderson and Michael D. Schulman

I n the early twentieth century, the Southern textile industry's labor force, recruited from impoverished farms, was overwhelmingly white and unskilled.[1] Many white women worked in the textile mills, and, like their male counterparts, labored for low wages and long hours in these hot, noisy workplaces. Mill villages, while often a step up from the hardships of farming, were dominated by paternalistic mill owners who attempted to control their workers by integrating work and community life into a single system of deferential social relations.[2] Mills were typically located in rural areas where the company constructed and owned the surrounding town, thus controlling the political, social, and economic spheres of activity. Company managers and owners sought to orchestrate village social life, providing housing and welfare activities and sponsoring community organizations. The dominant ideology within the mill village portrayed workers and owners as organically bound together into a single "family."[3]

Despite the pervasiveness of paternalistic control, female and male textile workers developed a comradeship at work and in the social life of the community that provided them with the solidarity needed for labor resistance. As evidenced

91

by mobilizations during the 1920s, the General Strike of 1934, and recent unionization attempts, mill workers have not been passive victims of oppressive rule. Rather, they have exhibited significant amounts of solidarity, intraclass cohesion, cultural autonomy, and agency.

Historians have produced a great amount of scholarly material on the history of Southern mill villages and the lives of female textile workers.[4] However, the current struggles of Southern textile women seem relatively neglected in comparison to the focus on the earlier industrialization era. Perhaps the current preoccupation with the effects of global economic restructuring has led scholars to assume that employed Southern women are either high-end professionals battling the glass ceiling, service workers burdened with the double day, or members of Third World communities fighting sweatshops and global labor sourcing. In short, while Southern female textile workers may no longer be hidden from history, their presence in contemporary discussions of class, race, and gender seems obscured by the apparent logic of the emerging global economy.

Global economic restructuring has indeed altered the work, family, and community life of women textile workers, but it has certainly not eliminated such women from the South. Their communities display outward vestiges of the old system of paternalism. Mill houses, uniformly painted white, still surround the factories. Mill owners' names remain visible on the dedication plaques of recreation centers, high schools, and libraries. However, mill villages have become incorporated towns, where the textile industry may no longer be the chief employer. Regional economic diversification has brought new industries and jobs to the piedmont of Virginia, North Carolina, South Carolina, and Georgia, areas that were once the heart of the Southern textile industry. Diverse people from other regions of the United States and even the globe move into these areas, find employment in mills and other workplaces, and permanently alter local cultural dynamics and community life.

Global restructuring also entails transformations in the economic and social organization of the textile industry itself. Family-based firms merge into multinational conglomerates. Gone is the paternalistic mill owner who sought to preside over his company town. Plant shutdowns, modernization, and computerization accompany the corporate reorganization. The local mill, if it still exists, uses new technologies and labor processes, resulting in significant job losses, intensified work effort, fluctuating wages, and radically altered relationships among workers.

How have major transformations in the textile industry altered the work relations and community life of women textile workers in the South? The purpose of this chapter is to answer this question by drawing upon results from a multilevel case study of a textile community and its associated firm in North Carolina. Our analysis stresses the embeddedness of women workers in a web of social sites and relationships—their households, their local community, the dominant firm, the U.S. textile industry, and the global economy. In particular, we explore the changing dynamics of intraclass relations as shaped by the reorganization of the firm, the workplace, and the community.

The Case of Fieldcrest Cannon

The firm selected for this extended case study, Fieldcrest Cannon, is especially appropriate for analyzing the social consequences of restructuring in the community and workplace. Cannon Mills, established in 1887, was a stereotypical paternalistic employer that provided workers with mill housing in the unincorporated town of Kannapolis, North Carolina. The town developed as a result of the aspirations of James Cannon, an early Southern entrepreneur who built a city around his industrial plant.[5] From 1905 to 1910, he bought farmlands and spent thousands of dollars (in the form of donations, loans, and gifts) to build mills, houses, churches, stores, schools, and buildings for local businesses. Workers, recruited from nearby farms, lived in white clapboard houses owned by Cannon. The houses surrounded the mill in a circle, a spatial organization that facilitated travel to work and close supervision at all times. All the mills were located within a twenty-mile radius of one another, and the CEO's office was only a few steps away from Plant Number 1, allowing extremely close supervision. Power relations in the mills were also reflected in the spatial organization of the county: workers lived in the unincorporated town of Kannapolis, while owners and managers lived in the nearby town of Concord, the county seat.

In 1921, ownership of the Cannon mills passed to Charles Cannon, the son of James. Known as "Mr. Charlie," he ran the company for the next fifty years. During this period, Cannon Mills maintained its dominant position in the U.S. towel market, regularly producing half of all towels purchased. The economic success of Cannon Mills was due to a combination of paternalism, control of workers on the job, technologically efficient production practices, and state repression. The firm led the industry by vertically integrating production, from the cotton spinning to the finished product.[6] Cannon was also a leader in developing new products for the home furnishings segment of the textile industry.

Paternalism was embedded in the civic and economic organization of the community. As an unincorporated town, Kannapolis had no mayor, town council, or legal charter. Cannon Mills paid for the community's police and fire services, and was responsible for its water and sewage system, trash collection, and street maintenance. The company also owned approximately 1,600 houses that it rented to mill employees. Cannon owned virtually all the property within the one-square-mile business district.[7] Described by a community leader informant as a "benevolent dictator" and as the "daddy of the town" by a worker informant, Cannon would not allow any other industry into the area. A worker who violated the "family" norms of the community (e.g., by public drunkenness) could be fired and evicted from his or her company home. When traditional paternalistic control failed to prevent worker protest or mobilization, state power could be called upon to restore order. For example, the state militia was used to suppress strikes in 1921 and 1934.

In 1982, Cannon family members sold the firm to David H. Murdock. A California corporate raider, Murdock altered work rules, closed plants, modernized technology, and raided the company pension fund.[8] A bitter unionization struggle followed, and, in a 1984 National Labor Relations Board (NLRB) election, the union was defeated. Murdock sold his interest in Cannon to Fieldcrest that same year, and the mills in Kannapolis are now part of Fieldcrest Cannon. A second unionization drive culminated with a narrow defeat in 1991 in another NLRB election, although the results are being contested through litigation over charges of unfair labor practices. Changes in technology, labor processes, and work rules have continued. Fieldcrest Cannon has closed several antiquated mills in Kannapolis while building a state-of-the-art towel manufacturing facility in Alabama. The number of people employed in the mills around Kannapolis has declined from approximately 22,000 in the 1970s to approximately 7,200 in 1994.[9]

Today, Fieldcrest Cannon (based in Eden, North Carolina) is a leading designer and producer of a wide variety of home textiles, including sheets, blankets, comforters, and towels. Its products are sold to chain stores, department stores, catalog companies, warehouse clubs, home furnishing stores, and mass merchants, as well as other retail, institutional, government, and contract customers under private labels. As of the late 1990s, the firm had eighteen plants in the Southeast, two of which are in Kannapolis, and several more in the immediate labor market area. Although it is close to Charlotte, North Carolina, Cabarrus County, in which Kannapolis is located, historically has seen limited development of large-scale manufacturing, because Cannon Mills controlled the local labor supply. Fieldcrest Cannon is still a key employer in the community, but new service and manufacturing jobs have appeared in the post Cannon era. The labor market area has expanded in recent decades to include the major metropolitan area of Charlotte; workers commute in and out of the adjacent towns, providing the region with a larger, more flexible labor supply. No longer isolated in a mill village, members of the Kannapolis community are entwined in a wider network of diversified relationships and opportunities.

From Company Town to Global Village: Contemporary Kannapolis

Global economic restructuring has redefined and expanded the labor market around Kannapolis and the Fieldcrest Cannon mills. No longer an isolated, insular community governed by paternalism, Kannapolis is now integrated into a complex regional network of jobs, housing, and commuting. On the one hand, the end of a once tightly controlled labor market should benefit workers by providing a variety of new employment opportunities. On the other hand, the paternalistic community services (recreation, medical care, loans, housing, etc.) provided by the dominant firm no longer exist. Current workers face multiple needs and dilemmas—elderly parents who need care, insufficient income, layoffs, and unemployment—without this paternalistic cushion, at a time of shrinking social provision from government.

Other trends are similarly contradictory. Fewer textile jobs exist due to mergers, plant closings, and automation, but a greater number of job alternatives exist in the local area. For some, higher earnings can be obtained in manufacturing jobs in Cabarrus County. Opportunities for better jobs also exist in the Charlotte–Mecklenburg region, and many residents commute via the interstate. Economic growth and diversification have brought new people to this area, however, including those from racial and ethnic populations other than the traditional black and white, who join longtime residents in seeking employment. Job competition, plus inadequate transportation, child care or other problems, may keep longtime Kannapolis residents from taking advantage of new opportunities. For them, jobs in the immediate area paying below national averages are the alternative.

Economic restructuring thus entails profound social reorganization. Gone is the homogeneity of the company town. Neighbors in the working-class communities of Kannapolis do not necessarily work in the same industry, much less the same workplace; they may commute in different directions on the interstate. Similarly, those who work side by side in the mills of Fieldcrest Cannon may be from different towns and different racial and ethnic groups, and may even speak different languages. Gone is the density of relationships, the multiple overlapping ties, that once bound white mill workers together in the singular "occupational community" of the company town.

Economic restructuring is also evident in the mills of Fieldcrest Cannon, where women workers face the similarly contradictory trends of both new opportunities and hardships. Recently introduced automated machinery relieves workers of certain tasks; however, "stretch-outs," in which workers are responsible for increasing numbers of machines and/or jobs, are commonplace. The new management practice of organizing workers into teams disrupts traditional work relations and patterns of solidarity, but also tends to dismantle former inequities and distinctions based on gender. Regional economic diversification generates alternative job possibilities, but the decline in real wages necessitates multiple jobs and intensifies productivity pressures on those paid on a piece-rate basis. Kannapolis residents may now enjoy a diverse range of cultural and social activities in places like Charlotte, but twelve-hour shifts leave little time and energy for recreation, family life, or community involvement.

The remainder of this section describes these multiple, contradictory trends in work relations and the labor process at Fieldcrest Cannon. We utilize data from in-depth interviews with women textile workers, many of whom started their employment during the Cannon family era, to describe the changes in their daily work. Our analysis stresses the implications of these changes for intraclass relationships among workers in the contemporary textile industry.

Today, the production of textiles is becoming increasingly automated, but for women textile workers, this does not necessarily mean the alleviation of their workload. The economic logic of automation is to increase productivity, lower costs, and—in order to meet retailers' demands in a volatile and competitive global market—maximize flexibility. Corporate managers deploy new information technologies to facilitate a shift toward continuous processing, which is better able to respond to rapid changes in fashion and consumption patterns. Computerization, electronic control, and automation also reduce the number of textile workers needed and thereby lower labor costs.[10] For the workers who remain, however, these innovations often mean the intensification of work: they are responsible for multiple jobs and increased demands, all to be accomplished at a quickened pace.

What exactly does automation do to the production process? In general, the process is shortened as nonvalue-added steps are removed. A simple example involves doffing, the task of unloading yarn from machines and moving it to different locations throughout the plant. Doffing was once a separate job assignment performed by specialized workers. Today, one element of the doffer's job has been replaced by automatic transport systems that do not require human labor. The remaining aspects have been absorbed by other workers, whose job demands are thereby increased.

Diane,[11] a white woman who had twenty-five years in the mills, offers an example of how the elimination of doffers is associated with changes in the working conditions of clerks, whose sole responsibility in the past was making orders and overseeing the placement of goods on trucks for distribution. Today, clerks are also required to weigh the goods and physically take them to packing, for there are no longer doffers to carry the goods. They now are also expected to complete up to one hundred orders per night, a dramatic increase from previous expectations of twenty to thirty orders per night.

Fieldcrest Cannon's drive to compete in the global market leads not only to automation, but also to other production changes with direct implications for workers on the shop floor. Sue, a sewer, reported that her job has become more difficult as the firm has expanded sales of washcloths to Mexico. Trade regulations require multiple labels for brand and content information in the appropriate language; workers must now sew new labels (in Spanish for the Mexican markets) on each individual cloth. Additionally, as consumer tastes change, retailers require different cloth styles. Today, for example, washcloths are becoming larger and thicker. As a result, Sue's output of washcloths is no longer measured by the pound but by a computerized bar-code system that keeps track of how many she completes. Style changes cause problems for workers like Sue who are "on production," that is, those who are paid a base rate with extra pay for output that exceeds the base. They are expected to sew cloths at a steady rate; however, as Sue reported, because it takes longer to sew bigger washcloths, workers' production rates (and therefore their pay) decline.

Not all workers reported negative feelings about automation. Diane works on automatic winders in the spinning room of Plant 1. She spoke fondly of open-ended spinning, saying that it was "fantastic" and that she "loved it." According to her, the newer, automatic open-ended spinners require less maintenance than the previous machines. For example, before the new spinners were installed, workers had to insert bobbins into the spinning machines, a task that required detailed attention and effort. With automation, Diane says, "all you have to do is make sure the cans of roving [strands of cotton wound onto bobbins] don't run out." Automation also eliminates much of the physical labor involved with moving the cans. Diane, using hand motions to imitate the job, described the new, automated process as "beautiful."

Diane's appreciation for the new technology should not be interpreted as romanticism, however. She noted that shifts have been changed from eight to twelve hours and the workload increased. With the elimination of doffers, spinners themselves must doff, or remove the cans of yarn from their machines. Additionally, the number of machines maintained per worker has increased. According to Diane, "they have stretched it out . . . so many frames . . . it is too much to do."

Automation falls especially hard on older women who have spent much of their working lives at Fieldcrest Cannon. One informant, a white woman in her fifties who had worked in Plant 6 for nineteen years, recounted that older women in the hemming and sewing rooms were often unable to push the stiff, heavy towels through the new, automated machines. Some of these women were only one or two years away from retirement when they were faced with these changes in the technology of their jobs. Most refused to quit, needing the income and potential retirement benefits. Several interview respondents complained that it was unfair of David Murdock, who then owned the company, to do this to women who had given their lives to the mills. They believed that the Cannons would not have treated workers in this manner.

The intensity of work effort required in the automated mills leads to high turnover among new hires, which diminishes the potential for social cohesion across different generations in the workforce. Julie, a weaver, described great turnover on the twelve-hour shifts: "It used to be hard to get jobs in the mills. Now young people don't stay because they say the work is too hard." Julie claimed the company may hire as many as two hundred new workers a month and have only ten stay. People in their twenties may work for a year or two, but usually quit and seek less demanding jobs; older workers, according to Diane, are the only ones who stay.

These older workers form a cohort that shares a common history of lifetime work in the textile industry. On Julie's shift, for example, only two workers have been with the company fewer than fifteen years. The more experience a worker acquires, the less likely she or he is to leave. Older workers' tolerance for harsh conditions should not be attributed solely to personal endurance. Retirement and health benefits, although minimal, along with the fact that age discrimination reduces other employment opportunities, contribute to older workers' limited alternatives outside the mill. What changes will occur in the production process and labor-management relations when this older cohort retires remain to be seen.

One of the most controversial changes in the labor process, with significant implications for workers' relationships to one another, is the initiation of new work groups, or teams. Conceptually, teams appear to validate and encourage worker cooperation and cohesion. In practice, however, they are associated with intensified work, increased tasks, and, in some cases, diminished pay. The entire team must "meet production" in order to receive the expected pay rate; failure to do so tends to be blamed on the inefficiency of one or more team members rather than on management's pay structure. Further, management controls the composition of each team and can use that power to disrupt the informal work groups that workers themselves create.

Each team is centralized around modules (new machines) that perform multiple functions. Some of the newest modules on the shop floor may be found in the hemming departments of towel manufacturing plants. The module performs the multiple functions of hemming, cutting, and sewing, thus collapsing into one machine what used to require four or five workers to accomplish. Lisa, who works in the hemming department, reported that in the beginning there were numerous mistakes as workers learned to operate the modules; these have lessened with time.

The combination of new technology and the reorganization of workers into teams is redefining traditional gender boundaries. Working as a team with the modules requires employees to do multiple tasks, including fixing the machines. For the reorganization to function efficiently, fixers, usually male workers who attend to looms, make adjustments, replace broken parts, and conduct general overhauls, have to be able to hem, traditionally a female job. Lisa laughed when she said that "fixers don't like this and will threaten to quit." At stake are long standing hierarchical divisions in the labor process. Will the team concept break down gender boundaries? Or will workers rebel and refuse to participate? Lisa suggested that most workers will conform to team expectations if they hope to continue working for Fieldcrest Cannon.

At the same time as managers forcibly require team "cooperation," their control over the composition of teams tends to divide workers from one another, especially around issues of pay and workload. Diane offered an example from the packing area of the plant, where four people work on a line. The job is paid on a production basis, and workers can only make "good money" if they work together. "Sometimes you'll have two experienced packers teamed with two new ones. . . . The new ones can't keep up, and the others have to do all the work." Diane reports that this job, one of the lowest paid in the company, has a great deal of turnover.

Julie, a weaver, also attested to the divisiveness and lowered morale caused by forcing workers into teams. For example, in an apparent effort to maintain high productivity, management sometimes teams two "good" weavers with a "smoker" (i.e., someone who smokes tobacco products). This causes tension as the two nonsmokers have to cover for the smoker when she or he goes outside for a cigarette break. Julie claims that this happens "every fifteen minutes" and that "we resent doing her work." It is also problematic when an entire team is not present. Snow days are the worst, and "any weaver who comes into work ends up running a whole section of one hundred or more looms."

The association of teams with intensified work effort, or the "stretch-out," is a key source of worker resistance to the concept. Julie went so far as to state the team concept would not work. She cited an example in which the company dissolved two fixing jobs to reorganize the remaining fixers into teams. The fixers now work together and have to cover for each other rather than working independently. Julie's husband is a fixer. Before the team concept, he took care of 97 looms. Now, he works on 130 with no increase in pay. If a team member takes a break or is sick, the remaining workers have to cover for him. This creates a problem not only for fixers but also for weavers. Fixers are so scattered about the plant that they often do not see flags on broken machines. Weavers may have to leave their looms to find a fixer, and then wait as long as three or four hours for the machine to be fixed. As Julie notes, all this time the weaver is not meeting production quota. As weavers fall behind, they are written up by floor managers, and their wages are cut.

Finally, some workers argue that teamwork is being utilized to lower pay. Weavers working on their own may make $9.40 to $10.40 per hour, but on a team they end up making less than $9.00 per hour. According to Julie, the wage of a weaver is directly related to that of a fixer: "Weavers are not supposed to make more than fixers even though they work harder . . . Sometimes fixers only have to fix three looms in a day so they get more breaks than weavers. Still they make more." Julie explains that the difference supposedly exists because "they [the company] have [invested] more time in a fixer." However, weavers tend to be women and fixers tend to be men; as numerous researchers report, jobs dominated by men pay more than jobs dominated by women.[12]

In sum, the introduction of modules and the shift toward teams are dramatically altering the social organization of work. No longer specialists on a single task, workers must now be responsible for several operations on a single automated machine. The reorganization of certain jobs changes their gendered definitions in ways that may benefit women textile workers. At the same time, the elimination of other jobs, combined with management expectations of increased productivity, means that women's workloads have increased. Assembled by management into teams, some women must now work with others who have different work habits and levels of experience. Pay structures on teams are "collectivized," so that failure to meet a quota results in a penalty for the entire group. It is possible that textile workers will redefine these teams as a locus of cohesion and solidarity. However, whether and how they will accept, resist, or redefine these changes are unclear. Managers, for their part, seem quite serious about the team concept. They are requiring workers to complete classes on dispute resolution and attend periodic review sessions. According to interviewees, Fieldcrest Cannon has fired workers for not complying with the rules of team organization.

A final issue, discussed in many dimensions and implications by our interviewees, is the hours that the workers spend on their jobs. Their concerns centered primarily on the increased amount of time they spend at work and the irregularity of their schedules. Not only are shifts longer, but many of the workers hold more than one job. Dual-income marriages, with both partners in the textile industry, are not a new pattern, as the Southern wing of the industry was founded on family labor. However, many individuals are now working second jobs *in addition* to their fulltime mill work. Women working in the mills also hold jobs at Hardee's, grocery stores, and WalMart; some women *also* generate income and other resources outside the formal labor market (see Chapter 6). The increase in living costs, decline in real wages, and removal of services that were once provided by the company all require intensified efforts to maintain household resources.

An additional problem that many face is the insecurity in income due to irregular work. This may arise from machinery breakdowns or from periodic layoffs driven by the vagaries of the retail market. Diane notes that when machines break down, she and her coworkers must "do odd jobs, if there is any, or get sent home." She complains that "we never know what the schedule will be . . . We can't plan for things 'cause we don't know if we'll have to work." Unreliability may also occur in the form of increased work hours. When a large order is due, the firm will demand more time from workers. For example, Sue began our interview saying she was tired because she had "been working the ten-hour shifts, seven days a week to do a big order from Wal-Mart." This may be a welcome relief for some workers, such as Julie's husband, who was working overtime in anticipation of the time he would be off during Thanksgiving.

Irregular work is not limited to erratic layoffs or machine breakdowns. Shift work for some workers now entails four twelve-hour days, followed by three days off, then three twelve-hour days followed by two days off. New schedules such as the twelve-hour shift put pressure on families, especially those raising children, in their efforts to maintain households.

It was extremely difficult to schedule an interview with a twelve-hour shift worker. After several months, we finally secured an interview with Julie. She is a member of the "sandwich generation"—she takes care of her mother and two sons, and at times, her husband. During the interview, Julie continually expressed discontent over the twelve-hour shifts and blamed them for the behavior problems of her older son, who was a high school dropout and had been in trouble with the law. She said angrily, "You [Fieldcrest Cannon] destroyed my family life with the twelve-hour shift." She said she sees her children only twenty-four hours in a week, missing ball games and school functions. She sees them from about 6:00–6:30 in the morning, long enough to feed them and see the younger son off to the school bus, and then again after 7:00 P.M., long enough to feed them again and get ready for bed. The grocery bill is "way up" because she has to buy "microwave stuff they can fix for supper." Or, she has to cook extra food on her days off. They cannot have the extended family dinners they used to have unless everybody is laid off at the same time. Julie considers herself lucky, despite new shift demands, because she has a husband to help out. However, at the time of our interview, Julie said she and her husband "don't know whether to buy Christmas or not because we don't know whether we'll have a job in January."

Our interviews with women workers at Fieldcrest Cannon suggest that the economic and technological restructuring of the Southern textile industry has profound social dimensions. Workers' relationships with one another, both on the shop floor and in their now diverse communities, are undergoing radical change. No longer cohered within the occupational community of the company town, workers are geographically dispersed and socially decentralized. Increasingly, work relations are formally structured around teams, but the divisive aspects of this reorganization seem at present to overshadow the potential for cohesion. In their communities, workers' social relationships solidify around familiar institutions—schools, churches, extended families—when they can overcome the unpredictability of irregular work and the exhaustion of twelve-hour shifts. Complicating this social landscape is a crucial additional feature, race, which we address in the next section.

Race Relations

Race looms large in the history of the Southern textile industry. Until the 1960s, textile workers in the region were racially homogeneous, overwhelmingly white.[13] Some blacks did work in segregated areas of certain mills during the nineteenth century; however, with the institutionalization of Jim Crow at the turn of the century, the textile work force became exclusively white. (The exception was a scattering of black men in menial positions.)[14] This situation persisted well after World War II, until the civil rights movement broke the industry's color bar.

Prior to their employment in the mills, black women in the area of Kannapolis typically worked as domestics, both for white mill workers and owners. For example, Mae, a black woman in her eighties at the time of our interview, worked for the Cannons as a household servant from the 1940s to 1970s. For six years she cleaned offices in the mills, but later returned to household domestic work. Her husband, who is now deceased, worked as a janitor in the mills and cleaned bathrooms during the 1940s and 1950s.

Mae recalled the rigid segregation of those years, when blacks and whites could not use the same bathrooms or eat in the same locations. Her husband was not allowed to drink out of the water fountain at the mill, so he had to carry a water bottle. Emma, a thirty-eight-year-old black woman who has lived in Kannapolis her entire life and is now an organizer for a progressive local grassroots group, also recalled stories of the segregated mills. Racial integration occurred only in the gendered space of the "smoker," where primarily men went to smoke. Emma remembered that "certain things within the plant were for men— it was mostly men—to spit in and they had sawdust in them . . . And smokers, they were these wooden boxes. They were separated by race and gender . . . to keep black men and white women separate, you know. But they were side by side."

In the years after World War II, as industrialization in the South and the expansion of "pink-collar" jobs for white women led white textile workers out of the mills, the breakdown of legal segregation allowed blacks to enter them in significant numbers.[15] Racial integration did not signify equality among workers, however. Blacks were placed in the dirtiest, most difficult and hazardous jobs. As Emma explained, "The dirty jobs were more people of color, black men. And lint type of jobs. You would go through the plants from the opening room, where they open the bale of cotton and progressively, as you went through the mill, it got whiter, and whiter, and whiter and you'd get to the very top, which was clean. . . . it was always white."

Emma was careful to point out that mill work also brought new economic opportunities for blacks, especially for those on production who "were young and fast, and could produce." Her mother, for example, was able to purchase a mill house, so Emma, her siblings, and their mother lived in "the white section of town." So, although job discrimination persisted, the experience of mill villages was not uniformly negative for blacks, especially when they were able to elevate their standard of living, the case for many after 1964.

Mae also recounted the benefits for herself and her family when production jobs in the mills became open to blacks. Currently, Mae's daughter Sue and her husband Will live next door; both are employed in the Fieldcrest Cannon mills. Sue sews wash "rags." She has worked with Cannon for thirty years and was the first black woman to work with machinery in the washcloth room in the late 1960s. Will works in the bleach room, where he takes wet towels to be dried. Will, who is from Concord, North Carolina, started with Cannon in 1952 as a janitor, worked on the cotton platform, and then moved to the bleach room in 1966.

In a process that illustrates the adaptation of old-style paternalism to the new era of race relations, both Sue and Will benefited from Mae's association with the Cannon family. In the early 1960s, Mae was asked by management to recommend a black woman to work in the wash room. Her daughter Sue received a letter offering her the job the next day. The wash room is relatively clean, and the pay is one of the best for mill jobs. Likewise, after Will married Sue, Mae spoke to Cannon about him; he was soon moved to the bleach room, where he was one of three black men among many whites. This is also a relatively clean and well-paying job.

Did tensions between black and white workers arise with the integration of the mills? Sue said no, that the white workers had been warned by management not to say anything mean. The company held a meeting instructing whites to accept the new black workers. Sue said that it was still hard for blacks, however. At first, when she walked into the wash room, the whites stopped working and lined up against the wall to watch her for ten minutes or so. She could still recall how it felt being subject to their collective scrutiny: she became extremely nervous, her stomach tied in knots.

Today, racial dynamics in the Kannapolis area are changing dramatically with the arrival of new immigrant populations, primarily Latinos. Blacks represent the "old" or established minority in contrast to these new groups. According to U.S. census data, in 1980 23.1 percent of the population of the local labor market area (LMA), a nine-county area defined by 1990 census data on patterns of commuting to work, was black. There was little change by 1990: 22.6 percent of LMA residents were black.[16] In contrast, between 1980 and 1990, the Hispanic population in the nine-county area shot up from 0.73 to 9.0 percent. Other racial minority groups represented in the LMA include Laotians, Thai, Vietnamese, and Cambodian.

This racial diversification is linked to the process of economic globalization. There is now an international market for labor, and workers move across national boundaries in search of employment. Technological and economic restructuring of certain domestic industries has been accompanied by a transformation in the racial and ethnic makeup of the labor force. In the U.S. meatpacking industry, for example, the number of immigrant, refugee, and native-born migrant workers has increased significantly since the late 1970s. The development of flexible production methods allows these workers to be easily replaced, so high turnover is less of a problem for employers.[17]

In Cabarrus County, where Kannapolis is located, recent statistics show a rapid increase in the Hispanic workforce. U.S. census estimates placed the number of Hispanics in the county at 483 in 1990. By 1995, population estimates from social service providers, county activists, and local church leaders suggested that the number had risen to at least 3,500. Most Hispanics come to the area for production line jobs. Some migrate from Costa Rica, Guatemala, Mexico, and other Latin American countries; others come from U.S. states such as Texas and New Mexico. One community leader estimated that at least 400 Latinos work at a local poultry plant in jobs that pay minimum wage.

Hispanics have also moved into the textile mills. Compared to those in the poultry plant, mill wages and working conditions represent a form of upward mobility. Hispanic workers are usually hired in the packing rooms, one of the lowest-paid jobs in the mill. However, several respondents asserted that management recently began placing the new minority employees in better jobs, even starting them at higher wages than those at which other workers, both white and black, had begun. For example, Raymond, a retired mill worker, claimed that new hires (typically Hispanics) now receive $7.25 per hour. (This figure was confirmed in a Kannapolis newspaper advertisement.) This is a significant increase from the standard $6.00 per hour at which most whites started. These new hires at Fieldcrest Cannon now go through a training program for thirty-two to thirty-six weeks, during which they are not bound to any specific production quota. Interview respondents claimed that earlier hires had a much shorter training period.

More generous treatment of new workers in an expanding, indeed internationalizing pool of labor seems economically illogical, for companies presumably could pay immigrants well below prevailing wages. Raymond, who had been active in unionization struggles, felt that Fieldcrest Cannon's new hiring policy was a deliberate tactic to "smother the union." By paying workers higher wages and giving them longer training periods, the company hopes to show that workers do not need a union. Higher wages for new hires, especially those who are "new minorities," also divides them from older employees, thereby diminishing the potential for solidarity and successful unionization. Management may also use new minority workers to heighten existing employees' fears for their job security. For example, Lisa, an established employee and known union supporter, was required to train a Hispanic male to do her job. According to Lisa, the worker had no textile experience and understood very little English. As she put it, "I was supposed to train a foreigner to learn something that had taken me twenty-six years to do." She trained him, however, and tried to teach him everything she knew. She concluded her story by saying that the new worker quit after two weeks, complaining that the job was too difficult for anyone.

Many analysts assume that global economic restructuring means the transfer of U.S. jobs and industrial plants overseas. Fieldcrest Cannon and Kannapolis represent a different form of globalization: instead of moving plants to Third World locations, Third World workers are moving to the plants. In their new-found communities and workplaces, relationships within and among these "new" minority groups, between the "new" and "old" minorities, as well as between each group and whites, are complex and fluid; they involve dynamics of racism, racial-ethnic group formation, and nationalism, in which class and gender are also implicated (see Chapter 12). For women textile workers in the South, these new racial dynamics reinforce and complicate the trends toward intraclass fragmentation.

Conclusion

Global economic restructuring is transforming the work and community life of women textile workers in the South. The old system of paternalism, embedded in the cohesive but restrictive social organization of the mill and company town, has been displaced. Corporate reorganization and transformation of the labor process, economic expansion and the formation of a multicounty labor market, population growth and racial diversification—all bring profound social consequences. Undoubtedly, some women textile workers are "winners" in this new system: the expansion of the Kannapolis labor market and the growth of new industry have created new jobs and new patterns of labor market mobility. However, those who remain in the mills find that the security of work, family, and community that they struggled to establish has been disrupted by twelve-hour shifts, reorganized production practices, and new technology. Resistance has taken many forms, including individual attempts at upward mobility and collective efforts at unionization. In early 1997, the 4th U.S. Circuit Court of Appeals in Richmond set aside the union defeat in the 1991 election, and ordered a new vote after finding that Fieldcrest Cannon had harassed and intimidated workers.[18] UNITE (Union of Needletrades, Industrial and Textile Employees) lost the August 1997 election by 369 votes (2,563 opposed versus 2,194 for union representation). In addition to continued attempts at unionization, a nonprofit group has initiated a community-organizing project in Kannapolis that seeks to attract textile workers and others through issue-based organizing.

Although the social relations of Southern textile workers seem troublingly fragmented, with the prospects for unified and successful class action increasingly remote, it is important not to romanticize the past. The company towns of the Southern textile industry were places of social cohesion, but they were also sites of intense repression, racism, gender inequality, and class exploitation. Although the diversified neighborhoods and workplaces of today's textile workers may seem racially divided and socially decentralized, they also offer expanded possibilities. No longer insulated within racially exclusive occupational communities, women workers in the Southern textile industry are now black, white, and brown, part of a global economy that, for better or worse, links them in a common class relationship.

Notes

Acknowledgments: Support for this research came from U.S. Department of Agriculture, Cooperative State Research Service, National Research Initiative (USDA/CSRS NRI) Rural Development Grant 0166485 to North Carolina State University. Additional support was received from North Carolina Agricultural Research Service. The opinions expressed are those of the authors.

1. Michael D. Schulman and Jeffrey Leiter, "Southern Textiles: Contested Puzzles and Continuing Paradoxes," in *Hanging by a Thread: Social Change in Southern Textiles* ed. by Jeffrey Leiter, Michael D. Schulman, and Rhonda Zingraff (Ithaca, NY: ILR Press, 1991), pp. 3–20.

2. Dwight B. Billings, Jr., "Religion as Opposition: A Gramscian Analysis," *American Journal of Sociology.* 96(1) (1990): 1–13; Melton Alonzo McLaurin, *Paternalism and Protest: Southern Mill Workers and Organized Labor, 1875–1905* (Westport, CT: Greenwood Publishers Corp., 1971).

3. Jacquelyn Dowd Hall, James Leloudis, Robert Korstad, Mary Murphy, Lu Ann Jones, and Christopher B. Daly, *Like a Family: The Making of a Southern Cotton Mill World* (Chapel Hill: University of North Carolina Press, 1987).

4. Jacquelyn Dowd Hall, "Disorderly Women: Gender and Labor Militancy in the Appalachian South," *Journal of American History* 73 (1986): 354–82; Hall et al., *Like a Family;* Victoria Byerly, *Hard Times, Cotton Mill Girls: Personal Histories of Womanhood and Poverty in the South* (Ithaca, NY: ILR Press, 1986); Mary Frederickson, "Four Decades of Change: Workers in Southern Textiles, 1941–1981," *Radical America* 16(November–December 1982): 27–44; Harriet L. Herring, *Welfare Work in Mill Villages: The Story of Extra-Mill Activities in North Carolina* (Chapel Hill: University of North Carolina Press, 1929); Herring, *The Passing of the Mill Village: A Revolution in a Southern Institution* (1949; reprint, Westport, CT: Greenwood Press, 1977).

5. James Moore and Lewis Wingate, *Cabarrus Reborn: A Historical Sketch of the Founding and Development of Cannon Mills and Kannapolis* (Kannapolis, NC: Kannapolis Publishing Co., 1940).

6. This highly efficient process was not present in most textile mills until after World War II. See David Barkin, "The Impact of Agribusiness on Rural Development," *Current Perspectives in Social Theory* 3(1982): 1–25.

7. C. L. Collins, "Fieldcrest Cannon," in Paula Kepos, ed., *International Directory of Company Histories*, vol. 9 (Detroit: St. James Press, 1994), pp. 213–17.

8. Rhonda Zingraff, "Facing Extinction?" in Leiter, Schulman, and Zingraff, eds., *Hanging by a Thread*, pp. 199–216.

9. U.S. Bureau of the Census, *Statistical Abstract of the United States* (Washington, DC: U.S. Government Printing Office, 1996).

10. Trevor A. Finnie, *Textiles and Apparel in the USA: Restructuring for the 1990s*, Economist Intelligence Unit Special Report No. 2632 (London: Business International Limited, 1990), pp. 64–108; authors' interview with a professor of textile management at North Carolina State University, 1995.

11. All names of interviewees are pseudonyms.

12. See for example, Donald Tomaskovic-Devey, *Gender and Racial Inequality at Work: The Sources and Consequences of Job Segregation* (Ithaca, NY: ILR Press, 1993).

13. Schulman and Leiter, "Southern Textiles."

14. Joel Williamson, *The Crucible of Race* (New York: Oxford University Press, 1984).

15. Richard L. Rowan, *The Negro in the Textile Industry* (Philadelphia: Industrial Research Unit, Wharton School, University of Pennsylvania, 1970); Chip Hughes, "A New Twist for Textiles," *Southern Exposure* 3 (1976): 73–79.

16. For comparison purposes, the nine counties identified as the 1990 LMA are used for both 1980 and 1990.

17. See Michael J. Piore and Charles F. Sabel, *The Second Industrial Divide: Possibilities for Prosperity* (New York: Basic Books, 1984); Laura T. Raynolds, "Institutionalizing Flexibility: A Comparative Analysis of Fordist and Post-Fordist Models of Third World Agro-Export Production," in Gary Gereffi and Miguel Korzeniewicz, eds., *Commodity Chains and Global Capitalism* (Westport, CT: Greenwood Press, 1994), pp. 143–62; Louise C. Johnson, "New Patriarchal Economics in the Australian Textile Industry," *Antipode* 22(1) (1990): 1–31.

18. Shannon Buggs, "Cannon Employees Reject Union," *The News and Observer* (Raleigh, NC), August 14, 1997, A1.

6

A Coalfield Tapestry

Weaving the Socioeconomic
Fabric of Women's Lives

Ann M. Oberhauser and Anne-Marie Turnage

Throughout the coalfields of central Appalachia, working-class people are engaging in alternative means of economic survival. For many, the region's endemic poverty is now worsening as tremendous job losses in coal mining diminish the historic source of employment for working-class men. In order to secure the necessities of life for themselves and their families, working-class women are not only entering the paid labor force but also turning to unregulated forms of income generation that lie outside the formal, wage-earning economy.

This chapter examines the involvement of rural, working-class women in central Appalachia in home-based work and other informal sector activities as part of their strategic response to economic restructuring. It situates these activities within the context of the informalization of work, a global phenomenon that is being extensively investigated and theorized. Utilizing both historical data and the findings from interviews with eighty-two homeworkers in rural West Virginia, the chapter illustrates the barriers to women's participation in the formal economy and the gendered dimensions of their informal income-generating activities. Of particular importance to this volume is the way in which these informal sector activities create new relationships between women from lower income households in rural areas and higher income women in urban areas.

Informalizing Work Across Cultures

The informal economy encompasses those forms of economic activity that escape regulation in a society where similar activities are regulated.[1] The broad array of alternative economic activities that are considered informal includes home-based arts and crafts production, contract work as an industrial "outsource" (producing parts and supplies for sale to companies that previously manufactured the items in-house), and self-employment. Informal activities may entail both barter and monetary exchange.

Analyses of the informal economy tend to pay particular attention to the socioeconomic and institutional contexts where these activities occur. In many developing regions of the world, for example, informal activities are carried out by the members of individual households, yet they are also interrelated with the formal national and international economies. Global restructuring has contributed to economic conditions (declining wages and increased unemployment, for example) that have forced many people in both developing and developed countries to engage in informal economic activities. In reinforcing the dynamic nature of informalization and its connection to broader socioeconomic and political structures, Manuel Castells and Alejandro Portes maintain that we need to understand it as a process rather than as an object.[2]

A growing body of literature on the informal economy examines the link between the informal economy and household survival strategies, the relationship between local informal activities and broader economic processes, and the diversity of informal income-generating activities.[3] Extensive reviews of this literature appear elsewhere and are not repeated here. Rather, in this chapter the informal sector is analyzed as an important component of economic strategies among women in semiperipheral regions such as Appalachia. Here, as in similar locations around the world, people are experiencing significant economic shifts as traditional forms of production and formal work opportunities are replaced by more flexible production methods and contingent (e.g., part-time, temporary) work.

This reorganization of production is accompanied by other social and economic dynamics that loosen the singular, formal ties between employer and employee and produce more flexible and fluid work situations.[4] Production is becoming more decentralized in terms of both control and organization.[5] The once centralized corporation, with production and workers concentrated in massive factories in a few locations, is now becoming a global network of offices and subcontractors. This vertical disintegration of firms is made possible by the practices of outsourcing, homework, and other more flexible forms of employment, which are facilitated by technological advances in communication, transportation, and production. Thus, informalization is a widespread and growing phenomenon that is both the source of and a response to the marginalization of workers brought about by more insecure forms of income generation and decentralized processes of production.

Cross-cultural studies are particularly useful in analyzing and comparing informal income-generating strategies in different geographical contexts. For example, women in rural Appalachia and Third World regions often engage in similar economic strategies that involve the informalization of work. Cross-cultural studies of the informal sector, however, often have urban biases and tend to focus on Third World regions such as Latin America, Asia, and Africa. For example, Lourdes Benería and Martha Roldan's analysis of industrial homework among economically marginalized women draws largely from research in Mexico City.[6] Other studies from Latin America demonstrate the interdependence of formal and informal sector activities in urban areas of Peru[7] and the influence of locally contingent structures on the informalization of work in Ecuador.[8] In contrast, Lauren Benton's research highlights the important, yet largely invisible, role of industrial homework in the shoe, textile, and electronics industries in rural regions of Spain.[9] An emerging body of literature recognizes that the informalization of work is not limited to developing regions, but is increasingly important in developed regions of the industrialized world as well.[10] Maria Patricia Fernández-Kelly, for example, has made significant contributions with her research on global restructuring and informalization of work among Hispanic immigrants in the United States.[11]

These analyses of alternative economic strategies in diverse cultural contexts often counter the prevalent image of informal sector workers as destitute people living on the margins of society. Instead, engaging in informal activities can be seen as a strategic economic activity among people who are active agents of change.[12] Castells, Portes and others demonstrate that in some cases unregulated income-generating activities have contributed to increased living standards among participants and rapid industrialization in certain semiperipheral regions.[13] In the Emilia-Romagna region in Italy, for example, flexible production networks include a significant amount of informal activities that rely heavily on women homeworkers. This region is noted for its artisanal tradition that has led to regional specialization in ceramics, food processing, shoe production, textile and clothing manufacture, and knitwear.[14] In recent decades, productivity, wage levels, and investment per employee have risen dramatically in this area compared to the rest of Italy.[15]

The economic restructuring and informalization of labor outlined above involve several interrelated levels (or scales) of activity and rely on gendered social relationships. Although national and global shifts in production and marketing have influenced localities and households, these broad economic changes have in turn been shaped by socioeconomic structures and dynamics at the local and household scales. This dialectical relationship is critical in analyzing the process of informalization. Additionally, gender relations and gendered divisions of labor influence the types and conditions of informal sector activities in diverse geographical contexts. Women may seek home-based work, for example, as a means of fulfilling their simultaneous and overlapping responsibilities for household income generation and caregiving. Benton reinforces this point in her analysis of the gendered nature of industrial homework and its link to household responsibilities in rural Spain.[16] Finally, analyses of economic restructuring, scale, and gender are useful in demonstrating the somewhat unique process of informalization in rural areas, given the spatial barriers, lack of social capital, and economic hardships associated with rurality. Specifically, producers in rural settings, especially women, are often isolated from markets and other producers. Inadequate social capital in the form of skills and training, coupled with reduced economic resources and access to financial capital, also affect their informal activities. For example, rural producers frequently engage in barter exchange or seek external markets to sell their goods and services.

In sum, this discussion demonstrates that the informal economy is not a rare or isolated form of income generation, but rather is inextricably bound to the dynamics of the formal economy. The informal economy has developed or expanded in response to ongoing economic restructuring in many regions of the globe.[17] This theme of interconnection also extends to the public and private spheres of work. These arenas are often presented as dichotomous, yet in reality they are closely connected, especially in income-generation strategies.[18] Finally, both the historical process of industrialization and contemporary forms of economic restructuring have depended upon the construction of distinct gender roles that have marginalized women from and within certain types of income-generating activities. The following analysis applies these conceptual themes to the central coalfields of Appalachia. We suggest that the region's history of social and economic exploitation has contributed to working-class women's contemporary marginalization and shaped their informal sector activities over time.

Women and Work in Appalachia

During the late nineteenth century, industrial capitalism penetrated central Appalachia's predominantly agricultural economy in the form of timber, oil, gas, and coal industries. Many small subsistence farmers were forced to relinquish their land to absentee corporate owners and thus became rural industrial workers.[19] Although the social and economic changes associated with the creation of an industrial labor force have received considerable attention from scholars of the region, gender relations have often been neglected.

Recent scholarship on the history of Appalachian women confirms that they were actively involved in many spheres of economic activity, including agrarian work.[20] Yet employment in the central coalfields of Appalachia includes a stark history of job segregation based on gender. As extractive industries developed within the region, production became a sphere of male domination; men directed the ownership and management of land, natural resources, technology, and capital. New jobs within the region's primary industries were considered "men's work."[21] The establishment of company towns offered limited opportunities for women to engage in waged work, but the types of jobs available stressed women's roles as caregivers and nurturers, essentializing criteria that segregated them in nursing, teaching, and domestic work.[22]

While some women engaged in waged work, the region's physical geography left many isolated in rural areas. Their engagement in the informal economy was vital in a region where employment was based upon the boom and bust cycles of extractive industries, especially coal mining.[23] Several of these informal economic activities reinforced the relationships among women of the same and different economic classes within the region. For example, many working-class women in coal camps generated income by performing domestic work such as laundering, housekeeping, and child care for more socially prominent families in the camps.[24] Others raised chickens, tended gardens, sold butter and eggs, and took in boarders for income. Recent immigrant women in the camps baked bread in communal ovens,[25] while women who were native to the region provided traditional health-care services by working as midwives as well as herbal healers.[26] Bartering for these goods and services was an important aspect of the informal sector, since many households did not have abundant access to cash.

Finally, many families in the camps lived in overcrowded and unsanitary housing. Lack of garden space meant that the only source of food for many families was the company store. The payment of wages in scrip (nonlegal tender accepted only at the company store), inflated prices, and low wages meant that many families became deeply indebted to the store.[27] The informal exchange of goods and services allowed working-class women to avoid this economic exploitation while establishing and strengthening intraclass relations within the camps.

In sum, the informal networks of production and distribution in which women participated were integrally linked to the formal market, operated within and beyond family groups, and were "based on [systems] . . . of reciprocity."[28] Women's participation in these alternative economic strategies within the coal camps reveals how the formal and informal sectors are inseparable. Although the gendered division of labor within Appalachia's primary industries often excluded women from certain types of public work, it did not prevent them from engaging in economic strategies within the public sphere of their communities.[29] Informal work, however, is not just a historical phenomenon specific to the Appalachian region's industrialization, for contemporary studies indicate that informal-sector activities remain important economic strategies.[30] The next section analyzes the relationship between contemporary economic restructuring and women's informal economic activities in Appalachia.

Gender and Home-Based Work in Rural West Virginia

The globalization of capital has contributed to the loss of jobs in manufacturing and mining and the rise of the service sector in Appalachia. The region has functioned as a layover on capital's flight to cheaper labor and resources,[31] as "industries fleeing the [U.S.] South are purchasing one-way tickets to Taiwan and other exotic destinations just as readily as they used to depart Akron, Ohio, for Opelika, Alabama."[32] The increased mobility of firms has left laid-off manufacturing workers with bleak prospects for obtaining new jobs that have similar levels of security, wages, and unionization.[33] Although residents of the region have historically been subjected to the erratic cycles of the mining industry,[34] increased capital mobility has only heightened the insecurities associated with periodic layoffs and plant closings.

As a result of the dramatic unemployment within manufacturing and mining, many residents of the area, especially working-class women, have turned to employment in the service sector and continued involvement in informal economic activities.[35] The changing composition of Appalachia's workforce is related to the gendered nature of economic restructuring within the region. Since the early 1970s, economic shifts have reduced many male-dominated positions. In West Virginia alone, nearly 70,000 jobs in manufacturing and mining were eliminated between 1979 and 1987.[36] While those jobs averaged $20,000 to $36,400 annually, they have been replaced by retail and service sector jobs that pay $13,500 to $15,000 a year and specifically target a female labor force.[37] Many women in the Appalachian coalfields are entering the paid workforce in response to mine layoffs.[38] The flexibility of work in the service sector has been especially attractive to working-class women who maintain the majority of household responsibilities. However, the positions many of these women find as secretaries, schoolteachers, waitresses, and nurses tend to offer low wages and few, if any, benefits compared to male-dominated occupations. Furthermore, service sector jobs are not readily available in the region's more rural areas.[39] The lack of social capital or social support systems in rural areas, particularly day care, often prevents women from seeking employment in those jobs that do exist. Lack of access to transportation, domestic responsibilities, inadequate job training, and lack of previous work experience also deter many working-class women in Appalachia from entering the formal workforce.[40] In response to such barriers, many of these women continue to rely on the informal sector as an important component of their household's economic strategies.

This case study examines women's home-based work in the central Appalachian coalfields, drawing from in-depth interviews with eighty-two women in West Virginia. The analysis identifies the types of work women do as well as the various reasons they choose to engage in home-based work. We argue that gender relations in the household influence women's decisions to participate in informal, home-based work and bring rural Appalachian women into contact with other women as they seek markets for their goods and services.

Numerous women interviewed in this study cite domestic responsibilities as a primary factor in their decision to work for income at home rather than engaging in formal outside employment. Household responsibilities also tend to dictate where and when women do their homework. In response to questions about how she juggles domestic work and her home-based business of designing and making costumes, Cindy[41] replied, "I can still stay with my children. I stay up later at night. . . . Like if I have a job to get done and it has to be out the next day, I'll stay up 'til four in the morning to make sure it's done. 'Cause the kids are used to me doing *their* thing. And I don't want to take away from them, so that's what I do."

Pamela is involved in a quilting cooperative and shared similar feelings about the importance of being available for her children: "I've always been able to work around my kids' schedules. I've never had to be gone, you know, away from 'em. And I don't want to start now. Teenagers need you. The jobs that I've had have usually been with them. Or, you know, I wasn't gone a long time. So, that was big for me, because I could be there when they got home." Since household tasks such as child care, cleaning, laundry and cooking typically fall on women's shoulders, female homeworkers often adjust their work schedules and activities to household demands.

The undervaluation of women's work—often by family members—is a major obstacle to raising women's material and psychological well-being. For example, it was common for family members of women who participated in this study to refer to their activities as a "hobby" or an extension of their domestic tasks. Cathy, who sews garments and crafts for sale in a local cooperative, feels as if her family regards her primarily as a housewife: "They see me as a homemaker. My husband comes home and does nothing. I feel I put in an eight-hour day, just like he does. Maybe I'm not doing the physical labor that he is, but I have mental stress. I'm doing labor. I'm working the same way."

An important factor in these women's decision to engage in homework or other informal sector activities is the barriers to formal employment that stem from their remote rural locations. Several women cited the lack of access to reliable transportation, such as private vehicles and public buses, as contributing to their decision to work for income at home. In many cases, if there is a vehicle in the household, the man uses it for his work, leaving the woman without a means of transportation.

Some of the women have lost jobs in the formal labor force due to economic restructuring. For example, Patricia describes her experience working at a textile plant in her town before it closed: "Well, basically, the past eighteen years I had worked at Kelwood. We made curtains and shower curtains for Sears. Then Sears did their thing. We did 70 percent of our business with Sears catalog." After the factory closed she began to work in her home for a knitting cooperative that was just beginning to operate in the area. She has been a knitter with the cooperative for three years, earning approximately half of her household's total income.

Despite the remote nature of many of these women's locations, informalization of work often brings women of different socioeconomic backgrounds and geographic locations into contact with one another through the buying and selling of goods and services. The exchange relationship among these women underlines the multifaceted dimensions of informalization, connecting formal and informal activities, local households and global restructuring, production and reproduction, and buying and selling commodities and services between women of different classes. The biggest markets for rural women engaged in homework are urban areas that have a larger and wealthier clientele. Several of the women interviewed for the study sold their handicrafts or agricultural goods in urban areas at festivals, farmers' markets, or craft shops.

In the case of informal work such as child care and house cleaning, women in rural or semirural areas tend to prefer urban clients who are more likely to be able to afford these services. However, they are not necessarily able to access these markets. For example, Rebecca lamented the fact of living in a rural area and not being able to charge higher rates for her typing services.

> Around here I don't think I could have gotten $2.50 a page. I don't think there is any way someone would pay me that much to do typing. People in Chicago are going to be able to command a lot more money than I am going to be able to in this area. People tell me I'm selling myself short, but I feel like when I started, I couldn't go and ask for big amounts of money.

Another woman in the southern part of West Virginia who bakes cakes and caters parties commented that she could do better business in a higher income area. She is attempting to establish more clients in the town of Beckley, forty miles away, but distance and transportation difficulty deter her from pursuing that market.

Through the exchange of services in their homes, women of diverse class backgrounds enter into economically functional, but also socially embedded, relationships with one another. For example, women who care for other people's children are often seen as "substitute" mothers or are considered "part of the family." One woman who runs a preschool in her home related to the children as if they were her own: "I feel that I am taking over what the parents cannot do. I am helping right now and I am really where I like to be. I really have a love for children because I'm giving them the environment . . . because this little girl feels like she's home. I'm not just giving them a class environment, I'm giving them a home environment."

Finally, relationships among women engaged in informal activities are often shaped by organizations that bring women together as both producers and consumers. Many of the women interviewed for this study collaborate with other women in producing or marketing their goods through some sort of network or cooperative. These networks are a critical part of the connection between the informalization of work and economic restructuring. Flexible production in locally based networks is designed to adapt quickly to shifting demands for a company's or network's products. Two examples of economic networks comprised primarily of women that can be found in this region are a quilting cooperative, Cabin Creek Quilts, and a knitting network, Appalachian by Design.

Cabin Creek Quilts, located in Malden, West Virginia, has been in operation since the late 1970s and currently has nearly 220 members from around the state.[42] Each member specializes in a particular component of quilt-making. For example, someone pieces a quilt, which is then sent to the training center for inspection before being given to a quilter to be quilted. It is then returned to the center for inspection before being sent to the customer or displayed in the main store in Malden. Pieces and material are shipped back and forth from the sales shop to the members largely by UPS, thus avoiding the need for these women to travel. Besides being sold in the main shop, quilted items are marketed through catalogs such as Land's End. As with many other quilting cooperatives in the United States, Cabin Creek is having difficulty competing with imported quilts, especially Chinese quilts made with less expensive labor. The handcrafted Appalachian quilts are usually sold for hundreds of dollars, thus attracting relatively high income clients. In contrast, the socioeconomic background of the homeworkers is modest, representing lower income women from largely rural areas. Their earnings from quilting are based on what they sew, so those who work efficiently earn equivalent to minimum wage; some are extremely efficient and can earn well above minimum wage.

Appalachian by Design (ABD) is a nonprofit, flexible manufacturing network that coordinates over fifty self-employed women who produce knitwear in their homes. The staff of ABD connects the home knitters with national and international markets, and helps them develop their skills as artisans and small business owners. They have had contracts with Esprit and other catalog firms that sell this knitwear for mostly upscale niche markets. Most of the women in the network are in low income households that also operate family farms or have other income-producing ventures.[43] Production of the knitwear requires computerized knitting machines that the women purchase or lease. This technology makes their work more efficient and adaptable to quick shifts in the design, yarn, or style of goods produced.

ABD forms a complex social and spatial web of knitters who produce pieces in their homes and send them to a center in Lewisburg, West Virginia, to be seamed before they are shipped to the buyer. The buyer often supplies the yarn, which is shipped to individual knitters. They are connected via a telecommunications network that coordinates the orders and troubleshoots for any difficulties these women might encounter in their production of the knitwear. Although the women who produce goods for both the quilting and knitting networks rarely come in direct contact with the people who buy their products, their livelihoods are closely intertwined through the social and economic dimensions of this exchange.

Conclusion: Gender and Diversity in the Informal Sector

Informalization is a growing phenomenon, reflecting the increasing diversification of work that is taking place with global economic restructuring. The informal sector is linked to multiple scales of economic activity: isolated rural households are connected to local and regional economic processes, which in turn are affected by global restructuring. Despite its neglect in the literature, gender is central to the processes of informalization and global restructuring. Not only is the gendered organization of households affected by shifting demands for waged labor, household gender arrangements also influence men's and women's involvement in both the formal and informal workforces.[44] By directly addressing the household scale, researchers can better understand how economic restructuring is related to women's engagement in informal income-generating activities, especially home-based work.

The case study presented in this chapter illustrates the interrelationships among women that are being created through the informalization of work and economic restructuring in the central Appalachian coalfields. Women in this region face a long tradition of marginalization from the formal workforce, partially due to its history of resource extraction and coinciding cultural dynamics. This legacy means that women's labor-force participation is relatively low, that they work under extreme occupational segregation, and that they experience high rates of poverty. In addition to the traditional marginalization of working-class women, households in this subregion now confront heavy job loss in relatively well-paying, male-dominated employment sectors such as manufacturing and mining. Within this social and economic climate, many working-class women are turning to alternative forms of income generation.

Through several flexible networks, low-income rural women produce goods and services for consumption by urban people who represent a different socioeconomic class. Quilting cooperatives, child care, and other examples of home-based income generation connect working-class women who earn money by producing goods and providing services in their homes with more privileged women who are able to purchase these goods and services. The lives of these women are thus intertwined in a complex material and social web. Women separated by class and geography are by those very same distinctions structurally linked: rural areas are connected to urban areas, household strategies are connected to regional economies, working-class women are connected to middle- and upper-class women. These economic linkages are imperative to understanding the relationships that connect diverse Southern women not only to one another, but ultimately to women all over the globe.

Notes

Acknowledgments: Funding for this research was provided by the National Science Foundation Grant SBR-9309275 and the West Virginia University Regional Research Institute. Their support is appreciated.

1. Manuel Castells and Alejandro Portes, "World Underneath: The Origins, Dynamics, and Effects of the Informal Economy," in Alejandro Portes, Manuel Castells, and Lauren A. Benton, eds., *The Informal Economy: Studies in Advanced and Less Developed Countries* (Baltimore: Johns Hopkins University Press, 1989), pp. 11–37.

2. Ibid.

3. Ibid.; Enzo Mingione, *Fragmented Societies: A Sociology of Economic Life Beyond the Market Paradigm* (Oxford: Blackwell, 1991); Brian Roberts, "Informal Economy and Family Strategies," *International Journal of Urban and Regional Research* 18(1) (1994): 6–23.

4. See David Harvey, *The Condition of Postmodernity: An Enquiry into the Origins of Cultural Change* (Oxford: Blackwell, 1989).

5. Ibid.

6. Lourdes Benería and Martha Roldan, *The Crossroad of Class and Gender: Industrial Homework, Subcontracting, and Household Dynamics in Mexico City* (Chicago: University of Chicago Press, 1987).

7. Maureen Hays-Mitchell, "The Ties That Bind: Informal and Formal Sector Linkages in Street-Vending: The Case of Peru's *Ambulantes, "Environment and Planning A* 25 (1993): 1085–1102.

8. Victoria A. Lawson, "Work Force Fragmentation in Latin America and Its Empirical Manifestations in Ecuador," *World Development* 18 (May 1990): 641–57.

9. Lauren Benton, *Invisible Factories: The Informal Economy and Industrial Development in Spain* (Albany: SUNY Press, 1990).

10. Portes, Castells, and Benton, eds., *The Informal Economy.*

11. Maria Patricia Fernández-Kelly, "International Development and Industrial Restructuring: The Case of Garment and Electronics Industries in Southern California," in Arthur MacEwan and William K. Tabb, eds., *Instability and Change in the World Economy* (New York: Monthly Review Press, 1989), pp. 147–65.

12. Portes, Castells, and Benton, eds., *The Informal Economy.*

13. Michael Piore and Charles Sabel, *The Second Industrial Divide: Possibilities for Prosperity* (New York: Basic Books, 1984).

14. Enzo Mingione, "Life Strategies and Social Economies in the Postfordist Age," *International Journal of Urban and Regional Research* 18(1) (1994): 24–45.

15. Allen J. Scott, *New Industrial Spaces* (London: Pion Ltd., 1988).

16. Benton, *Invisible Factories.*

17. Portes, Castells, and Benton, eds., *The Informal Economy;* Mingione, *Fragmented Societies.*

18. Dorothy Helly and Susan Reverby, eds., *Gendered Domains: Rethinking Public and Private in Women's History* (Ithaca: Cornell University Press, 1992).

19. Dwight Billings, Kathleen Blee, and Louis Swanson, "Culture, Family, and Community in Preindustrial Appalachia," *Appalachian Journal* 13 (1986): 154–70; Ron Eller, *Miners, Millhands, and Mountaineers: Industrialization of the Appalachian South, 1880–1930* (Knoxville: University of Tennessee Press, 1982); Sally Ward Maggard, "From Farmers to Miners: The Decline of Agriculture in Eastern Kentucky," in Lawrence Busch, ed., *Science and Agricultural Development* (Totowa, NJ: Allanheld, Osmun, 1981), pp. 25–66.

20. Mary Beth Pudup, Dwight Billings, and Altina Waller, eds., *Appalachia in the Making: The Mountain South in the Nineteenth Century* (Chapel Hill: University of North Carolina Press, 1995).

21. Mary Beth Pudup, "Women's Work in the West Virginia Economy," *West Virginia History* 49 (1990): 7–20.

22. Ibid.; Sally Ward Maggard, "From the Farm to Coal Camp to Back Office and McDonald's: Living in the Midst of Appalachia's Latest Transformation," *Journal of Appalachian Studies Association* 6 (1994): 14–38.

23. Patricia Beaver, *Rural Community in the Appalachian South* (Lexington: University Press of Kentucky, 1986); Rhoda Halperin, *The Livelihood of Kin: Making Ends Meet "The Kentucky Way"* (Austin: University of Texas Press, 1990).

24. Janet W. Greene, "Strategies for Survival: Women's Work in the Southern West Virginia Coal Camps," *West Virginia History* 49 (1990): 21–36.

25. Ibid.

26. Sandra L. Barney, "Accepting the Findings of Medical Science: Gender, Class, and the Political Economy of Health Care in Central Appalachia, 1880–1935" (Ph.D. diss., West Virginia University, 1995).

27. Greene, "Strategies for Survival."

28. Paul Salstrom, "Appalachia's Informal Economy and the Transition to Capitalism," *Journal of Appalachian Studies* 2(2) (1996): 228.

29. Ibid., 223.

30. Ann M. Oberhauser, "Gender and Household Economic Strategies in Rural Appalachia," *Gender, Place, and Culture* 1(2) (1995): 51–70.

31. John Gaventa, "From the Mountains to the *Maquiladoras*: A Case Study of Capital Flight and Its Impact on Workers," in Phillip J. Obermiller and W. W. Philiber, eds., *Appalachia in an International Context* (Westport, CT: Praeger Publishers, 1994), pp. 165–76.

32. James C. Cobb, "The Southern Business Climate: A Historical Perspective," *Forum for Applied Research and Public Policy* 2(1) (1986): 98.

33. Gaventa, "From the Mountains."

34. Ronald L. Lewis, "Appalachian Restructuring in Historical Perspective: Coal, Culture, and Social Change in West Virginia," *Urban Studies* 30 (1993): 299–308.

35. Mary Anglin, "Engendering the Struggle: Women's Labor and Traditions of Resistance in Rural Southern Appalachia," in Steve L. Fisher, ed., *Fighting Back in Appalachia: Traditions of Resistance and Change* (Philadelphia: Temple University Press, 1993), pp. 263–81; Gaventa, "From the Mountains"; Ann M. Oberhauser, "Industrial Restructuring and Women's Homework in Appalachia: Lessons from West Virginia," *Southeastern Geographer* 33 (1993): 23–43.

36. U.S. Bureau of Labor Statistics, *Employment and Earnings, States and Areas* (Washington, DC: U.S. Government Printing Office, 1990).

37. Ibid.

38. Maggard, "From Farm to Coal Camp."

39. Cynthia Rogers, Kimberly Mencken, and F. Carson Mencken, *Female Labor Force Participation in Central Appalachia: A Descriptive Analysis*, Research Paper 9532 (Morgantown: Regional Research Institute, West Virginia University, 1995).

40. Ann M. Oberhauser, Chris Weiss, and L. Waugh, "Gender Analysis and Economic Development in West Virginia," *The West Virginia Public Affairs Reporter* 13 (1996): 2–13.

41. The names of the women in the study have been changed to protect their confidentiality.

42. Dan Davenport, "The Fabric of Life," *Mature Outlook* (1996): 26–27.

43. "Creative Solutions Woven by Rural Communities," *Economic Development Digest* 5 (2) (1996):1.

44. Nanneke Redclift and Enzo Mingione, *Beyond Employment* (Oxford: Blackwell, 1985).

III

SUSTAINING COMMUNITIES

1

Finding a Voice

Latinas in the South

Loida C. Velázquez

lthough it is not known for the diversity of its population, the South is now home to a variety of ethnicities and races. In this chapter I shall focus in on one of the fastest growing of these groups: Latinas, or women who trace their origins to countries colonized by Spain. As new arrivals in historically biracial locations throughout the region, Latinas must intentionally create an ethnic identity and community for themselves.

Although Hispanic women share a history of Spanish colonization and communicate primarily in the language imposed by the Spanish conquerors, Puerto Rican, Cuban, and Mexican women come from distinctive nations and cultural groups, and have had very different experiences upon their arrival in the United States. Moreover, the experiences of Latinas settling in Florida or Texas are, for demographic and historical reasons, very different from those of Latinas settling in North Carolina or Tennessee. Florida and Texas were initially colonized by Spanish-speaking settlers and have long had thriving Hispanic populations. Latinas in both states have been able to establish traditions and create organizations that address issues of common concern. Tennessee and North Carolina, on the other hand, are just beginning to experience the impact of Hispanic immigration. Hispanic women living in these states have yet to experience the support and strength emanating from their new ethnic identification as "Latinas."

125

Latinos, as a distinct population in the United States, have gained national minority group status, which combines the notion of an ethnic or racial group with that of a minority group.[1] An ethnic or racial group is distinguishable from the dominant society because it shares distinctive cultural characteristics; a minority group plays a subordinate role in a stratified society as a result of its race or ethnicity. The culture that distinguishes a national minority group is not static and passive but fluid and intentional. Indeed, Samuel Betances defines ethnicity as "the ability of people from a similar region of the world [or with similar cultural experiences], who find themselves in a hostile environment, to see the urgency of harnessing their numbers under a common identity so as to operate as an interest group for the purpose of removing barriers to social progress."[2]

Ethnicity, in this sense, is the invention of people who share a common experience of rejection and who agree to define themselves collectively as agents of change. Until very recently, Latinas in areas of the South other than Florida and Texas were geographically scattered and too small in numbers to exert any impact at the local level. This is changing very rapidly, and at this moment their ethnic identity is in formation.

Nationally, the Hispanic population has increased considerably during the last two decades. In the 1980 census Hispanics totaled 6.4 percent of the population; by 1990, their numbers had increased to 9 percent. It is estimated that by the year 2000 Hispanics will exceed 31.2 million, or 11.6 percent, of the total U.S. population. Due to this rapid growth, demographers predict that by 2020, Latinos will be the largest minority group in the United States. Composed largely of four principal groups—Mexican Americans, Puerto Ricans, Cubans, and Central and South Americans—the size of the Latino population is expected to surpass that of the African American population.

This study focuses on Latinas who have moved into two Southern states, North Carolina and Tennessee, where the Hispanic population historically has been negligible. In North Carolina, the 1990 census showed a 26 percent increase from the figures in the 1980 census; however, the consensus is that Hispanics in this state were drastically undercounted because of their mobility, language barriers, and legal status. Most professional Latinos come to these areas of the South trying to escape the social problems endemic to large cities. Attracted by the growth of agribusiness and industry in these states, both migrant workers and blue-collar Latinos are also relocating. For example, a large number of Latino migrant workers who had made Florida their home base lost all their belongings after a series of hurricanes there and have subsequently relocated to Tennessee, North Carolina, and South Carolina. As a result of such trends, North Carolina is predicted to become the state with the fourth largest number of Hispanic migrant workers—after California, Texas, and Florida—and the number of Hispanic residents in Tennessee has more than doubled in the past five years.

Everywhere one can notice signs of this growth: North Carolina has a biweekly Spanish newspaper, *La Voz de Carolina,* and Tennessee grocery stores are beginning to carry produce and canned goods that are unique to the Latino diet. In a rural community in Tennessee, a Latina has founded a grassroots organization to advocate for the rights of migrant workers. The Knoxville diocese of the Catholic church has an active Hispanic ministry. Spanish-speaking Protestant churches are beginning to appear in the upper east Tennessee region.

The impact of this expansion on every aspect of social and cultural life in the South has yet to be considered or researched. It was this concern that motivated me to conduct a study of Latinas during the early spring and summer of 1996. I was primarily interested in discovering how Latinas in the South are negotiating a sense of personal identity, what accommodations they have made to integrate into Southern culture, and how they have constructed an ethnic identity as Latinas.

The Study: Questions of Identity, Culture, and Belonging

Through semistructured interviews and informal conversations, I collected data from two groups of Latinas in Tennessee and North Carolina: ten professionals in science, communications, and education careers, and ten migrant farmworkers. All of the study participants traced their family origins to one of the four major Hispanic groups in the United States.

The group of professional women was the most diverse and included at least one participant from the four major Latino subgroups: two Mexican Americans, one Mexican national, one Colombian, two Cubans, and four Puerto Ricans. The group of migrant workers was composed entirely of Mexican and Mexican American women. The median age for both groups was thirty-five years; the youngest was twenty-two, and the oldest was fifty-one.

The interviews were facilitated by my nineteen years of residence in Tennessee and my ten years as the director of a federally funded program serving migrant and seasonal farmworkers in Georgia, South Carolina, North Carolina, and Tennessee. Once I announced my intent to conduct this study, it was not difficult for me to find Latina lawyers, psychologists, engineers, public relations specialists, and educators to participate. I had done previous research within the migrant communities in both Tennessee and North Carolina, and had good friends who facilitated the interviews with the female migrant workers. The conversations with most of the professional women were conducted in a fluid mix of English and Spanish that moved easily back and forth between the two languages to find the sentence or phrase that best expressed the intended meaning. Spanish was the preferred means of communication by the female migrant workers.

My previous research within migrant communities in western North Carolina and eastern Tennessee had awakened my interest in comparing the experiences of Latina migrant workers with those of nonmigrant Latinas, yet I entered the study without expectations and open to following a path of inquiry driven by the meaning each participant placed on her own experiences. My experience with ethnographic research had taught me that people engage in a continual process of constructing and interpreting meanings in their social interactions as they try to make sense of the world from their own perspective. I intended to discover each woman's understanding of her world by observing and listening with as few interruptions as possible. I wanted to uncover the meaning these two groups of women made of their experiences rather than impose my own. However, I did take along the following four groups of open-ended questions to assist me in developing a conversation:

1. Tell me about your family and how they came to the United States.
2. Tell me about living in the South. Have you lived in other regions of the United States? How did they compare?
3. Tell me about your cultural traditions. What traditions from your country of origin do you still practice? Would you like your children to keep these same traditions?
4. Tell me about your plans for the future. Would you stay in the South? Would you like your children to grow up here?

I had purposely selected two very different groups of Latinas to be able to compare and contrast their experiences. While listening to their voices I found marked differences yet also striking similarities. Whether their experiences were expressed in the sophisticated phrases used by the professional women or in the colloquial terms of the migrant workers, both groups told me of their daily quest to clarify a self-image, improve interpersonal relations, and find a voice and place in society. They were women negotiating an identity and a sense of belonging within a cultural context that was sometimes fascinating and enticing as well as threatening and confusing. For many of them the process of cultural adaptation came with a huge personal cost. They were dealing with conflicting cultural and personal values, and often felt torn and dissatisfied. Others had successfully negotiated the cultural differences, developed an ethnic identity, and found a voice.

Patricia Zavella has suggested that researchers should pay close attention to what she calls "social location"—the social space created by the intersection of class, race, gender, and culture—when trying to understand differences among various groups of Latinas.[3] Another important consideration is generation. Whether Latinas are members of the first generation born in the United States, part of a subsequent generation born in the United States, or recent immigrants has implications for language, cultural knowledge, and self-identification. A Latina's generation affects whether she feels a sense of identification and solidarity with other Latinas, whether she feels marginalized, and whether she feels more "American" than Latina. While analyzing the data, I looked for social location and generational differences as guiding points.

Ambivalent Acculturation

External Barriers

Acculturation (now sometimes termed "transculturation") is an adjustment that takes place when an individual from a different culture comes into continuous and direct contact with a new, dominant culture.[1] No two individuals of the same cultural background go through the process in the same way and at the same rate. Acculturation is experienced as a series of changes and choices that include how to live, what to eat, what language to speak, how to behave toward relatives and friends, and whether to follow a pattern of behavior dictated by the culture of origin. The acculturation process of Latinas—their quest to clarify a positive self-image, improve interpersonal relations, and find a voice and place in the new society of the South—has involved serious external and internal barriers.

One obvious and significant external barrier to Latinas' successful adaptation is their stereotypical image in popular culture. Most study participants expressed concern about this stereotype, which assumes that all Hispanic women share common cultural traits, values, and behaviors. The popular image is that of a submissive, family-oriented, unassertive, and poorly educated woman. Such stereotyping complicates Latinas' already difficult acculturation process: they must negotiate between their native culture, the dominant culture, and the dominant culture's representations of their culture. A migrant woman said to me, "They think they do, but they don't know who we are or where we come from."

The professional Latinas tended to view themselves as highly acculturated and expressed a greater degree of ambivalence toward their native culture than the recently immigrated migrant females. Discrimination in the form of lack of promotion, denial of access to staff development opportunities, or assignment to projects that were of low importance and thus not conducive to job recognition were particularly painful for them. They believe that, as professionals, they have much more to offer an organization or institution than merely "providing the Hispanic point of view." One of them expressed this feeling as follows: "It is such a burden to always carry your culture on your shoulders. You cannot be you, you have to be that idea they have of you. You have to always think that the way you act is going to be used to judge your culture." These Latinas' acute ambivalence toward their native culture and American representations of it may be related to class distinctions in the meaning and context of acculturation. For the professional women, occupational success is predicated upon their degree of acculturation and English proficiency. The social context of migrant life, however, requires the perpetuation of Latino culture while at the same time undermining it.

The migrant workers spoke of feeling isolated and marginalized. Their community is composed of other Hispanic farmworkers: they socialize only among themselves, sometimes travel across state lines to go to a Mexican store for staples, and communicate mostly in Spanish. Their values, cultural traits, and behaviors are patterned after the country of origin, which for this particular group is Mexico. Some of the migrant women are striving to develop in new directions as individuals but are finding obstacles both within and outside the home. Several spoke about how their marriages have been affected when they try to assert themselves. To these women, asserting themselves means making decisions on how to use part of their paycheck, refusing to share their home with some of their husband's friends or relatives, or contradicting their mate in front of his friends. As a result, their marriages have dissolved, or they have been victims of domestic violence.

Although domestic violence is common in migrant homes, going to women's shelters is not an option for the victims.[5] Most of the Southeastern women's shelters I contacted while trying to assist Candida, a study participant who had been battered, were not equipped to assist Hispanic migrant women; staff were ignorant of the Hispanic culture and unable to communicate in a language other than English. In addition, migrant women often will not look for outside help since, like most victims of domestic violence, they find ways to justify the violence as something they brought upon themselves.

Candida was born in a rural town north of Monterrey, Mexico. She married Francisco when she was fifteen years old. They already had two sons when they joined his brother, who had migrated to western North

Carolina. There they became a part of a household that already included three other families: some blood relatives and others who were friends. Candida and Francisco were hired by the same farmer to pick apples and began making the adjustment necessary to integrate into the culture of migrancy. They stayed in North Carolina until the apple harvest ended and then migrated to Florida for the winter crops. Candida expressed her loneliness and isolation as follows:

> Sometimes I want so badly to go home and see my pa and ma that I cry and cry. North Carolina is not bad, but I hate going to Florida. I don't like the people we stay with there but if I complain, Francisco gets mad and we end up fighting. I don't want to be a bad wife, and I have those two children to think about. I miss the church celebrations, the town fairs, the Three Kings Day celebration, and the family *bautismos* parties. We had many occasions where the whole family would get together and there would be a lot of food and music. I miss that the most. I try to keep those traditions, and I build an altar to the Virgin wherever I go.

Candida and Francisco separated for a while. After they had a violent fight, she went to live with another migrant family, but there were so many people in the household that she decided that it would be better for the children to return to Francisco. (At least at their uncle's house there were mostly blood relatives who would provide child care while she was working at the canning factory.) As of this writing, Candida continues to seek an identity for herself in the shifting cultures and places of her migration.

Regardless of social location, all of these Latinas face significant external barriers to successful acculturation. From the occupational discrimination faced by the professionals to the constant social adjustments required of migrant women, class differences shape—but for more privileged women by no means eliminate—the difficulties of acculturation. Ambivalence and conflict characterize their common effort to create a social space between American culture and their culture of origin.

These and other similarities should not reinforce erroneous assumptions that Latinas are members of a coherent group with common values, norms, customs, rituals, symbols, and experiences. In reality they are as diverse among themselves as they are different from the majority group. Different social classes, countries of origin, generational locations, and forms of acculturation produce individuals who, even when claiming ethnicity or speaking as a member of a group, are also demanding recognition of their uniqueness as people. Indeed, the tendency to pigeon-hole them as a racial-ethnic "type," thereby eliminating their individual humanity, may be one of the more harmful external barriers that they face.

Internal Barriers

Cultural traditions provide a framework of purpose and identity for a person's life, both individually and as a member of a group. Yet Latinas throughout the United States recognize two voices within themselves: one that accepts without frustration inherited cultural patterns, and one that wants, and more importantly needs, to reshape those patterns in new ways.

Even the most isolated and marginalized of the migrant workers noticed a profound clash between expectations of women in the United States and in their country of origin. For acculturated Latinas, the prospect of having choices in life is exciting but also terribly threatening. Words like "guilt" and "frustration" kept coming into the conversation. The role of a "good" woman was described by most of the migrant workers as follows: a good woman always puts her family first. She sacrifices everything for her family. The family is her sacred duty. Professional middle-class Latinas do not escape this pressure. A Latina civil engineer, who by all accounts is very well acculturated, said: "I don't know where it comes from but I need to have everything in its place. In my house everything has to look perfect."

The sources of guilt and frustration varied for both groups but they always were related to breaking traditional patterns of behavior for the "good" mother and wife: putting children in day care, not serving meals on time, traveling for business, not calling a mother often enough, openly criticizing her husband, talking about personal problems (especially to someone outside the family), wishing for more personal time, or expressing feelings.

"Marianismo" is the term used by some analysts to denote the ideal role of the Hispanic woman. Rosa Maria Gil and Carmen Inoa Vazquez described marianismo as follows:

> Marianismo takes as its model of perfection the Virgin Mary. Marianismo is about sacred duty, self-sacrifice, and chastity. About dispensing care and pleasure, not receiving them. About living in the shadows, literally and figuratively, of your men—father, boyfriend, husband, and son—your kids and your family. . . . In the Old Country, it affords a woman a level of protection as a wife and mother, gives her certain power and much *respeto* as well as a life free from loneliness and want. In today's North America marianismo is the invisible yoke which binds capable, intelligent, ambitious Latinas to a no-win lifestyle.[6]

Estela Herrera calls marianismo the essence of womanhood in the Latin world.[7] According to her, the term is derived from the cult of the Virgin Mary that developed during the Middle Ages, when the horrors of wars and pestilence caused people to beg for a kind mother to mediate between the misery of humanity and the wrath of God. Coined in the

1970s for use in the mental health profession, marianismo retains the medieval connotations of virginity, self-sacrifice, boundless generosity, submission, and loyalty expected of "good women."

Gil and Vazquez view marianismo as the other side of the coin to machismo. Both are gender roles closely linked to the development of patriarchy worldwide. When Latinos immigrate to the United States, they bring with them these traditions of gendered distinctions and divisions. As acculturation proceeds, these traditions may be discarded, but remnants filter in, causing pain and confusion. Most acculturated Latinas consciously reject their ingrained values and beliefs about gender, but, nonetheless, these traditions continue to guide the behaviors and inform the beliefs of many. Many of the study participants expressed ambivalence about competition, power, and independence, which some interpreted as the cornerstones of the feminist canon. They explained their ambivalence by saying, "I was not brought up to act that way."

I read the literature on marianismo in an effort to understand the paradoxes expressed during my conversations with Pilar, a beautiful Puerto Rican woman who seems always perfectly dressed and coifed. She has a master's degree in industrial engineering and has been employed at a federal government agency in east Tennessee for the last five years. Despite her physical appearance, she is tense and gives the impression of being under a lot of pressure. Since finishing graduate school in Puerto Rico, she has accomplished most of her life goals: she married, moved to the United States, was hired by the federal government and given the management of an important project, bought a nice home, and had a child. Yet she feels very insecure and confessed that she always looks for outside validation to achieve a sense of self-worth. Any small mistake Pilar makes at work becomes a nightmare she cannot erase from her mind. She is in therapy and considering leaving her job and staying home to take care of her child. As a "marianista" she is compelled to be the perfect employee, wife, and mother, and cannot feel good about herself if she fails in any way at any of these roles. As with many Puerto Ricans, she travels to the island often to visit her family. She misses the sense of family she finds there at every level, where, she says, "No matter what you do you know you are among friends and it will be accepted." She expressed her feelings this way:

> I miss the warmth and personal interest everybody showed to you. I am not sure I want my son to grow up here. I want him to feel protected by the same support system that gave me security and encouragement. I cannot stand the pressures anymore. It is too much for me. I have some pressures at work, but I know that most of the tension I feel comes from inner pressures, from my need to do everything and do it well, my need to feel accepted and secure.

My own experience as a Puerto Rican woman echoes that of Pilar. I am a late bloomer, as is typical of women of my generation. I married early, had four children, and stayed home until the youngest was in school. I knew all along that one day I would finish my education and have a career. I had married after my third year of college and spent eleven years completing my undergraduate degree by taking university courses sporadically while caring for my family. My husband and I left Puerto Rico looking for better educational opportunities for our children, and I was determined to wait until they were in school to seek professional fulfillment. I went back to school the same year my youngest child started kindergarten.

While completing a master's degree in counseling, I took the Myers-Briggs Type Indicator Test. I recently took it again nineteen years later, having completed a doctoral degree and pursued a career as an administrator of adult education programs. The test results revealed that I had changed from an Extrovert-Feeling type to an Introverted-Intuitive-Judger type. The test administrator was surprised when I shared with her the different results. They revealed the adjustment in personality I had had to make to meet the challenges I faced as an education administrator, as a Latina leader in my community, and as a wife and mother. According to the test, an extrovert woman guided by her feelings is approachable and easily engaged by friends, but makes a poor leader because she always needs affirmation from superiors and subordinates.

The most painful adjustment I have had to make has to do with what Latino sociologists call "familismo." Families tend to be very important in much of Latin America. Extended family, friends, and neighbors are paramount when people have to depend on each other for survival. The incorporation of friends into your family is taken for granted and is extended sometimes to people at work. I still remember the day I realized my coworkers were not my friends but people with whom I shared tasks and responsibilities. This revelation filled me with great sadness. Some of them, with time, have become friends that I treasure, but that initial realization took away the spontaneity and informality that were traits of my personality.

Unlike Pilar, I have come to reconcile my culture of origin with that which I found in the United States. Like her, and many others, however, I know that this process of adaptation has come at a high price in personal pain, anxiety, and sadness.

Finding a Voice

The relative success of Latinas in their quest to find a voice in the South is exemplified by the stories of two of my study participants: Liz, a thirty-year-old former migrant worker, and Matilde, a forty-five-year-old lawyer. Although they live in different social classes and generations, both have become leaders; they strive to create a sense of ethnic community within the Latino population and to make connections with the community at large.

Liz came to western North Carolina more than a decade ago following the eastern migrant stream, an identifiable path of migrant workers moving from Texas to Eastern states with a large agricultural base. She was born in Austin, Texas, and was a third-generation migrant worker. Her husband, a Mexican national, had become a migrant crew leader, but she wanted to leave the fields and start a more stable life in North Carolina.

Like many migrant women, Liz dropped out of school when she became pregnant for the first time; she later decided to complete her high school education by enrolling in a federally funded program specially designed for migrant adults. She also had a desire to help other migrants who wanted to settle in North Carolina. Liz passed the high school equivalency test and, with the help of her husband, opened the first Mexican *mercado* (market) in western North Carolina. Benefiting from the visibility that the store gave her within both the migrant and local communities, Liz started to become a leader of, and a voice for, the Hispanic migrants. She began writing letters to the editor of the local newspaper on migrant issues, volunteering at schools for cultural presentations, and organizing the appearance of the first Hispanic float in the Apple Harvest Festival parade. Soon the newspaper began coming to her when it wanted to publish the perspective of a local Hispanic, and community leaders started asking for her help in organizing activities. Liz has also served on the boards of the local health center and of various charitable foundations. During the summer of 1996, she, with six other community leaders, was recognized as one of her county's outstanding women.

Matilde came to east Tennessee from New Mexico in 1985. Her family had settled in the Southwest before it became United States territory. Before "Latinos" became the politically correct term and even before "Hispanic" became the approved U.S. census nomenclature for Americans of Latin origin, her family called themselves Spanish Americans.

As a child of the 1960s, Matilde is committed to social justice and equality, and became a lawyer when there were few Hispanic lawyers and even fewer Latina lawyers. Upon her arrival in Tennessee, she became involved in organizing the growing east Tennessee Hispanic community. Through Matilde's efforts, the Hispanics of the area have become an integrated community involved in social and educational issues. Until very recently, she provided legal counsel to the manager of the region's largest federal energy research facility.

The community-building activities of Latinas like Liz and Matilde bridge the social distance that separates the new wave of immigrants from each other and from local residents. By constructing an ethnicity as Latinas, they have located a collective social space for themselves and other Hispanics without removing themselves from the dominant culture. Rather, they have effectively created and used ethnic group identification as a strategy to foster communication and relationships of solidarity among themselves as well as mutually respectful interdependence with the larger community.

Conclusions

Latinas in the Southern part of the United States, like Latinas all over the nation, must find a voice and place for themselves within multiple, sometimes conflicting, cultures. They struggle to create a new self-image while at the same time preserving a healthy image of their culture of origin. As Latinas develop a voice in the South, researchers must pay attention to their personal histories, to the paths of their migration, to how their local communities were formed, and to the key structural differences among them. It is also important to consider how each woman's generation, age, and process of acculturation affect her construction of a social identity in general and an ethnic identity in particular.

Of the Latinas interviewed for this study, recently arrived migrant women's social location seems the most marginalized, their experiences and opportunities the most constrained by class, race, gender, and culture. Candida's story gives us a good insight into their plight. Although Pilar's class background and other factors make her process of adaptation different from Candida's, she too is dealing with cultural conflict. Despite the stress produced by its norms and values regarding women, the Hispanic culture provides her with a sense of identity that she cherishes and that is constantly reinforced by visits to her family in Puerto Rico. Significantly, Liz and Matilde, who were born in the United States, have been able to construct a new, hybrid ethnicity stemming from their shared historical experiences as both Americans and Latinas. Acculturated but not completely assimilated, they have been able to transcend most cultural barriers, both internal and external. They foster an appreciation of diversity and improve interpersonal relations by building bridges between the local Hispanic and white communities. They have found a voice and constructed a place for themselves in the South.

The difficult process of acculturation is not unique to immigrants or people of color in the United States. By sharing the findings of this study with a white co-worker who has Southern roots, I discovered that my process of acculturation, of constructing a new social identity, has much in common with her experiences as an educated rural Southern woman still influenced by "remnants of Baptist hellfire and brimstone." This realization serves as a reminder: we have much work to do in order to understand both commonality and diversity among all Southern women, and to encourage solidarity among women at different social locations.

Notes

1. See William I. Robinson, "The Global Economy and the Latino Populations in the United States: A World System Approach," *Critical Sociology* 19 (2) (1992): 29–59.

2. See Samuel Betances, "African-American and Hispanic/Latinos: Eliminating Barriers to Coalition Building," in Stanley Battle, ed., *The State of Black Hartford* (Hartford: Urban League of Greater Hartford, 1996), p. 1.

3. See Patricia Zavella, "Reflections on Diversity Among Chicanas," in Steven Gregory and Roger Sonjek, eds., *Race* (New Brunswick, NJ: Rutgers University Press, 1994), pp. 199–212.

4. "Transculturation" and other terms are increasingly used to indicate the syncretism and dynamism of cultural interaction and adaptation. See Fernando Ortiz, *Cuban Counterpoint: Tobacco and Sugar* (Durham: Duke University Press, 1995); Carolyn Martin Shaw, *Colonial Inscriptions: Race, Sex, and Class in Kenya* (Minneapolis: University of Minnesota Press, 1995); Faye Harrison, "Rehistoricizing Race, Ethnicity, and Class in the U.S. Southeast," in Carole E. Hill and Patricia D. Beaver, eds., *Cultural Diversity in the U.S. South: Anthropological Contributions to a Region in Transition* (Athens: University of Georgia Press, 1998), pp. 179–89.

5. See Loida C. Velázquez, "Migrant Adults' Perceptions of Schooling, Learning, and Education" (Ph.D. diss., University of Tennessee, 1993), p. 75.

6. See Rosa Maria Gil and Carmen Inoa Vazquez, *The Maria Paradox* (New York: G.P. Putnam's Sons, 1996), p. 7.

7. See Estela Herrera, "Marianismo," *Si Magazine*, Summer 1996, pp. 40–43.

Doing Good
While Doing Well
Professional Black Women
in the Mississippi Delta

Cynthia M. Duncan, Margaret M. Walsh,
and Gemma Beckley

ississippi's Yazoo Delta has long been a two-class society comprised primarily of well-to-do whites and poor blacks. The region was settled in the 1830s by wealthy, ambitious planters from other areas in the South who had the resources to clear the swampy, snake-infested land and buy slaves to cultivate cotton in the fertile soil. Their ability to maintain a lifestyle of conspicuous consumption and meet the economic requirements of growing cotton in this harsh environment "was wholly dependent on their success in retaining and controlling a large supply of black labor."[1] Following emancipation and the Civil War, Delta planters retained control over their laborers through the sharecropping system. Disfranchisement of black men in the late nineteenth century further eroded opportunities and options available to blacks in the Delta.

During the 1930s psychologist John Dollard and sociologist Hortense Powdermaker documented the rigid class and caste

Based on material from *Worlds Apart: Why Poverty Persists in Rural America*, forthcoming from Yale University Press. Reprinted by permission of the publisher and the author, Cynthia M. Duncan.

138

stratification imposed by the Delta's white elite.[2] They showed that planters maintained domination over their black laborers and share-croppers not only in the workplace, but also in crucial social institutions such as schools and churches. New Deal agricultural policies and postwar minimum wage laws eventually induced planters to mechanize and re-duce their workforce in order to save on labor costs. Nevertheless, they maintained control over the laborers they continued to use on tractors, in fields, and in work on cotton gins.

Many black residents of the Delta responded to the extremity of racial oppression and the promise of greater opportunity elsewhere by moving out of the region. During the 1950s and 1960s, the second Great Migra-tion to Chicago and other Northern cities swept these rural communities. Most of those who stayed behind relied on a combination of seasonal farm labor and welfare programs to survive. The latter, although estab-lished by the federal government, were also tightly controlled and ma-nipulated by the local elite. Economic historian James C. Cobb found that "although the cumulative influences of the New Deal and World War II brought dramatic changes to the Delta's economy, the transformation of Delta agriculture left the region's planter-dominated social and polit-ical framework fundamentally intact."[3]

What is the class structure of the Delta today? Does the rigid system of class and caste stratification persist? We sought to answer these and other questions through interviews with 160 men and women, black and white, from all social classes in two Delta counties with a combined population of about 18,000 in the 1990s. Forty-five of these interviews were with members of the black middle class, and it is on them, particularly black middle-class women, that we focus in this chapter.

The Legacy of the Civil Rights Movement

Despite the danger of violent repercussions in these small, segregated communities, many rural blacks in the Delta took part in civil rights demonstrations during the 1950s and 1960s. Cobb recounts reprisals against civil rights activists throughout the region, including an incident in which everyone who signed a National Association for the Advance-ment of Colored People (NAACP) petition in favor of school integration lost his or her job. The relentless and devastating punishment white em-ployers could inflict on blacks who supported civil rights forced the NAACP to be less outspoken. As a result, the NAACP came to represent what Cobb describes as "a conservative, middle class orientation," and what many of our interviewees call an organization of "Toms" who go along with the white community's desire to maintain the racial status quo.[4] Today the NAACP is regarded as out of touch and ineffectual. As one Delta leader explained:

> We end up leaving them [NAACP members] behind because they have lost their way—the vision of what the organization is about is in limbo. They're just holding on to something of the past and they haven't been able to modernize the organization to get with the times, to be the kind of organization they should be in this day and age. And so we have sort of taken the spotlight, in a sense, in terms of people seeing it as a viable organization helping low-income people, Afro-Americans, in the community. The NAACP in our county, for all practical purposes, is dead.

During the 1960s many manufacturing plants moved from America's increasingly troubled urban areas to job-hungry rural communities where they could pay lower wages. However, in our study counties both whites and blacks cite specific examples of factories interested in locating there being turned away by planters because they would not agree to bar blacks from production work. The handful of factories that did come in during this period reportedly hired blacks only as janitors up until the late 1970s. Most black men and women continued to do agricultural and domestic work, supplemented with public assistance during the winter. Thus there was little year-round employment available for blacks.

One-fifth of the population in our two study counties migrated out of the region in the 1960s. The men and women interviewed for this study describe how planters continued to maintain tight, even ruthless, control over economic and political life to ensure continuity of their privilege and power though the 1960s and into the 1970s. When integration threatened the well-established caste system, whites set up separate private institutions to replace public ones, including schools, recreation facilities, and clubs. These separate worlds largely persist to the present. As a local minister put it, "Everything here is segregated. There is no social interaction between the races, and no trust. Whites say you can't trust blacks, and blacks say the same thing about whites."

In the 1990s there were 6,000 households in our two study counties, 2,500 in the white minority and 3,500 black, a demographic fact with far-reaching political and social implications. The poverty rate has been over 50 percent for decades, and over 80 percent of blacks are poor. Altogether, about 1,200 black families with children live in poverty, while about 150 white families with children do. Per capita income for whites is nearly five times that of blacks—over $15,000 compared to $3,500. Nearly 3,000 households received Food Stamps and Medicaid in the early 1990s—indicating that over half the population are poor, including those dependent entirely on government assistance and those who are employed.

But these counties also have many wealthy households; some local sources say there are more millionaires per capita here than in any other counties of the United States. Over the last thirty years farms have become larger and ownership more concentrated. These thousand-acre farms receive very large federal subsidies—as much as $20 million in both counties combined in some recent years, twice the amount of federal grants that comes in for the 3,000 families on public assistance. Since large farmers disperse ownership among family members to increase the subsidy for which they are eligible, some wealthy farm families have received more than $85,000 per year. A white farmer explained, "The big corporate farms that you have around here, they're still family farms. It's just the corporation is made up of the patriarch or matriarch of the family, and the sons, and as many people as they can scrape up for government purposes." In one notorious case that hit national newspapers, a local planter with over 14,000 acres in a neighboring county claimed over a million dollars in federal payments through his various corporations and family trusts.

So there has been great wealth for the few, deep poverty for most, and, until very recently, virtually no middle class. A white schoolteacher stated flatly, "There are four middle-class white families here." A storekeeper says, "I think there are three or four of us now." A black schoolteacher reflected that "our black middle-class are those who have left for the cities." Indeed, census statistics show that in 1960, when there were twice as many farms, there were no families in a middle-income range around the median; even by 1990 the proportion was very small. This inequality, with its glaring racial dimension, has been the dominant factor shaping social relations and determining prospects for mobility and change. For over a century, the plantation economy produced and maintained a social structure consisting of two classes—the wealthy, powerful white farmers and the black poor who worked for them and depended on them for every aspect of social life. The black middle class was small, in many ways still vulnerable to the demands of the white elite in these segregated rural communities.

The Shifting Character of the Black Middle Class

Dollard and Powdermaker were among the earliest social scientists to examine the class structure among African Americans in the rural South, which consisted of a tiny upper class, a small middle class, and a large lower class.[5] While the origin of upper-class black families may have been rooted in the lightness of their skin and their history of domestic work during slavery, middle-class men and women distinguished themselves by their education, behavior, and social connections rather than their heritage.[6] Up until the 1960s, the black middle class consisted mainly of ministers, teachers, nurses, and an occasional small landowner or businessman.

It was rare for the black middle class to be recognized as successful among whites, but its members usually enjoyed high visibility in churches and prominent leadership positions within their own segregated communities.[7] They achieved upward mobility by adhering to the norms and values of the white middle class: high educational aspirations, high income, and high personal standards of morality and sexual restraint. They were prepared to get along with—and sometimes compete with—the white middle class. Status distinctions between lower-class blacks and middle-class blacks were evident in their outward behavior and attitudes toward each other.[8]

Membership in the "old" black middle class required more than a proper education and moral code; they also had to find a niche for their skills. In these rural counties only a few higher status professions were open to blacks—school teachers, some nurses, preachers, and funeral directors. Family connections to occupations were passed along between generations of funeral parlor directors, school principals, and clergy.[9]

In our study area a few blacks from this group acted as intermediaries between black sharecroppers and their white bosses, and emerged as a kind of black middle class, with a few assets, some skills, and some education. Ownership of a small amount of farm acreage also was an important characteristic of middle-class families in our two Delta study counties. Most of the black professional women we interviewed came from "old" middle-class families, although some had escaped poverty, gone to school, and attained a professional occupation. In every case there are important differences between them and their predecessors in both their identity and their relations with others in these communities, including the white elite and the poor black majority.

The late 1970s and 1980s brought changes in opportunities for blacks, even in the rural South, and consequently a new professional black middle class is emerging. As professionals, they are part of an occupational stratum with a long history in the United States.[10] They enjoy the kind of independence and autonomy that, according to sociologists of work, characterize a professional career—aspects that would especially appeal to those who have seen their families dependent and vulnerable for decades.[11]

The black middle-class participants in our study generally did not come from a well-to-do background. But their guardians, one or both parents, grandparents, or other relatives tended to have some kind of assets—physical capital or human capital—that gave them greater independence and higher expectations for their children than most rural blacks in this region. Their parents or their grandparents may have owned a small farm or trade-related business, had a special skill such as a carpenter or mechanic, or served in World War II and taken on responsibilities in their black regiment; they may have migrated to an urban area and worked in a factory, or, most often, been a schoolteacher. One woman's father had worked on the railroad and periodically had taken the family on train trips. In other words, the adults in their families had some basis for economic independence, such as their own business or land, as well as wider cultural exposure to other social worlds, perhaps through the military, migration, or teaching.

The families worked hard, sometimes even at low-status jobs like chopping cotton or domestic work, and generally everyone pitched in. Even those who were poor describe how their parent or guardian "was a good provider," saying they did not "want for anything." In most families education was valued by someone, and in most sacrifices were made so that children could complete school. These children, who now are middle-class adults, also often benefited from some kind of community work program during the summer—sometimes in distant Chicago or St. Louis, where relatives hosted them, other times in these rural communities. Although a few who became professionals did come from a poverty background, most were raised in what were considered "name-brand" families—families with some assets, some education, and a good name in the community—and their children tended to know one another growing up. But whether or not their origins were middle class, in the modest terms such status was possible in these tightly controlled and rigidly segregated counties, they each had someone who looked out for them, who was hopeful for them, and who was demanding of them. They recognize this influence, and deliberately set out to have the same effect on young people in their community.

All but a handful of these middle-class men and women have had some college training, and most have college degrees. In many cases they did not go straight through the university after high school; some took detours to marry, have children, or work. Even for those with a middle-class background, getting a college education took extraordinary commitment and effort, especially when they chose to attend institutions further away than local community colleges. When they were growing up the great majority of black children were expected to leave school during crop planting and harvesting time to help on the plantation. Despite such obstacles, several have graduate training and master's degrees that they completed while holding full-time jobs.

We shall discuss the social origins and work, both paid and volunteer, of four representative black professional women to show how they cooperate to develop their professional skills and to carry out their role as middle-class leaders in their Delta communities. They invest in crucial public institutions like schools and health clinics that serve both their own families and the large number of black poor in the community, and they create new programs that help the poor gain the skills they need to participate in the mainstream. Much of their community focus is on the young people, whom they prod and encourage. We argue that the confluence of their class interests, as black adults raising children in middle-class families, and their personal interests, as ambitious, conscientious professionals, gives weight and permanence to their civic work to improve opportunities for the poor in their communities.

Their efforts are often difficult and frustrating, however, for in these Delta counties, economic and political power remains tightly intertwined. Political activists who work hard to organize the black community find themselves thwarted by the economic dependency that undermines their political rights. As one leader put it:

> It's going to take years to change this. People don't understand that. When you've got people that has been in politics for years and years, you can't just come in and vote them out that easily just by having a black running. I mean, they're ingrained in the community, in the black community. They've got a large share of black people depending on them for housing, for jobs, for Christmas bonus. In other words, they can provide things to these black people that they need. Black people figure if you put Mr. So-and-So out of office, they feel like they're cutting their own neck off. It's economic power. How can you defeat a guy that has got half of the people working for him or that benefit from him, whether through a job, living in one of his houses, or going through him making loans? How are you going to defeat him? They just feel obligated to him because they've worked for him or he's provided them jobs.

Until very recently, most members of the black establishment—such as teachers, preachers, and funeral directors—appeared to cooperate with the white power structure and were scorned as "Toms" by the more radical social activists who wanted to see equity and opportunity rather than accommodation and the status quo for the black community. Politically, the black community was divided into these factions, and whites effectively used the dissension about political goals and strategies to maintain their own control. In this context of scarce opportunities and arbitrary power wielded by the white elite and those who worked for them, distrust and jealousy often characterized relationships outside families. Steadily employed members of both the establishment and the so-called radical leadership groups were derided or, as they say, "labeled," as "uppity-ups" by the poor black majority. Between this distrust and the long-standing dependence on white planters, organizing for social change has been difficult.

But the growth of a new professional class of social welfare workers, health-care professionals, and school personnel is changing this dynamic. Newly elected black officials are beginning to act more independently, backed by the growing expectation of accountability from black professionals. The more liberal white merchants and professionals see new opportunities to work with their black counterparts on antidrug programs, Habitat for Humanity projects, or even in business. White merchants have always depended on blacks who are members of the working poor as customers, but the growth of the black professional class and casino businesses in neighboring counties has opened opportunities for black entrepreneurs as well.

Most of these new professionals, as we shall see, combine economic resources with cultural resources to achieve a kind of new independence from the white bossmen. They come primarily from families that had modest resources in a region where most families had no resources at all, and many have had exposure to worlds outside this segregated and oppressive rural Delta setting. As Carol Stack demonstrates in her account of black return migration, women who have been trained and worked outside the rural South can become a potent political force for change and empowerment on their return (see Chapter 9).[12] They have a different vision of what is possible, as well as experience running programs that can be employed in their professional and volunteer work back home. Their interests as ambitious, conscientious professionals coincide with what their communities need to fight the isolation and dependency of the chronic poor. This is in distinct contrast to their predecessors in the black middle class, who were constrained by the all-encompassing power of a white elite whose interests were in keeping the black poor powerless, both individually and collectively.

The women in our group began thinking about their career path in college, but it was not until they went on the job market that they knew what type of work was—and was not—feasible if they wanted to stay in the area. Some found work in their chosen professions right away, but others "fell into" their jobs at welfare agencies, health clinics, and schools, and learned they were suited for them. They all have made some professional "compromises" for choosing to be near home, but they mostly feel content with their jobs because they see themselves as professionals who are "doing good" in their communities. Here we profile four professional women whose backgrounds, circumstances, and perspectives are representative of that group: Linda, a nurse practitioner; Sarah, a court clerk;

Diane, an educational leader; and Patricia, a social worker in protective services.

Linda

Linda is a thirty-three-year-old nurse practitioner who is married with two sons, aged nine and five. Both her maternal and paternal grandparents owned their own farms in the northern part of the county, a resource and experience that gave them independence. As one interviewee explained the significance of land ownership to Delta blacks:

> Theoretically you have control of your own destiny. You own your own land so you can think of how best to utilize your resources. When you're staying on somebody else's plantation, you move at their will. You know they don't want you; they can discard you like some of the assets that they own. And living on the plantation is just one step up from slavery. You're really still a form of slavery. It just depend on how the plantation owners felt about you, as to how much money they take from you from year to year. When you own your own land, you don't have to worry about that. You learn, you are an entrepreneur, you have to do all these things yourself. You have to learn to take care of your own business. And you get a chance to pass it on to your kids.

When she was two years old Linda and her sister went to live with their aunt and uncle in the Delta. Her uncle farmed the family land, and her aunt worked as a schoolteacher. After finishing grade school in the 1950s, her aunt had been sent away to a boarding school to become a teacher. Thus Linda's family was part of the solid middle class—well-educated property-owners who put a high value on education for their children. They were strict but supportive, she says.

Linda enjoyed school and was involved in activities and clubs. She did not have to work during high school, but after graduation did have the opportunity to get a job in the local welfare department through a summer youth program. The family assumed she would follow her aunt's path and become a teacher, but as a sophomore in high school she decided that she wanted to work in medicine instead:

> It was just something I wanted to do. We had physicians here, but at that time no black physicians and I just wanted to do something different for my community. At that time, the hospital still had blacks on one side and whites on the other side. I always wanted there to be a change.

With her aunt and uncle's help, Linda went away to college in the state capital, a step taken only by a few in her class. At college she joined a sorority and completed a degree in nursing, planning all along to return home to practice her profession.

Sarah

Like Linda, Sarah, now in her early thirties, was born to relative privilege. Her grandmother was a well-regarded teacher in this community, and her parents emigrated to St. Louis, where she was born and lived until she was six. When her parents divorced, she returned with her mother and brother to the Delta, but she always spent summers with her father in the city. Both her parents finished high school, and both held good supervisory jobs in factories. While her mother's parents were sharecroppers, her father's were middle class—her grandfather was a mechanic who had his own business, and her grandmother was a teacher.

As would be expected of a child of her class background, Sarah was heavily involved in high school clubs and teams, and received good grades that put her at the top of the class. When she became pregnant at sixteen, at the end of her sophomore year, she dropped out temporarily at her mother's insistence, had the child, and then returned. No one in the family would have considered an alternative to returning.

> I didn't want to drop out. I never even thought about it. I wanted to further my education. I'm still thinking about it now, going back to school. And my mother and grandmother wouldn't have heard of it—no way! And with my grandmother being a schoolteacher, there was no way I could have dropped out even if I wanted to.

Although she has had a child out of wedlock, she has not been completely a single parent in practical terms. Her daughter's father lives nearby, pays child support, and has stayed involved with their daughter.

Sarah went on to junior college, taking her daughter with her, and after finishing with a degree in business, she returned home to find work. Like many others, she took whatever work she could get in this job-scarce home county, reestablishing contacts, confirming her family's reputation for hard work, and waiting for a more challenging opportunity to emerge. After only a year in a part-time position selling clothes, she saw an advertisement for a newly created judicial position as county court clerk. The clerk would be an administrator to the elected judges, who handle all fines, traffic tickets, misdemeanors, civil cases, and small claims. She applied and was selected for the position by the County Board of Supervisors, who saw her record and her family background as advantages. She and the new judges were trained in this new system at a judicial college in the state capital. There she learned not only how to do the work of a county clerk, but also something very important in this community dominated by white planters accustomed to feudal-like control: that she had professional support from the statewide group if her work were challenged for political reasons.

Diane

Diane is a thirty-six-year-old schoolteacher and educational program co-ordinator who is married with two children. Unlike Linda and Sarah, she grew up very poor. She was one of three children born out of wedlock to a woman who had eleven sons and daughters altogether. When her mother married and moved to town, Diane and her brother stayed in the country to be raised by her great-grandfather who worked as a day laborer on a large farm. He was known and respected as a good worker by the powerful whites in town, and Diane describes him as a good provider: "You know, he may have suffered, but we never went without."

When her mother died in childbirth, her great-grandfather contacted the fathers of the three out-of-wedlock children, and Diane's father stepped in and took an active role in her life. Although her mother and great-grandfather were very poor, her father had a steady truck-driving job in Chicago, where he had a wife and other children. When Diane was growing up, she spent summers visiting her father and his wife in Chicago. There she had the advantages of both living in a new world with "more to do" and being exposed to her stepmother's commitment to ed-ucation. Her stepmother had gone back for her high school equivalency certificate and then went on to nursing school. She believed education was all-important. "She was a big incentive for all of us," Diane said. Through her stepsisters, she learned about summer opportunities for teenagers in Chicago and applied for any available jobs: "I was always able to get on these social program projects that they had. . . . just about every summer I would always walk into a job." These early experiences in Chicago offered more than just a chance for employment, for in the city she also attended cultural events, performed in a choral group, and learned about career options: "It was just a whole other world to me, and I looked forward to doing something else." She went straight through high school to the local state college, majoring in business education.

Patricia

Patricia, thirty years old, comes from a family more like Diane's than Linda's or Sarah's. Her grandparents worked on white planters' farms, chopping weeds and picking cotton, and in their homes, cleaning and baby-sitting. She was raised in a large family of eight children by a mother who worked three and four jobs in a day as a maid in white people's houses to support her children. Her father died in a fight when she was only two. Her mother briefly remarried and had her eighth child, but by the time Patricia was six, her stepfather had left. Like Diane, the family lived in a two-room shack, girls in one bed, boys in another. Her mother was very, very strict—so strict about curfews and not going out that it would sometimes drive Patricia to tears.

Although Patricia's mother had only completed eighth grade when she had to quit school to work, she believed passionately in education. She worked to send her younger sister to college, and all eight of her own children were expected not only to finish high school but to go on either to college or the military. When one would get through college, he or she would be responsible for helping the next one to go.

Like the other women in this group, Patricia was active and successful in high school. Through her high marks and a watchful guidance counselor she had an opportunity to attend Upward Bound at a nearby junior college, where she says she learned how to be independent and develop self-discipline. She played two instruments in the high school band, and after graduation she and a few friends followed this band teacher to Texas, where he had a new job at a college. This experience of attending college in a new environment opened her eyes as she met students from all over the country. She had majored in broadcast journalism, but really wanted to come back home to work. Like Sarah, when she returned she took "all kinds of crazy jobs to start out with. I was a telephone sales person, worked in a furniture factory, worked with U-Haul, worked at the Internal Revenue Service." She had applied to work in the local social welfare office, but others were called before her, a fact she attributes to their better connections: "It's a small town, and you have to know someone." Eventually she did make the right connections, having established a reputation as a good, hard worker in other jobs, and she became a social worker who checks on foster children, adoptions, and abuse cases.

Doing Well: Establishing Professional and Social Identity

Professional women in these two counties work in education, health care, social welfare, and the legal system. They are teachers, nurses, or other health-care professionals, employed in either social work or government-sponsored community programs. Although sometimes referred to as "semiprofessions," in these job-scarce areas where most jobs are controlled by a few powerful whites, semiprofessional work carries not only a professional badge of honor but also real independence from the whims and potential repercussions of the white elite. Those who work in the schools generally were handpicked by the former white superintendent—a wily political operator renown for his racism and sexism, but also savvy about identifying workers with potential. Those who work in the social welfare agencies were hired either by the former, fairly liberal, white supervisor or her black male successor, again employers looking for reliable, professional staff. In these small communities where everyone knows all the local families, workers in health care and county government would be hired by people they have known all their lives. Certainly they are beneficiaries, if belatedly, of affirmative action as well. Beginning in the 1970s more and more of those doing the hiring for growing numbers of public sector jobs in these rural counties would select blacks. In the previous generation those with the ambition, skills, and education needed for such jobs would instead have been teachers or emigrants to urban areas where opportunities were greater. But the combination of a growing professional services sector and the impact of civil rights legislation in the 1960s began to change the rural landscape for black middle-class job-seekers.

The professional women we interviewed take deep pride in their work and hold strong principles about how their work ought to be carried out. At the same time they are savvy about the politics, both racial and personal, that pervade the community. Each grew up chafing under the complete segregation and inequality in her community, and has taken deliberate steps, some open and some quiet, to bring about social justice. They do so in part through their activities in their chosen profession, and in part through their volunteer work in churches and programs for the disadvantaged. Even when they "fell into their profession," as did Sarah and Patricia, they speak about their work with pride, conscious of the obligations and skills it requires.

Linda

Linda married at twenty-two, just as she was completing her bachelor's degree. Her husband was a computer specialist in the military, and she found a good job as a staff nurse in a hospital in the city where they lived, about an hour from her hometown. During this time she also commuted back home to work part-time in the local hospital until it closed. Her two children were born when she was twenty-four and twenty-nine, and shortly after the second child was born she began studying for her master's degree. After completing it, she was looking for a new, better position when a private health-care provider asked her to help set up a new clinic in her hometown. She moved back home with her husband. He has had difficulty finding work for which he is qualified and has held a number of low-skill jobs in recent years. She is in demand at the clinic.

People come to Linda because they know her and trust her, she says, but she finds she really needs to reach out to the poorer residents: "Sometimes you have to carry your programs to the people in a place like this. They don't come to you." One of her achievements has been to form the

Health Coalition, a group of workers in the health department and welfare department who share ideas about what the community needs and coordinate their various programs.

Linda is seen by others and sees herself as a community health leader—several other interviewees mentioned her as an example of a leader whom they admire and work with—and she plans to start an after-hours health clinic to serve the poor in these Delta communities: "I thought about doing an evening clinic on my own with some of my physician friends in Memphis, to come two or three days a week." She feels confident that her idea will work and is now investigating funding sources:

> Because I grew up here, everybody knows me, and they know that I've been doing this type of work all the time. So I think they trust me a lot because I'm from here. It is not really hard. I knew what the community needed and that is the reason I wanted to do it, not so much for just the money, but because there is a need.

Linda plans to undertake a project that will enhance her own professional skills and future while also serving the community by improving health education among women. Recognizing the need for better assessment in her programs, she plans to conduct a survey that will give her data on women's knowledge about their own bodies: "What I want to do is ask: Do they really know how to check for breast cancer and things like that? One woman I treat has tumors, and it's so far gone you can't do anything for her." This research would connect her interest in health practices with her desire for further education and research experience. Although she enjoys her work and is full of ideas for new programs, she is also ambitious and at times regrets her decision to become a nurse instead of a doctor: "Sometimes I wish I went on to medical school."

Sarah

Sarah has been in on the ground floor of the new court system in her home county, and she has considerable responsibility. At the training program in the state capital where she learned the procedures and rules of the new judicial system, she also learned about her professional obligations and her rights on the job.

> We basically deal with the public and their small complaints, do preliminary work for the grand jury, handle these smaller court cases. I have all the administrative duties of the court system. I take affidavits, assign cases to the judges—basically I do it all except hear the cases.

Naturally, in this context where powerful white planters are accustomed to having their way in public as well as private matters, she has been pressured to accommodate their wishes on these small criminal cases. Indeed, many blacks we interviewed in these communities complain about the lack of accountability and legality in police work. But Sarah learned in her training that she has support in the state capital if she is pressured and that it is to those higher judicial bodies that she must answer if justice is not done; she has withstood pressure from even the most powerful, and reputedly racist, planters in her area.

She is proud of the way she, and the judges she supports, work. And she is flattered that several leaders have suggested that she run for judge herself. She does plan to go on for further training, perhaps for a job as a legal aide. "I just feel like no matter what, the more you know, the better you are. I am always pushing my girls to learn as much as you can. It's heavy on me now to go back to school, to study more, to learn more." In the meantime she runs her office professionally, spends time with her teenager daughter and her niece, whom she has adopted, and works with Linda and others on teen recreation projects.

Diane

When Diane completed college she married her high school sweetheart. After a brief time living and working in large cities in neighboring states, they returned home. He wanted to get involved in politics and work for change, and she always planned to live near to home so she could easily help care for her great-grandfather. "Papa's been old ever since I knew him. He's kept me here." One of her summer jobs in Chicago was in a financial institution, so when she first returned she went by the banks for an application. It never occurred to the bank officials that a black woman would seek employment with them, so they brought her a loan application. She left a job application "on file," but never pursued the matter. Today, with affirmative action reaching even these relatively remote Delta counties, each of the local banks has one black female employee.

Diane was trained in business education, but like the others, she took what work she could get, and when there was an opening for a secretary in the school system, "I borrowed a car from a friend and drove down one Monday morning and talked to the principal about it. He told me, 'Yeah, if you want it, you can have it.'" After one year of working as a secretary, an English teacher retired, and Diane was first in line for the job. She applied for her emergency teaching certificate and completed the required courses during the next summer. She worked as an English and remedial studies teacher for ten years, and then assumed the position of local director of a large federal education and training program.

She sees her role as teaching students not only the content of courses but also *how* to be successful. She tries to show them the value of discipline and hard work by prodding them to push themselves and listening:

I spend a lot of my time just trying to talk with young men and young women. Not trying to push any ideas on them or anything, but just talking with them and trying to see what they have on their minds. When you hear something that suggests she's going to fall into the same trap that her other sisters did, you try to talk to her and gear her toward other things. I'm sure that other people are doing this counseling as well. You try to bring in all kind of programs and topics and speakers and people and— you just try to make them see that it has to start right here. I tell them, "You have to get this first. If you're going to get anywhere, you have to get everything that we can give you right here first."

She establishes good rapport with her students and expects a lot:

Now, as far as my classroom and discipline go, I have very few problems. I don't have any kids who will not do what I say or will not try to stick to my schedule. Some people have that problem, I understand. But, I just don't have that kind of problem with my kids for some reason. And I think maybe it is because I do not just see these kids at school. I see them in the community. I see them at church. I'm not sure if that has any effect, but I kind of think it does sometimes—because I can see them and I can speak to them in church about something that's going on. Or, I can see them at school and I can say, "Yeah. I saw you sing in the choir yesterday. You know, you all really sounded good."

Diane worries about the way so many of her older students, especially the welfare mothers she works with in state-mandated summer literacy programs, are easily satisfied living with very few resources:

They just don't realize that there's something else out there. They think, "I'm kind of happy where I am; everything around me seems just fine." And then by the time they're older and they start to realize the cost of it, it's too late, they've gotten into the trap. It's like . . . I see a lot of ladies, even the ladies in this class with me every day, they sit here and they talk about their child-care check or the little check they get for going to school. Like this is what I'm supposed to be getting. It's not like . . . "Okay, I can get me a job paying $15–$30,000 a year." They see that they're going to get this check Friday and the world is fine.

But Diane does not despair entirely; she thinks that, over the long term, working with these women will have a positive effect on their children:

One reason I think we're going to change is because I think we are getting through. Education is going to be the most important thing. Just like all these women are having to come back to school now. . . . Hopefully, they're going to instill a little more into their children. They will say, "Hey, get it while you're there. Go ahead and make sure you get your education." So, we're hoping that education is the first phase of it.

She knows that education is the key for the future of these women and of the young men who refuse to do field work:

> I'm thinking that it has more to do with the changing of the times that these young guys, young black guys, aren't finding jobs. Maybe they're uneducated or undereducated. Most of these guys in that group, I think, just don't *want* to do farm work. Not that they couldn't find a little bit every once in a while. They just don't want to do that. Because I've heard guys say, "I'm not working for no minimum wage." Okay! But you don't have a high school diploma. What else can you work for? Others could be not working because they just don't . . . what?, don't worry about it. A lot of times in that age group . . . from I'd say thirty and under . . . if they're not still at home with parents, then they're with one of these women in low-income housing. They are still not worried about a roof over their heads. So they, I mean, they're eating. These ladies all get food stamps and checks, so they're eating. So a lot of them just don't, at least it's just what I think, a lot of them just don't . . . bother to work.

Although Diane does not let the welfare recipients or young men who drop out of school "off the hook," she does see the root of the problem in the plantation system and the bossmen's ability to keep their workers ignorant:

> Lack of education is one of the things that probably held this community back for so long. For a long time, the farmers just did not want industry in this county because they felt like it would take away all their farmworkers. Which, I'm sure it would have. And so, they just . . . never encouraged or even wanted it. And they resisted education of "their people."

Patricia

As a foster-care social worker, Patricia feels deeply for the children who are her official charges because something is going wrong in their lives. She aches with them, and she looks for ways to keep them with their families if the abuser can be removed:

> The worst thing I've ever had to do in my life is remove a child from a home. As long as I've been doing this here, it tears me up inside; even though you know you're removing them for the right reasons, to protect them, it still hurts. You know, no matter what a parent does to a child, they still love their parents. They still love their moms and daddies.

But she is also tough-minded.

> Most of my cases are sexual abuse cases. There is better reporting now. Not many people knew much about abuse in the way that they could report it. Now, the least little things neighbors see, they call and report it, which is

good. Most of the time if the perpetrator is in the house, we have to remove the child unless the perpetrator leaves. It's often the boyfriend, and
the mother is divorced, or even fathers. But I've been lucky though. Most
of them do jail time. They go here and they admit it. They plead guilty so
they won't have to go through the humiliation of the court. They know
they did it. I say, "Take me on," because I know I would beat them. . . .
Then they're in there a long time. Hopefully the child would be grown
when they get out, and they can protect themselves.

Community Volunteer Work

Black women in the Delta who work in helping professions find themselves in a unique position as leaders in their own communities. They
have the benefit of knowing the economic and political landscape where
they live and are savvy about how to get things done; they may be trusted
by both the poor and the powerful. They have a sense of moral obligation to their community as members of a middle class relatively unfet-
tered by the white elite, and they have a kind of "self-interest" in making
this community a better place for their own children. Doing so, in this
still-segregated Delta, means investing in poor blacks as well as in those
who are better off. Both men and women volunteer substantial time to
work with young people—overseeing scout troops, starting a Pathfinders
group, establishing and coaching out-of-school sports teams, and raising
funds for a recreation center. The men have formalized their organization as the Dahlia Men's Club, while the women work together on an informal basis as friends and through their churches. Linda, Sarah, Diane,
and Patricia are among these volunteer change agents, and like their
friends and co-workers, they often combine outreach with some level of
political involvement, whether to improve black turnout at the polls, hold
elected officials accountable, or prod for greater political participation.

Linda

Although Linda's professional work is in health care, she devotes a good
deal of her community volunteer work to education and teenagers, in
part because she sees the results of idle teens in her clinic when young
pregnant girls come in, and in part because she has her own teenager.
She reaches out to what she has seen elsewhere for ideas about how to
help her community, most recently in terms of how to motivate young
people. She recalls that when she was growing up the only role models
for black youngsters were in the schools:

> We have black public officials now, on the county board, in the sheriff's of-
> fice, but when I was growing up we did not have any. When I was growing

up your role models were inside the school system because becoming a teacher was about the only professional option at that time. And now you have a lot of blacks working in administrative positions, like the Welfare Department. So I guess things are changing.

Linda has plans to show young people in this poor community that they can make something of themselves:

What I have planned is to try to get some motivational speakers and maybe some people to come do a little workshop. I am going to try to contact someone from the radio station to see if they can get some well-named person to come do a free concert. Students would earn bonus points to go to this concert. They would have to attend certain classes and keep their grades up in order to go. So I am going to work on that. I am going to try to get the hospital to help me with the funding and different things like that.

She is concerned that so many people look down on those who are not educated. She hears even her own friends make disparaging comments about people whose parents were only farmers, and she recognizes that this stigmatization is part of what prevents country people from aspiring to more education and better jobs. In her work with both patients and teens, she combines a respectful but demanding approach with practical solutions. For example, although more than three-quarters of her clients are on Medicaid, the other one-fourth who lack insurance may get her personal help. She uses her own discretion about whether to charge patients:

When I get people [who are poor and uninsured] I try to charge them the lowest amount. . . But if I know the person and I know the situation sometimes I would not charge [at all]; they probably won't like it, but I just throw the bill away.

Linda uses her contacts in other places for ideas about how to improve the schools and encourage parents to be more involved:

We're going to start a PTA meeting, start a parents' and a mothers' club, and try to help our kids. This is what we really need. But the parents got to be helped too. A lot of them are really young, and they just don't understand. Sometimes they probably don't even understand the homework themselves, so they can't help their children with it. My cousin who lives in Chicago, they started a program where they would go out and just teach the parents in the home; being a part of the family, they help the kids with their work. So maybe something like this has to happen here. I think this would be a good thing. A lot of them [parents] dropped out of school or when they were in school, they were just there, they were not really trying to learn.

Linda pushes all the groups she is involved in to do more outreach—her church, the school, her teen recreation projects, and, of course, her own clinic. She has seen such organizations work effectively in the community in other places, and she brings those higher expectations for participation and inclusion to her own activities in this more remote rural setting. She and her husband were taking their son to a city some distance away so he could participate in scouts, but last year they started a local troop through their church. In these ways she is expanding the base of resources for the poor in the community, both as a professional and as a concerned parent and resident.

Sarah

Sarah works with Linda and others on the teen recreation program that helps keep teenagers occupied, exposed to challenges and new ideas, and out of trouble:

> It's a program that was started almost eight years ago. A woman in the school system, an assistant teacher who works in the system and sees what goes on, just took an interest up with the kids. And during the summer, she takes a group of kids places and does things with them. Eventually the word spread about what she's trying to do. And she has organizations that are helping her now. It's been chartered now. I'm on the board of directors with them. It's a nonprofit organization. But we're having a problem finding a place to really set it up. Land is so hard to get.

Diane

Diane also looks to examples she hears about or has seen in other communities, and recently she took a few people to a conference so they could see alternatives for themselves: "I think the change has come through those people who have gone out and saw what other communities have. . . . And they say to themselves; 'Why not in our community too?'" She thinks strategically about social change through politics because her husband is an elected official in the area who has been in office longer than most other blacks, and she has seen remarkable changes.

> Black and white. It's such a divided community. I mean, it has only been the last two elections where blacks have really gotten into the political part of the government in this county. Before then there had never been a black on the Board of Supervisors, and as a consequence you never did have any idea what was going on. You knew *nothing* about how they were making decisions, about what opportunities you *could* have had, had somebody put forth a little effort, and what not. So at least now we know some of the barriers and some of the opportunities for programs, for improvements.

Patricia

Patricia also sees the political changes that have occurred, including a growing awareness, even among the less educated blacks, that their votes are now private and that they can vote for their candidate and not their bossman's:

> They finally figured out that they can vote for somebody, and they [whites] wouldn't know who voted for them. A lot of them thought that, "Mr. John is going to see my ballot," or "Miss Mary is going to see my ballot," and "Don't tell so-and-so." But they know now that nobody can see it.

And she sees the increasing number of blacks in positions of authority as reassuring the more fainthearted that they can indeed vote their choice:

> Blacks know now that they've got the power. They've got the power, because there are more blacks in this county than there are whites. We've got the power, now all we've got to do is use it. And now they know that they can make a change, make a difference. It's just like—okay, like knowing we've got a black sheriff, we've got a black service clerk, and had it been ten years ago, no way, you know? No way it would have happened.

But Patricia is not a political activist, since she works for the state, and her community involvement is a combination of extra help to clients and volunteer work with programs through her church:

> I feel very happy when somebody will walk up to me and say, "You're the one who helped somebody." I feel good when I help a client, or when I can organize a group to accomplish some good thing. Like at Christmas time I worked with a local program and I had two days to come up with gifts for forty-five kids. I called around to the local businesses and the rich farmers. Everybody came through and that makes me feel proud. When I saw those little kids' eyes light up with those fifty-dollar dolls—that makes me feel good when I help somebody. When I see a child that's been so pitiful and so, you know, moved around, neglected, and everything, and then when I see them okay that makes me feel good.

Conclusion: Implications for Social Change

These four women we have profiled are not unique—their stories were repeated over and over to us, by both women and men, with differences only in details. There is a new middle class in the rural Delta, made up of black professionals in the social services and public sector, who know their jobs, know their rights, and have higher expectations for their communities and their own roles in them. They have personally experienced racism, understand the power of the white elite, and recognize the source of poor blacks' feeling of vulnerability. But they see some changes in opportunity, and they are working to make a difference.

Whereas their predecessors were often constrained in what they could do to initiate change because their livelihood and status ultimately depended on the white elite, these new middle-class women are not so vulnerable. There are cases when whites have the power to stop efforts to bring about change: they certainly have succeeded in maintaining control over land to prevent the development of crucial middle-class and low-income housing as well as a youth recreation center and black-owned businesses. But the fruits of the civil rights movement are gradually reaching even these isolated communities, and the sacrifices and investments of an earlier generation of working- and middle-class black guardians are bearing more fruit in the good works and important contributions their children are carrying out as adults.

Barrington Moore, Jr., in *Social Origins of Dictatorship and Democracy,* and Daniel Chirot, in *Social Change in the Modern Era,* are among those who argue that democracy emerges where there is a strong capitalist middle class who oppose political authoritarianism because it infringes on their own liberties and their children's future opportunities.[13] Many students of development around the world have shown that "potentially" middle-class families ally with elites in underdeveloped societies because such alliances serve their self interest when economic power is concentrated in the hands of a few.[14] What makes a difference for political freedom, and thus social change, is economic freedom. Professional work in human services and the public sector offers a kind of economic freedom in rigidly stratified and segregated rural Delta counties. The women described here, like the women in Carol Stack's *Call to Home,* are changing the face of the South by carrying out their jobs professionally and investing in inclusive institutions in their communities.

Notes

Acknowledgments: This work was supported by the Ford Foundation's Rural Poverty and Resources Program and, through a subcontract with Pennsylvania State University, by the U.S. Department of Agriculture.

1. James C. Cobb, *The Most Southern Place on Earth* (New York: Oxford University Press, 1992), p. 28.

2. See John Dollard, *Caste and Class in a Southern Town* (1937; reprint, Garden City, NY: Doubleday, 1957); Hortense Powdermaker, *After Freedom* (1939; reprint Madison: University of Wisconsin Press, 1993).

3. See Cobb, *Most Southern,* p. 207.

4. See Cobb, *Most Southern,* p. 232; Sidney Kronus, *The Black Middle Class* (Columbus, OH: Charles Merrill, 1970), who developed a typology of middle-

class blacks in which he defined "Uncle Toms" as blacks who are pro-white and anti-black. Our interviewees used "Toms" to describe blacks who accommodate whites' wishes even at the expense of blacks.

5. See Dollard, *Caste and Class*, pp. 220–49; and Powdermaker, *After Freedom.*

6. Ibid.

7. See Daniel C. Thompson, *Sociology of the Black Experience* (Westport, CT: Greenwood Press, 1974), pp. 227–28; Powdermaker, *After Freedom*, pp. 223–24.

8. See Powdermaker, *After Freedom.*

9. See Thompson, *Black Experience.*

10. Much of the research on the American middle class has been historical, tracing its self-conscious emergence in the eighteenth and nineteenth centuries. Robert H. Wiebe (*The Search for Order, 1877–1920* [New York: Hill and Wang, 1967]) focuses specifically on the growth of self-conscious "occupational cohesion" among health, education, and social welfare professionals at the turn of the century, while C. Wright Mills's classic study *White Collar: The American Middle Classes* (New York: Oxford University Press, 1951) lays out the transformation of the middle class from a petit bourgeois and artisan base to a white-collar class of middle managers in the early twentieth century. See Melanie Archer and Judith R. Blau, "Class Formation in Nineteenth-Century America: The Case of the Middle Class," *Annual Review of Sociology* 19 (1993): 17–41; Stuart M. Blumin, *The Emergence of the Middle Class: Social Experience in the American City: 1760–1900* (New York: Cambridge, 1989). Also see Mary P. Ryan, *Cradle of the Middle Class: The Family in Oneida County, New York, 1790–1865* (Cambridge: Cambridge University Press, 1981).

11. Joanne Miller, "Jobs and Work," in Neil J. Smelser, ed., *Handbook of Sociology* (Newbury Park, CA: Sage Publications, 1988), pp. 327–59.

12. Carol Stack, *Call to Home: African Americans Reclaim the Rural South* (New York: Basic Books, 1996).

13. Barrington Moore, Jr., *Social Origins of Dictatorship and Democracy: Lord and Peasant in the Making of the Modern World* (Boston: Beacon Press, 1966); Daniel Chirot, *Social Change in the Modern Era* (San Diego: Harcourt Brace Jovanovich, 1986).

14. Paul Baran, *The Political Economy of Growth* (New York: Monthly Review Press, 1957); Eugene Genovese, *The Political Economy of Slavery* (New York: Vintage Books, 1967).

9

Holding Hands

*An American Struggle
for Community*

Carol Stack

The exodus of rural African Americans from the South to Northern cities had all but ceased by the 1970s. Since then, in a little-noted but highly consequential turn of events, the process has reversed: black Americans have been leaving an urban Northern economy that failed them and returning South. The South has regained from the cities of the North the half-million black citizens it lost to northward migration during the 1960s. For many, the destinations are rural communities that by all statistical measures can only be assessed as some of the least promising places in the United States—places the U.S. Department of Agriculture calls "persistent poverty counties."

The story of this return migration is one of hardships—of starting over, of poverty, of rural life—but it is also the story of how people came back intent on applying hard lessons learned up North to build new lives. Going home requires reworking established relationships between men and women, parents and children, blacks and whites—and between those who never left the South and those coming back. Such sweeping readjustment is always emotionally and socially perilous.

It also offers all sorts of disturbing reflections on current thinking and policy-making on poverty and race. In the now fashionable term used by Robert D. Putnam, the returnees are engaged in "social capital formation" as they create networks of mutual support and build institutions for community action.[1] But these activities have brought the returnees into a collision course with the established white hierarchies. For years, it turns out, white officials in these hard-scrabble rural counties have been withholding federal entitlements from those entitled to them.

The communities to which these people return share a certain statistical profile. They are located far from big cities and from Sunbelt industry, rank way below national and even state averages for income, are linked historically to the traditional Southern cash crops, and are skewed demographically by generations of out-migration. Black people have traditionally made up the majority of the population in such places, although all the decades of black exodus have sometimes changed the local racial balance.

In researching the story of the return to these places, I crisscrossed nine counties in the Carolinas from the 1980s through the 1990s. But there are many other communities like them, in all the Southern states. I talked with white public officials across the region, but my study was primarily conducted among a broad cross section of African Americans who had returned to rural Southern homeplaces in the Carolinas: professionals, workers, unemployed workers, landowners and people who had lost their land, Vietnam veterans, people starting small businesses, and experienced but out-of-work bureaucrats. Some people were drawn home by rootless, jobless urban decay. Others, made stronger by the uncompromising demands of urban life, came back South acting on an obligation to help their kin or even a sense of mission to redeem a lost community.

But what these migrants experienced on their return has to give pause. The local power structures in the communities where returnees have sought to establish themselves have done everything in their power to thwart efforts at institution building. The same public officials who would administer block grants in rural counties are setting up obstacles to thwart community and civic action at its best.

Chestnut County is a highly rural and not particularly progressive setting.[2] In 1980, census-takers counted fewer than 1,000 people in the county seat, Chowan Springs, and just 467 in Rosedale, the next largest town. Nonetheless, by 1981 three women believed that the time had come for a group that would try to tackle the problems of Chestnut County hands-on, by creating an organization called Holding Hands.

In the setbacks imposed upon it by local power-holders, Holding Hands differs little from other new organizations in the regions I studied. County by county, the assault on such groups—MAC (Mothers and Children, Inc.) and CATS (Chestnut Action for Teenage Students) in Chestnut County, AWW (Alliance of Women Workers) in Powell County, and CEO (Coalition for Employee Ownership) in Poe County, to name a few—continues into the 1990s.

Holding Hands was founded by three returnees: Collie Mae Gamble, who had had a job in Camden, New Jersey, processing bids on government contracts; Isabella Beasley, who had worked for a state agency in Newark, New Jersey, that administered federal funds for Head Start; and Shantee Owens, who brought home experience with public bureaucracies in the Bronx. Such backgrounds established these women locally as people to be contended with. Those who had never left Chestnut County had also formed organizations around social issues, but never with the same scope or the same effect.

Back home by the early 1980s, these women began talking about local social conditions and the poverty surrounding them. The direct inspiration for Holding Hands can be traced to a backyard barbecue in late October 1981, but the origins actually went much farther back, as any of the women involved could explain, to painful lessons they had begun learning in 1979, when the first of them moved home again from the Bronx. Even earlier, in the 1960s and 1970s, the women had developed ways of dealing with the world while they were working their way through school, selling Amway products and life insurance, moving to the city, raising families, running PTAs and scout troops, and working in corporate offices and government agencies. Even more fundamentally, the roots of Holding Hands had been planted back in the 1950s, when the women were growing up as the daughters of sharecroppers and as best friends who just knew that everything was going to work out all right.

The aims of their project could hardly have been more basic. If there was somebody without heat, they would bring them a load of wood or lend them a down payment for a tank of oil. If somebody's porch steps were broken, or if their children needed coats, or if they needed a ride to town to see if they could get food stamps, or if they needed a sack of groceries to get through the month, or if they just wanted to learn to write their name—well, Holding Hands could help with that. The club could help when there was an old person who couldn't get around any more without a walker but couldn't afford the walker. And in the winter, for the people living in those little old houses that had no ventilation, where the air would get so hot from the stove that you could see the heat waves ripple around the room, Holding Hands would supply a fan. The organization did things as simple as that—little things that would make a difference.

Isabella recalled an organization in Newark called Helping Hands, which led them to their name: Holding Hands. This was exactly its fundamental mission: to hold their neighbors' hands, to help out at a basic level. They would just do what they could do, but of course they would do everything the right way—they would need bylaws and dues and fundraising strategies and goals and objectives. They would need another meeting.

Holding Hands got off to a decidedly businesslike start. Dues were set at ten dollars a month, and the initial membership goal was one hundred women in each of three counties—Chestnut, Powell, and Harden. By the end of 1981, Holding Hands was incorporated as a tax-exempt, nonprofit organization. On Martin Luther King's birthday in January 1982, the club held a memorial ceremony at the newly refurbished community building in New Jericho. By the end of 1982, they'd reached their goal of one hundred members in Chestnut County, and had signed up fifty-eight members in Powell County and thirty-one in Harden County. Because cutting wood had become a major club activity, the bylaws were amended to admit men as members. The maximum grant for a family was set at two loads of wood plus one hundred dollars, which usually worked out to fifty dollars in cash and fifty dollars in food. They would also supply sheets and pillowcases, a high chair, toys, a kitchen table and chairs—whatever people needed. Families whose houses had burned, for example, received one hundred dollars, plus household items and food.

At the end of the second year, Collie Mae wrote a grant application for Holding Hands and applied for funding from the Z. Smith Reynolds Foundation:

> A couple of weeks before we got our first grant, I got three phone calls in one day from people who would not identify themselves. They threatened that we better watch out, we're asking for trouble. Instead of hanging up on them, I asked, "Now, who is this 'we' you're talking about?" And they said, "You just keep your hands to yourself—keep your hands to yourself." In other words, the "we" was Holding Hands.

Isabella got calls, too, and she also got letters: "There were at least three letters we know about that were sent to social services to try and discredit us." Members found notes on their cars. "White folks don't want us organizing, but then they never stop talking how we can't do for ourselves. But I say let's just keep going—'cause we're helping."

Isabella, meanwhile, was taking her Amway products to every town, every hamlet, every crossroads for miles around. Anywhere she knew anybody—which was virtually everywhere in Chestnut County's six hundred square miles—she sold her wares and visited with the folks and learned about what was going on. One thing she learned was why she was having such a hard time finding a job, including one for which she seemed perfectly suited.

The county social services department had advertised for someone with expertise in administering federal funds. Isabella had gotten an interview, but the director had brushed her off immediately, saying that her background was not at all what they needed. She'd been baffled by his rejection until she'd traveled the backroads of the county for a while and realized that Chestnut had no projects whatsoever funded by the federal programs she had been working with in New Jersey. No Head Start and no day care—zero federal dollars. Locally, the only federal money that the social services office administered went for food stamps and Aid to Families with Dependent Children (AFDC), even though there were other federal programs designed specifically for areas with high levels of poverty, a description that fit Chestnut County if it fit anywhere. Isabella hadn't yet heard all the explanations for this situation from local officials, but she had seen enough to realize that they preferred not to provide the poor people of the county with such services as day care, even if they could be offered without spending a penny of local money.

About 20,000 people lived in Chestnut County, 60 percent of them black. Almost 40 percent of the population—nearly 8,000 people—lived below the poverty line. Unemployment was high, but there were many more people working than not working, which to Isabella meant that demand for day-care services must be strong. And most of the jobs in Chestnut and surrounding counties paid minimum wage or thereabouts, and offered nothing or next to nothing in the way of employee benefits, which to Isabella meant that unsubsidized day-care services must be far beyond what most working people in the area could afford.

While working her Amway territory, Isabella made a point of visiting all the day-care centers she could find, and there were a few, scattered here and there in private homes, run-down storefronts, and church basements. Conditions in most of the centers shocked her: at one overcrowded private operation, called The Three Bears, she noticed missing stairboards, a broken window with jagged glass at the children's eye level, a jug of bleach sitting on the bathroom floor, filthy rags used and reused for diaper changing, and Kool-Aid instead of milk served at mealtime. Such a place could never pass even a fire inspection, much less meet minimal safety and sanitary standards for a facility jam-packed with young children—and *it* had a waiting list.

Isabella knew, however, that the federal government had money available precisely for quality day-care in communities too poor to afford it. She knew the money was there, she knew the criteria for obtaining it, and she knew the procedure for applying for it. And even before Collie Mae pointed it out to her, she knew that she was in a position to make a big difference in the lives of her friends and neighbors. She began by documenting the situation. Two food-processing plants in Chestnut County employed more than 1,000 workers, and three other such plants in nearby counties employed 2,000 more. A sewing factory employed 210 people, and a furniture-maker employed more than 400. Wages in all these industries averaged just over five dollars an hour.

Isabella talked to parents, and she spoke with public officials, who admitted to her face what she had begun to suspect: that they turned back these funds year after year. "One lady told me she didn't believe in government subsidies at all, even though her office manages AFDC and food stamps." In another office the director said it was a point of pride for him that in his county they served very few of the eligible families—many fewer than in a lot of places—and that poor people have more dignity and self-regard for it.

Isabella believed she could organize an effort to bring Title XX day-care funds to Chestnut County, and she knew the people to call upon; she was not alone. She called on Collie Mae, of course; and on Eula Grant, who had become a vice-president of Holding Hands; and on longtime community activist Menola Rountree and on somebody else recommended by Shantee, a woman named Maude Allen, who worked as director of CATS, Chestnut Action for Teenage Students. Maude was someone who could make things happen.

At the first meeting, Isabella reminded everybody that government bureaucracy moved slowly. They gave their organization a name—MAC, or Mothers and Children, Inc.—and they set up a timetable for preparing for the mandated preliminary inspection of their model day-care facility, with Collie Mae in charge of site selection.

When Maude Allen asked how they planned to obtain the necessary application forms, Isabella smiled; such a question demonstrated sophistication about the hard realities of local politics. The only way was to circumvent the local social service agencies altogether; MAC would have to drive all the way up to the state capital and request the packet of forms in person.

Collie Mae arranged for MAC to use the old Shell gas station in Chowan Springs for their initial demonstration project. They wouldn't have to pay rent, but every inch of the building needed repair and renovation. The fund-raising that followed was like shaking money out of the bottom of the piggy bank. The women from the Working Women's Curb Market, a produce stand on the highway outside of Chowan Springs, provided MAC with "office" space—a card table and a rusty filing cabinet in the storage shed behind the stand.

Working across county lines, MAC focused all its efforts on establishing one single model day-care center. They wrote a grant application, and then, eager to lay the groundwork for a close working relationship with state officials, they took a preliminary draft in person to the chief deputy director in the Day-Care Section of the Department of Human Services in the state capital.

He reviewed their work; they made a point of calling him about every detail, consulting him on the dotting of every "i" and the crossing of every "t." After eighteen months, they received official notification of their first grant award.

And that was when the trouble began. Notice of the grant was also sent to the county director of social services in Chowan Springs, a Mrs. Beard, who immediately announced that every penny of that money would be returned to the state. Isabella went over Mrs. Beard's head to her new friend in the state capital.

> I worried the chief deputy director to death trying to find out what happened to our funds. We had renovated the building and completely furnished it. There were all the little tables and chairs, and the mats, the toys, the playground. We had interviewed day-care teachers and assistants, and we had begun training. We had checked eligibility and assembled a group of children—not all black children, either—it was strictly on income. We had everything but the funds.

The chief deputy director again sent the funds to Chestnut County. This time, the social services department passed the buck to the county commissioners, who were supposed to approve all funds coming into the county.

At the commission meeting, Mrs. Beard made no secret of her department's opposition to public support of day-care. Most of the commissioners were like-minded, but Maude Allen, anticipating the precise tone of the meeting, had made a move that seemed able to break the logjam: MAC packed the meeting room with all the little children who were set to attend the new center. The children sat together in the first three rows of adult-sized chairs, squirming and occasionally whimpering, and the parents and ministers and MAC board members who had come prepared to speak never had to say a word; officially, day-care funding was approved by a murmured voice vote.

From then on local opposition to MAC was limited to behind-the-scenes tactics. Bureaucrats stalled, politicians filed to reduce the allocation, clerks said they couldn't locate the funds, officials forgot about appointments and forgot to file papers and forgot how to write a check. Eventually, the commission informed MAC that the funding was secure, but that it would be administered by none other than the county director of social services, their good friend Mrs. Beard. The MAC women learned to work through her by maneuvering around her and by becoming accustomed to delays, broken promises, unmet deadlines, and the unfulfilled needs of parents who trusted them.

After three years, MAC was able to pull the political levers that changed the process of funding so that money could be allocated directly to their projects. But local attempts at sabotage continued, and the endless attention they consumed ate at the organizers' hearts and nibbled at the nerves of civic engagement. Shantee told me:

> When I was coming up, I gave things my best shot. But better than any teacher, even better than my Amway lessons, time is the best teacher, time makes the difference!
>
> Our saving grace was that we created alliances across at least three counties. When this all got started we could have been in, you know, competition. But then we started helping one another out. If one group was having trouble getting the money—political problems—well, one of us from another county would call the state capital for them, help them out with our direct contacts. We began to train board members in how they could help. We approached our state representative. Only the strong survive.

By 1986, MAC was operating three day-care centers in Chestnut County, one in Powell County, and two in Harden County. Rose Towers, Sunshine Center, Toddlers Club House, Lady Bug, Children's Wonderland, and Teddy Bear Town were all safe and sanitary child-care facilities, with trained staffs, developmentally oriented curricula, parent participation on the boards, and a sliding fee schedule. More than three hundred children were enrolled. Fifty new full-time jobs and a couple of dozen part-time jobs were created directly to staff the centers. Many parents could now hold jobs. Isabella became MAC's paid director. Shantee Owens was hired to manage Lady Bug Day Care Center.

Holding Hands and MAC represent a new type of organizing activity in poor rural communities. As efforts in grass-roots mobilization and self-help, they cannot fail to impress. But clearly, serious and sustainable services in desperately poor rural counties require funding that turkey raffles and fish fries can never provide by themselves. Nor will the contributions from the tiny handful of black business and professional people in these communities suffice. The projects might be aided to a degree by local tax support, but political resistance is unyielding. They also might be helped significantly by large industries employing local people, but the precedent is not auspicious. Corporations in places like Powell and Chestnut counties have never supported local organizations in the black community.

People who return and get involved feel they have to go it alone.

The new Old South isn't the old Old South, but distrust, fear, and hostility persist. In the midst of so much bitterness and ill will, outside money is a critical resource. Dogged self-help, with no reliance on government funding, can support some small initiatives, such as Holding Hands, but even Holding Hands eventually needed outside money, for which they turned to charitable foundations—and even a hundred Holding Hands can't do it all.

Where large numbers of people lack the minimal necessities of life, public funds make a difference. Organizing by black women and men to help provide obviously needed services—firewood, say, or safe child care—is perceived by "the white community" as threatening rather than helpful. An outsider might suggest that within the white community are surely as many nuances and varieties of opinion as exist within the black community. But it often doesn't sound that way to a black person listening to discussions at county commission meetings or to the current government debate over what the poor need.

In the mean-spirited, antigovernment mood of the 1990s, indeed, everyone seems eager to pronounce on what the poor really need. What they need, people tell us, is not government handouts but the sort of social capital that can only arise from their own individual or community self-reliance. Let government withdraw from the affairs of the poor, then. Or, if there is to be any federal role in supporting the poor or the weak, let it take the form of block grants, lump sums given to the states. The good folks there are closer to "their people," the story goes; they will know better than Washington bureaucrats how best to use these resources.

This rhetoric fuels the ideological fires of those who were never much concerned about the well-being of out-of-work and needy citizens in the first place. But the experience of those returning to their rural roots lays bare a dismal reality.

Block grants—that is, welfare payments in one lump sum—are headed in the wrong direction. They are on their way to the states and from there to the counties. No one has wrestled with the political implications of local control over block grants, especially in rural regions of the Southeast that remain battlegrounds of distrust in the 1990s. In these localities the people who proclaim most loudly the urgency and legitimacy of self-help—the bureaucrats and politicians—are the same people who, when faced with actual self-help organizations in their home communities, work to thwart them. The social consequences of decentralization can be predicted before this new intervention hits the streets—or America's back roads.

Notes

Acknowledgment: This article is adapted from my book *Call to Home: African Americans Reclaim the Rural South* (New York: Basic Books, 1996).

1. See Robert D. Putnam, "The Strange Disappearance of Civic America," *The American Prospect* 24 (Winter 1996).

2. Most people have never heard of the towns or counties where I did my research, but out of respect for the privacy of the people who shared their lives with me, I have changed both the place names and the personal names in this chapter.

10

Women and Revolutionary Relations

Community-Building in Appalachia

Monica Kelly Appleby

There is more than one *I* in these words. I write in the first person, singular and plural. *I* am Monica Kelly Appleby, a member of FOCIS, the Federation of Communities in Service. *We* are FOCIS. FOCIS is a nonprofit, community-building organization in Appalachia; it was created in 1967 by forty-four women who organized as a group to leave the Home Mission Sisters of America (Glenmary Sisters) of the Roman Catholic Church. For some thirty years, FOCIS members have lived in local communities throughout the mountains of Appalachia, seeking to create relationships and social change from the bottom up.

This chapter explores how FOCIS people, mostly women, live and work in local communities, what patterns have emerged in our efforts, and what we have learned about community life and work. While beginning the larger research project of which this chapter is a part, an article by Coleman McCarthy appeared out of the blue on Christmas Day, 1996, in the *Washington Post*. It reminded me of the original context of our formation. In the article, "The Revolutionary Mary," McCarthy likens us to Mary as she is depicted in the Magnificat (Luke 1:46–55):

> Mary sings of her God, who has "scattered the proud in the conceit of their hearts. He has put down the mighty from their

thrones . . . " This is the tone of a woman who has a taste for the revolutionary, a woman of impatience who sees the overthrow of the rich as a cause for celebration. . . .

In the 1960's, both the Immaculate Heart of Mary Sisters of Los Angeles and the Glenmary Sisters of Cincinnati came up against the male-centered conservatism of local bishops. Empowered by the renewals of the Second Vatican Council, large numbers of Sisters in both these orders left to form their own communities and directly serve those of low degree.[1]

Revolutionary Relations

The "revolutionary" emerges in relation to a certain time and place in history. In a sense we, during the Glenmary to FOCIS transition, were in such a time and place in Appalachia. The dynamics that pushed us to leave Glenmary and start FOCIS involved both the institutional male-dominated hierarchy of the Roman Catholic Church and our personal differences within the community. The place, the time, the institution, and the people all played a part in the decision to form FOCIS in 1967.

We were "creating something new," and that meant finding words for ourselves. Here is one way we tried to describe ourselves: "FOCIS members live in local communities as inside-outsiders, residents of Appalachia who have come from other places. With this identity they live as neighbor, friend, interested citizen, professional worker and community participant." These words were written in 1968–69 as part of a report on the grant-supported program Discovery, Expression, Communication—An ARTS Approach to the Problems of Appalachia. The report was entitled "Stay with Us. Don't Go 'Way."

I have lived in southwest Virginia since the summer of 1959. And I am still learning about what it means to be a neighbor, friend, citizen, worker, and participant. The organization we named FOCIS has changed through these years as a consequence of what we learned in the local and regional communities of southern Appalachia. Interviewing others involved in the same experience has helped me see our different perspectives within a more whole picture.

The information that appears in this chapter is part of a much larger book project of which I have been the coordinator. Helen Lewis will actually put the words together for the book *Changing Habits: A Community of Sisters Tells Its Story*. So far, we have twenty-two transcribed oral history interviews, written answers to survey questions, results from focus groups and reflection groups, observations from celebrations and meetings, networking diagrams, and maps. We have documents, photographs, poetry, music, visual art—and stories.

The Glenmary Sisters

Why would an active young woman want to become a Catholic sister? Why a Glenmary Sister in particular? In the 1960s there were compelling reasons (which have not been the same since):

> I really wanted to be a religious. *It meant being a woman of power.* The women I saw who were religious did something more important than other women I knew. My only figures of women were my mother, aunts, sisters and my teachers. Sisters always had something important to do. They were important people, important to the church; people showed them respect, they talked about important things, and talked about other places I didn't know existed. They were broader than my world, so I guess those were the attractions. (Beth Ronan)

> Social researchers say that women who attend all-women colleges are more likely to end up in leadership positions. The convent was certainly an "all-girls" school and my institution of higher learning. It was perfect for me to be the strong decisive woman I am. (Geraldine Peterson)

> I found that the Glenmary Sisters group had interest in us as individuals, and it was a priority with them and they wanted to be in touch with us. They wanted to learn about you. This was new territory for me. Years later I learned an expression by Mary Daly, "that women need to experience their own experience." I was beginning to sense the implications of that. (Margaret Gregg)

Becoming a Glenmary Sister was an experience of developing as a person and finding out about the institutional church from the inside. We were given the opportunity to do things we had never done before, never even dreamed of doing. Through experiencing our own personal power we came to be at odds with the institution of the church and left to "create something new," as Margaret Gregg said.

The Federation of Communities in Service

In 1967, with the breakup of the Glenmary Sisters in Appalachia, forty-four women joined to form the Federation of Communities in Service. FOCIS, as we call it, is a nonprofit, tax-exempt organization with no formal connection to the institutional church. The charter of its incorporation states the purpose: "to participate in the life and culture of the people of Appalachia through community development and the arts and through charitable, religious and educational activities."

Anne Leibig, one of our group, wrote, "We left Glenmary and created a new organization rather than confront and change. I sense that we have been women who want to create what we believe in rather than confront and change the other. In looking at all the corporations I have helped form I would say I rather create than confront."

The women who created FOCIS had in mind the goal of continuing to work with the people of Appalachia. That was more important than remaining a religious sister. For many of the women who joined FOCIS, the prime attraction was the other women themselves:

> The FOCIS group were the ones that made me think differently. . . . I didn't feel I was doing a bad thing, just that I was challenged by this group of women. (Beth Ronan)

> I am sure I got exposed to a lot of things through FOCIS that, had I not been connected, I would have missed. It was a real growth experience for me. I think the friendships that came out of that are so strong and solid. (Mary Herr)

> I have a broader perspective because of the [FOCIS] relationships than other people who live in Big Stone or Wise County, [Virginia]. . . . There was this long connection. (Kathy Hutson)

By moving to communities, FOCIS people brought with them their history of relationships and their ability to create organizations and programs that meet real personal and community needs. It was natural for us to create locally based and in many instances regionally connected organizations where we lived. From our beginnings as Glenmary Sisters, we were different from other groups of sisters in that we were "noninstitutional"; in other words, we did not run schools or hospitals. We were more inclined to find people we could connect with and then work with them around something that was needed in the community.

In the first year after the founding of FOCIS we started a program, funded by the Irwin Sweeney Foundation, called the ARTS Approach to Community Development. Teams of community artists—musicians, photographers, graphic artists, filmmakers, cooks, drama people—entered communities where FOCIS members were living in rural eastern Tennessee and southwestern Virginia, Knoxville, Chicago, and Cincinnati. During the summer of 1969, they helped form local community arts groups, some of which still exist.

We learned from this experience that we didn't want to enter communities as an outside organization with staff and funds. That did not fit the way we wanted to live:

> We would raise the money as FOCIS and we were controlling how it was spent. So, after we did that for one year, we decided rather than the money coming through FOCIS and us sending out these teams, communities could decide what they wanted to do within the parameters of the art expression of building the community. . . . After that, we raised money directly for communities. (Monica Appleby)

During the early 1970s, partly as a result of the popular upheavals of the previous decade, several philanthropic organizations changed the way their funding was controlled. The Commission on Religion in Appalachia began to include community groups in grant-making decisions. The Campaign for Human Development (the funding arm of the Catholic Conference of Bishops) developed the stipulation that representatives of the community must constitute the majority of the board of the grantee. FOCIS, too, has continued the practice of directing its fundraising efforts toward community groups rather than our own organizational programming. These changes made it possible to create and sustain community organizations for longer periods of time:

> There is a much stronger feeling of community organization that happened in Appalachia over the past twenty-five years. When I first came here there were no organizations. There was the family and the church. There weren't any organizations that had names like the Dungannon Development Commission or Appalachian Women Empowered or the Black Lung Organization. They were mainly begun by women. . . . It was women who mainly did it. The people who actually do the work are women. Sometimes you will find men who seem to be elected to the Boards. But the glue and hard work is always women. (Monica Appleby)

> I think that is one of the contributions we made in communities: we helped other women create their own organizations. So that they could do what they wanted to do in their community. We had to create our own organization. That is one of the things I learned about the change from Glenmary to FOCIS: we had to create ourselves. (Monica Appleby)

The rest is in the stories. What follows is the story of the beginning of the Bread and Chicken House, a workers' cooperative that was run by women in Big Stone Gap, Virginia, for seventeen years until competition from fast-food operations, an economic recession, and management difficulties put it out of business. It is a poignant example of what happens when:

- Relationships are created with women across class, race, religious, and geographic lines.
- There is access to resources such as funding and ideas beyond what is available in the community.
- There are the energy and experience to create something new.

The Bread and Chicken House

Most of the long quotations that follow are the words of Catherine Rumschlag, who was our Mother Superior in the Glenmary Sisters. For thirty years she has lived in Big Stone Gap, where she runs the homeless shelter known as Appalachian Family Ministries. I lived in Big Stone from 1959 until 1970. In the early years I mainly organized summer Bible schools and visited families in their homes. The women I got to know wanted to earn money to feed and clothe their children as the mines were automating and many men were losing their jobs. The women made cloth dolls and banners that we helped sell through our church networks. Later, some of the women from several of the hollers, coal camps, and towns got together to form Mountain People's Work, a craft group. The women came together because they knew us, not because they knew each other. They were black and white and of different religious backgrounds. There were class differences and distance factors as well. Some lived in town and others in hollers or camps. It was among this group that the Bread and Chicken House was born:

> I learned that a local restaurant had excellent bakery equipment that was little used. I went to the owner and told him of our interest. He suggested that I bake for him on a part-time basis. He would market the products and pay by the hour and I would gain some experience with baking in this area.
>
> I did this for some months and then he told me he planned to sell his restaurant. He also planned to sell a smaller business, Mr. D's Chicken House, which operated out of a small building behind the restaurant. He suggested that we take over the chicken carryout and combine it with the bakery business. Four of the women in the sewing group [Mountain People's Work] made a commitment to the project. We invited one more woman to join us. Oaklee had been the chief cook at Mr. D's restaurant and was living on unemployment compensation, since the restaurant was closed. We agreed to pay Oaklee the amount she was getting from compensation, while the other members would work as volunteers to get the business started. Two members were working full-time at a sewing factory, but donated time after work to the new business.
>
> The Bread and Chicken House was legally incorporated as a workers' cooperative. Founding members besides myself and Oaklee were: Illinoise Mitchell, a black woman who had been manager of the kitchen in the black school before integration. She had also been a cook and baker for private families at different times. She had jobs in the community action program, and when those funds were cut she worked in the sewing factory. Harriet Bush was also black. She was the mother of eight children. Her husband had been injured in the mines, and she worked in the sewing factory. Alberta Stanley lived in Derby, a mining camp. She was the wife of Jim Stanley, who played guitar and sang at many events sponsored by Glenmary Sisters and FOCIS.
>
> . . . The business opened March 11, 1971. The FOCIS group loaned $2,500 to the business to pay our first bills. None of the members had any capital. We paid our bills out of the day's receipts. . . . We were quite excited about having our own business.
>
> . . . Before long we were paying all workers an hourly wage, beginning

at somewhat less than minimum wage. . . . There was a good spirit of cooperation among the workers. During the first year we were having difficulty paying the bills, and the members of the cooperative volunteered to cut our own wages so that we could make it. We operated at a loss the first year, but after that we made a small profit during the succeeding years when we used the original building. . . .

. . . During the first year we learned of the Campaign for Human Development and its purpose of helping with developments among low-income people. We applied for $20,000 and received a $10,000 grant. That was a great help in meeting the demands of the business.

. . . After seventeen years of operation, the Bread and Chicken House closed. The five women who started the project continued until it closed, except for Illinoise, who retired (she was over seventy years old), and Oaklee, who died of cancer. . . . At the height of the operation we had from fifteen to twenty workers. Salaries were not much more than minimum wage, but we did try to consider workers' needs. There was usually a good spirit among the workers and I enjoyed the years of working there. In starting this business, I thought it would be more simple than being head of a religious community, simply working with women to make a living. When I was manager, however, I found that the administrative duties were surprisingly similar.

Reflections on Networking and Organizational Development

The Bread and Chicken House is only one of the many organizations associated with the community work of FOCIS. A story can be told about each one of the organizations listed on the following map. In order to view the dynamic relationship-building process of creating community, several people associated with FOCIS drew up the map in February 1997 at the Highlander Center in New Market, Tennessee.

The map was created by diagramming the places where individual FOCIS members have lived at different times. Through this process we identified the "hubs." At first, it looked like an airline map. Then we identified the local place names and wrote down the organizations that FOCIS people were involved in starting. Next we identified the regional organizations. At this point the map looked very messy. What is shown here is the more streamlined version.

We have identified the communities only in the southern mountains and have given the shortened names of the organizations. The groups in which we participated appear under the local place names. Seven areas and sixty-one organizations or programs are diagrammed. Most of the organizations were mobilized around issues or needs that are close to home—survival and safety, food, land, health, housing, education, work. The organizations in which two FOCIS-affiliated men played a major role

Networking and Organizational Development
Building Capacity and Accessing Resources Through Institutional Involvement of FOCIS Members

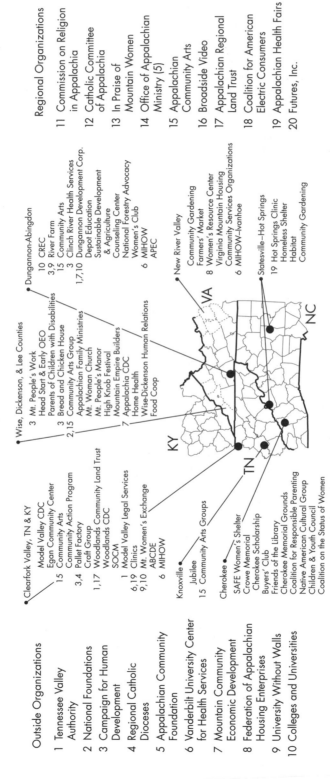

Outside Organizations

1 Tennessee Valley Authority
2 National Foundations
3 Campaign for Human Development
4 Regional Catholic Dioceses
5 Appalachian Community Foundation
6 Vanderbilt University Center for Health Services
7 Mountain Community Economic Development
8 Federation of Appalachian Housing Enterprises
9 University Without Walls
10 Colleges and Universities

Regional Organizations

11 Commission on Religion in Appalachia
12 Catholic Committee of Appalachia
13 In Praise of Mountain Women
14 Office of Appalachian Ministry (5)
15 Appalachian Community Arts
16 Broadside Video
17 Appalachian Regional Land Trust
18 Coalition for American Electric Consumers
19 Appalachian Health Fairs
20 Futures, Inc.

Clearfork Valley, TN & KY
Model Valley CDC
Egan Community Center
15 Community Arts
Community Action Program
3,4 Pallet Factory
Craft Group
1,17 Woodlands Community Land Trust
Woodlands CDC
SOCM
1 Model Valley Legal Services
6,19 Clinics
9,10 Mt. Women's Exchange
ABCDE
6 MIHOW

Knoxville
Jubilee
15 Community Arts Groups

Cherokee
SAFE Women's Shelter
Crowe Memorial
Cherokee Scholarship
Buyers' Club
Friends of the Library
Cherokee Memorial Grounds
Coalition for Responsible Parenting
Native American Cultural Group
Children & Youth Council
Coalition on the Status of Women

Wise, Dickenson, & Lee Counties
3 Mt. People's Work
Head Start & Early OEO
Parents of Children with Disabilities
3 Bread and Chicken House
2,15 Community Arts Group
Appalachian Family Ministries
Mt. Woman Church
Mt. People's Manor
High Knob Festival
Mountain Empire Builders
7 Appalachia CDC
National Forestry Advocacy
Wise-Dickenson Human Relations
Food Coop

Dungannon-Abingdon
10 CREC
3,9 River Farm
15 Community Arts
3 Clinch River Health Services
1,7,10 Dungannon Development Corp.
Depot Education
Sustainable Development
& Agriculture
Counseling Center
Women's Club
6 MIHOW
APEC

New River Valley
Community Gardening
Farmers' Market
8 Women's Resource Center
Virginia Mountain Housing
Community Services Organizations
6 MIHOW-Ivanhoe

Statesville–Hot Springs
19 Hot Springs Clinic
Homeless Shelter
Habitat
Community Gardening

KY

TN

VA

NC

Numbers next to the local/regional organizations indicate their connection to outside and/or regional organizations.

Abbreviations: ABCDE—Appalachian Based Communities Development Education; APEC—Appalachian Peace Education Center; CDC—Community Development Corporation; CREC—Clinch River Education Center; MIHOW—Maternal and Infant Health Outreach Worker; OEO—Office of Economic Opportunity; SOCM—Save Our Cumberland Mountains.

Cartography by Matt Servaites.

were more focused on distribution systems, advocacy, and confrontation. From the map it looks as though there is more opportunity to start new organizations in smaller, more rural communities.

What do you see when you look at this map? power in the connections? influence going in many directions? The way of friendship and relationship is surely evident. For me the map shows the dynamic of movement and rootedness—connecting and staying power. It shows that community is formed through a dense web of relationships with people and place. Community is not isolated, perfect, or clear-cut. It is very messy.

What does this way of relating within the community to organizations and people have to do with politics? with gender, race, and class? with the inside and outsider? with power? with community-building? From what I can see on the map and in the lives of the women, I would describe our position as follows: we were marginal to the church and to the communities where we lived; we were never part of the power elites. As with Mary in the Magnificat, this was our strength. We have found ways to support ourselves economically and to stay in the region or nearby. We do not depend on an outside organization to maintain us (as we did when we were Catholic sisters). We created not only new organizations but new programs within existing institutions, such as the first home-health program in the former Miners' Hospital in Wise, Virginia, and the first special education and art education programs in the schools in Wise County.

Even in our retirement years, one of our members is moving forward, spearheading the founding of a "lifelong living community" known as Futures, Inc.

Why is it that women are more likely to do community work or at least to do it in a more sustaining way? Marie Cirillo, a FOCIS member, was asked this question and answered with the following words:

> One of the major things is that I think women understand the connectedness of one thing to another better. . . . You know, you can sort of see where all the pieces are connected. So I think that's one of the major pieces: that women understand relationships better. And I think, because of that, they're more in tune with process than product. So they are better nurturers; I think it could be obviously something beyond what you've been trained or taught. . . . Women are more patient, many of them stick to things longer, they are more enduring when things would get discouraging and that's good for continuity in terms of nonprofits, and trying to keep it alive when there's nothing there. . . . And they network, and that's part of the connectedness to be sure. . . . They talk more.
>
> [As Glenmary Sisters, it has been natural for us continuously to create something new] because we were a new community, we had the experience of setting up our institutional capacities. . . . I was put in charge of re-

habbing these two old buildings for our institutional life and then I was in charge of setting up our art department. And what else? When the seminary first opened, I was assigned to the kitchen, so I had to set up the seminary kitchen. . . . And so I sort of understand, then, coming here, I understand a little bit about if you have nothing, what does it take to set it up.

We have strong connections with each other (and the "other" is much larger than FOCIS) and with many regional and national groups. This creative networking has made a difference in the communities where we settled. Resources have been accessible that may not otherwise have been. Most importantly, we have had influence through the long-term (and new) relationships we have built in local communities. We were able to empower ourselves and others, especially the women with whom we worked side by side by forming relationships as friends and co-workers. In the communities and within the organizations, we have had many roles—neighbor, friend, citizen, worker, and participant as well as mentor, catalyst, organizer, entrepreneur, and trainer. The most enduring and the most present, even now, is that of friend:

> From choosing to be in Big Stone Gap with Monica a lot was determined. It seemed to me a conscious choice of a friendship relationship beyond being Glenmary Sisters together. A friend is one who shares values, visions, can be called on when you need them, can call you to accountability, can have fun with [you].
>
> In looking back I think of Pat Rowland from Appalachia as a student who worked with us and became a friend. Helen Lewis, who asked questions, shared her values and vision, and became a friend. Susan Helton and Lynda Warner, who shared work and then created a workplace together and became friends. Nancy Robinson, Teri Vautrin, Carol Honeycutt, and Barbara Greene, who cared for the community and shared developing projects together and became friends. Jean Eason, who came to the region to be near her mother in Buffalo [New York] and became a friend. The FOCIS community, who has traveled together for thirty years and are friends. (Anne Leibig)

In fact, our spirit of friendship is so strong that a woman who interviewed us for a radio program she was producing slipped repeatedly and called us the *Friends* of Communities in Service rather than the *Federation* of Communities in Service. I felt that her slip of the tongue revealed such insight that I even tried to promote an organizational name change.

My experience of working with women in Appalachian communities has had its ups and downs, but there has been the constant theme of women fighting to make ends meet for their families and others in the community. Sometimes that fighting spirit has negative effects on projects, but it is nonetheless vital to our work. Actually—and here I sound like the older woman I am—I've come to believe that the project, the activity, is important because it sets a context for interaction and change; however, it is not as important as the development of ongoing relationships and the acknowledgment of differences that healthy communities allow and foster. Helping to create the contexts for those interactions and to foster the expression of different voices builds community. In Glenmary-FOCIS, I have experienced an upheaval of personal and community change that continues, but I have also felt the steadfastness of women's friendship that keeps me rooted in faith and the power of community.

Note

1. See Coleman McCarthy, "The Revolutionary Mary," *The Washington Post,* December 25, 1996, p. 23.

IV

CHANGING POSSIBILITIES IN THE GLOBAL SOUTH

11

Gender, Race, and Place

*Confounding Labor Activism
in Central Appalachia*

Sally Ward Maggard

n Appalachia, class oppression has long been the primary focus of activism and scholarship directed toward social justice.
Male coal miners have been viewed as the vanguard of
working-class resistance, their legendary labor conflicts the
premier examples of class struggle. Yet social inequality in
Appalachia, as elsewhere, has had multiple dimensions. Not
only have gender and race been the subjects of other, less
studied conflicts, but they have also influenced the character
and outcome of struggles focused on class.

This chapter, a case study of a strike at a hospital in Pike
County, Kentucky in the early 1970s, demonstrates how the
collision of class, gender, and race derailed one of the most
important union organizing efforts in the history of Appalachia.[1] The strikers were not all men but mostly women,
not industrial coal miners but service sector health-care workers. They represent the contemporary Appalachian working
class, and their struggle for workplace improvements illustrates many of the dilemmas facing women workers in the
postindustrial, global economy of the South. Class, gender,
and race *together* located the participants in this conflict in a
regional economic and social system, generated shared meanings of that system and of people's places within it, and

defined routine regimens of social life. This "matrix of domination" positioned people for their involvement in the class conflict.[2] It also shaped the subsequent course of events, including the workers' ultimate defeat.

Situational and Regional Context

The hospital strike occurred in eastern Kentucky, an area of central Appalachia where economic activity and social and political life have been dominated by the coal industry.[3] The livelihood of most residents is linked directly or indirectly to the industry, and other economic opportunity has been severely restricted ever since coal industrialists established their influence around the turn of the century. When fluctuations in the demand for coal and for coal miners' labor periodically throw miners out of work, local economies shatter. Everyone suffers. Problems caused by the volatile nature of the industry are compounded by high rates of disabling injury, fatalities, and occupational disease. Miners and members of their families live with the daily threat of economic uncertainty. As a result, even though mining wages and benefits improved through the twentieth century, mining families have remained vulnerable to recurrent and deep spells of poverty. Although great fortunes have been made in the region, the wealth generated by mining coal has not translated into local prosperity or community well-being.[4]

In the social system that developed with this economy, there is a clear demarcation of gender roles and a supporting gender ideology. Men are considered the "family wage earners." Most women depend on the income men earn and are responsible for the unpaid labor of managing households and family care. In the early coal camps, some women earned cash by providing services for more affluent households, and others took in boarders.[5] Over time, women moved into the low-waged secondary labor market, filling retail and service jobs in coal communities. No women were allowed in production jobs in the coal industry until the late 1970s,[6] and the women who became miners were soon pushed out by technological changes that shrank the size of the mining labor force, leaving only those miners with seniority (men). As a result of this mix of industrial history and culture, coalfield women and men occupy very different economic roles and enjoy divergent economic opportunities.[7]

Race and ethnicity also differentiate members of the working class in the region. Historically, men with varied racial-ethnic backgrounds made up the mining labor force. White men struggling in a faltering mountain agricultural economy were drawn into the mines by the promise of ready jobs and income, as were African American men fleeing discrimination and economic marginality in the South. They were joined by men from Eastern and Central Europe who came to the United States for new economic opportunity.[8] Blacks and immigrants were actively recruited to mining regions by agents of coal companies dispatched to the U.S. South, Europe, and the ports of entry where immigrants arrived in the United States.[9] Coal industrialists hoped that a "judicious mixture" of nationalities and races would divide workers and prevent union organizing.[10] To an extent, they were right: ethnicity and especially race divided miners. African American men filled the least desirable and most dangerous jobs in mining, and were among the first laid off when markets constricted or when automation reduced the need for miners.[11] Ethnic and racial enclaves in coal camps were clearly marked. In patchwork fashion, sections of the camps were set aside for African American, Hungarian, Polish, Slovakian, Italian, and other miners and their families. The lines of difference were most clearly drawn around African Americans. Segregated underground and in the schools, neighborhoods, and social life of the coal camps, they were a marginalized subclass within Appalachia's working class.[12]

Despite these divisions, the historic struggles to organize the United Mine Workers of America (UMWA) succeeded. Extreme exploitation inside the mines and shared difficulties of life in company towns drew miners and their families together across racial and ethnic boundaries. In a process one historian has described as "class over caste," ordinary working people collectively confronted powerful opponents, established a countervailing base of power, and improved working conditions and the standard of living.[13]

Most coalfield families have been touched directly by this history. They share a world view in which class is a fundamental social division; solidarity among union members, especially in disputes with the bosses, is a way of life. This cultural context influenced the hospital strike analyzed in this chapter. Workers at the hospital believed that if they organized, as the miners had done before them, they could improve their working conditions. Women and men, whites and African Americans, enlisted a union to represent them, signed union cards, and made their intentions known to the hospital administration. When it was clear that the administration would not recognize their union, they went on strike. They openly discussed racial divisions, drew on their history of setting these aside, and committed themselves to unity. They fully expected a broad base of local support, especially from unionized mining families. They fully expected to win.

What was not apparent to the hospital workers or to their union representatives were the ways that gender can fracture the working class, dividing people who have a rich history of union solidarity and a commitment to principles of unionism. This chapter exposes the pernicious effects of sexism and the hierarchy of gender, which pulled apart Pike County's working class and, in a surprising mixture with race, eventually defeated this strike.

Care Giving in a Mountain Hospital

The Pikeville Methodist Hospital (PMH) was created in the late 1960s when a business-oriented administration merged two existing Pikeville hospitals: a missionary endeavor built in the 1920s by the United Methodist Church and a hospital built in the 1950s by the United Mine Workers of America and staffed by a unionized labor force. The board of directors of the new venture envisioned a "true Medical Center for Eastern Kentucky" that would serve six eastern Kentucky counties and the borderland areas in West Virginia and Virginia.[14] Plans called for a new physical plant with new or expanded units in extended care, mental health, intensive care and coronary care, as well as expanded teaching programs. This required extensive capital investment. Local business and civic leaders captured federal development funds as well as grants and loans that were flowing into the region in the wake of the War on Poverty. They raised $7.5 million dollars and built a shiny, new, 225-bed facility.[15]

In December 1971, PMH opened with great fanfare on the site of, and literally swallowing up, the earlier UMWA hospital. Behind the glitter of the new eight-story concrete and glass facility, there was another story in progress. Employees were concerned about the consequences of consolidation and reorganization under a new style of management. Most of their fears were realized. The same plans that called for a greatly expanded health facility did not include plans to hire additional staff. Workers experienced a dramatic "speedup." Patient load nearly doubled for the nursing staff, and workers in other departments serviced many more people and cared for a much larger facility. Yet wages remained low.

The workers gathered a staggering list of grievances, all compounded by an unsympathetic administration that adopted increasingly coercive management policies. Specific complaints involved work schedules and overtime duty, discriminatory supervision and discharges without cause, no job security, promotion or seniority rights, and inadequate medical and unemployment insurance. Women who worked as nurse's aides were particularly concerned about being instructed to do work for which they were not trained, including dispensing narcotics. Above all, workers in every department complained of understaffing and unreasonable workloads, conditions that meant they could not provide quality care. One nurse's aide described the pressure she was under this way:

You work like a dog. Work for 89 cents an hour for years trying to raise six kids. Then $1.05. Then $1.10. We just all got tired. After we moved in that big hospital, so many patients and you couldn't get them all fed and bathed. You couldn't take care of the patients because the workload was too heavy. It just got till you couldn't handle it, and I guess it was [strike] or quit.[16]

Wages were very low. Among nonprofessional employees, the average wage at the time of the strike was $1.68 per hour. One nurse's aide was earning $1.87, after working thirty-one years in the hospital, when she went out on strike. Still, it was deteriorating working conditions and management practices, rather than wage scales, that finally pushed employees to organize.

The opponents the strikers faced were members of a small, very wealthy elite that dominates social, political, and economic life in the mountains. The strikers understood this, and they coined the slogan, "We're Fighting Millionaires!" Their opponents had little understanding of the lives of their employees, the nature of their work at the hospital, or their economic status and household need. A confrontation between the chairman of the board and a nurse's aide not long before the strike dramatizes this point. According to the aide: "I told him that I'd like to see him buy his groceries and eat on what I made. I showed him my check. He said, 'Well, that's not really very much, is it?' I said, 'No, that's not enough to pay my grocery bill, and I have bills to pay out of this, too.' He walked on off. He didn't have nothing else to say about it."

The people who struck the hospital all worked in nonprofessional positions. The men worked in maintenance, and as orderlies in the nursing department, watchmen, and janitors. The women worked in the housekeeping, nursing, and food service departments and in the business office and accounting. They were nurse's aides, clerks, housekeepers, kitchen helpers, technicians in the x-ray and operating rooms and the pharmacy, secretaries, cooks, dietary aides, and kitchen helpers. Many held multiple jobs, piecing together several meager paychecks to support their families. A nurse's aide described working three and four jobs at once, including at the hospital, to rear her four children: "I've did odds and ends work all my life. When I worked on the [hospital] day shift I used to work at a steak house in the evening three nights a week to make enough money for me and the kids. I have cleaned houses of an evening, . . . worked at motels, cleaned rooms, worked in kitchens, washed dishes. Just anything to make an honest dollar."

But interviews revealed that the average hourly wage of $1.68 the employees earned seemed fair to the hospital administration and board. Why?

In part, this can be attributed to the great social distance between eastern Kentucky's working class and local elite. This gulf was born with the development of the coal industry and exacerbated by the pattern of single industry dependence that discouraged economic diversity and independent entrepreneurial activity. This is the region of the country where for many years business leaders valued work animals, such as mine mules, more than human laborers. It took decades of collective action and the violent mine wars for which Appalachia is famous before miners were able to force change and curb the extreme labor exploitation that coal industrialists and their allies considered acceptable business practice.[17] Men who worked at jobs outside the coal industry, such as the maintenance men and orderlies at the hospital, had not had such collective success, and their wages were very low.[18]

But more is involved than social-class distance in explainig the wage scale at PMH. Answers also lie in the way class and gender intersect in this locality to rationalize compensation for different kinds of work. The hospital relied most heavily on the work of women. Cultural definitions of women's work and women's place in the labor force shaped wages at the hospital and the way the administration viewed its labor force.

First, in the coalfields women's wages have been understood as superfluous to men's, as supplementary or "extra." As a result, women's work has been systematically undervalued.[19] The assumption has been, and was at the hospital, that women didn't really depend on their jobs and that their "proper place" was at home. Research on the history of women's waged labor finds that such cultural assumptions are used to rationalize low wages for women.[20] Sexist ideology seriously constrains women's labor-force participation and earnings, supports a division of the economy into high- and low-waged sectors, and reinforces gender divisions among the working class. Work done primarily by women, like that performed by nonprofessional women at the hospital, is undervalued throughout the economy.[21]

Second, the specific kind of work the women did at the hospital is constructed within a gender ideology that functions to depress the economic status of women. The work of "caring"—in this case, nursing the sick, cleaning the hospital, and feeding people—is culturally defined as "women's work." The assumption is that such work is ordinarily done out of love, reponsibility, or some natural "impulse" to help others, rather than for pay. Research on the "caring professions" shows that defining caretaking in this way serves to depress wages.[22] For workers like the women at PMH, this creates a dilemma described by historian Susan Reverby as "the order to care in a society that refuses to value caring."[23]

In Pikeville, the class lens through which hospital officials understood the workforce was shaded by this gendered lens. Sexist ideology gave particular form to the class polarization between the hospital administration and employees. It contributed to the administration's inability to recognize grievances as valid and to the eventual outbreak of the strike.

The Strike

Two hundred twenty nonprofessional employees of the hospital went out on strike. Almost all, five-sixths of them, were women. The decision to strike is not easy for anyone, but it was especially difficult for these women. All the women in the study had worked at a variety of low-paid service and retail jobs, contributing a major part if not all of the incomes on which their households depended. They had sold shoes, cleaned motels, cooked in restaurants, pressed clothes, washed dishes, and the like, often holding multiple jobs to earn enough money to support their families. Compared to these marginal positions, a steady job at the hospital with some benefits and the chance of long-term employment was very attractive. In effect, these women had some of the best jobs open to working-class women in the tightly constricted and gender segregated labor market of the Appalachian coalfields. Still, they were willing to risk these jobs and wager they could win union representation that would improve their working conditions. As one woman said, "You get tired of people walking on you after a while, making a doormat out of you. . . . After you back something up in a corner so long, eventually it's going to fight back."

Pro-union employees asked members of the Communication Workers of America (CWA) who were installing telephone service in the new facility if their union would organize the hospital; the union agreed. Most of the nonprofessional, many semiprofessional, and some professional employees signed union representation cards. In its first official communication with the hospital, CWA informed the administration that over 90 percent of the employees had signed a petition for union representation. The hospital immediately took the position that "union representation is not consistent with the purposes of the institution."[24] Eight months later, on June 9, 1972, after refusing all requests to meet with the union, the hospital fired two employees for union activities. On June 10, workers walked off their jobs on the evening shift, and the strike began.

This was one of the first strikes ever to occur at a hospital in the region, and it turned out to be one of the region's longest labor conflicts, which no one predicted at the time of the walkout. Instead, as interview after interview revealed, the women expected the strike to be over quickly. One woman laughed at herself as she recalled her expectations: "In my wildest imagination [laughs] I didn't know what it would be like. . . . I had no idea it would last that long." First, the women believed their grievances were reasonable. As one woman said, "I really thought that they would go ahead and meet enough of our demands that would put us back to work. Because I didn't think the demands, you know—I really don't think that they were that unusual in the circumstances."

Second, they reasoned that their labor was essential, that the hospital could not function without them, and that their walkout would prompt recalcitrant hospital officials to recognize the union and introduce improvements. One of the women explained, "I didn't think it would last over a couple of weeks, and we'd be right back to work. Because usually hospitals can't work without the employees standing behind them and working."

Another said:

> I never dreamed it would be what it was. I figured . . . we'd be out there a week at the most, and then we'd go back to work. I guess I had a lot of stupid dreams about it, you know, like everybody else did. . . . We just assumed, you know, well, they needed us so bad. That's what you get for assuming. Nobody is indispensable. But we didn't [realize that]. We never dreamed it would last that long. I figured they would need us, and then they would take care of it and get us back. But it didn't work out that way.

For twenty-eight months strikers maintained a picket line around the clock. Then, just over two years into the strike, the National Labor Relations Act (NLRA) of 1935 was amended to extend coverage to employees of nonprofit health-care institutions, largely because of the strike.[25] At first, organizers believed this meant the union would win, and the union shut down the picket line. But subsequent interpretations of the amendments exempted the Pikeville strike from the changes, and for six more years the strike was fought in the courts.

Over the next several years a series of unfair labor practice rulings favored the strikers. The hospital Board, however, spent hundreds of thousands of dollars contesting each ruling, and even tried to take its side of the dispute to the U.S. Supreme Court. Finally, six years after the strikers had given up their picket line, the high court refused to hear the hospital's appeal. Eventually the hospital was forced to offer to reinstate the strikers and compensate them for economic losses. However, no strikers were back at work in the hospital until early 1981, and most never got their jobs back. Court-awarded back paychecks were not in strikers' hands until May 1983, just shy of eleven years from the night of the walkout.

In the end, the strikers finally outdistanced their powerful adversaries. Their back-pay settlement of $697,000 remains one of the largest in the history of strikes in the United States. Opportunities for service workers to organize unions were greatly expanded because of the strike. But the people who walked out of the hospital that night in 1972 did not win the right to a union.

Political Mobilization and Strike Direction

The social relations and ideology of gender influenced virtually all aspects of this labor conflict: the women workers' initial decisions to join the union and participate in the strike; the union's overall strike strategy and tactics of support; the response of others in the community to this unprecedented labor activism by women workers; and the eventual outcome of the strike.

Union organizing in Pike County had centered historically on the experiences of men in coal mines, and the decision by men to organize or to go on strike was not unusual in the area. But this strike was out of the ordinary in one central dimension: it involved hundreds of women. Further, participation in the strike cast the women in very public roles. Deciding to participate and to remain actively involved was difficult for many women.

Conditions at the hospital created the immediate crisis that led workers to organize, but individual decisions to participate were embedded in a web of other experiences. Since the income that women earned was essential in their households, many family members supported the strike and encouraged the women to participate. Some relatives had enjoyed union protection when they worked in coal mines or for the railroad, and others held strong pro-union attitudes. A few women had worked in unionized places themselves, at the previous miners' hospital, or in defense plants during World War II. Family relationships, family history, a commitment to the principle of unionism, and past experiences with unions all helped the women make sense of their problems at the hospital and translate them into imperatives for action.

Established routines, designed to integrate gendered obligations at home with jobs at the hospital, were equally important in facilitating women's activism. Because people had already arranged their job schedules around the needs of children, other dependents, and housekeeping, participation in the strike did not disrupt most households, whether they were headed by women or by married couples. Thus strikers did not have to devise a new balancing act between housework, dependent care, and the strike. As one woman said, it was "business as usual," with strike work replacing shift work at the hospital.

Apart from these internal household arrangements, however, it was not "business as usual" for women to be on strike and to take public roles in a controversial labor dispute. This strike not only threatened the hospital that many area residents used, it also catapulted into the public eye working-class women whose labor had been exploited and whose opinions and needs had rarely been considered. There was no local history of women's activism, comparable to the oral traditions valorizing coal miners' struggles to unionize, in which people could situate these new developments. The unease affected newly arrived union representatives as well as people who had lived in the area for many years.

CWA was determined to run a nonviolent, orderly strike. The union instructed the strikers to follow strict behavior codes that included picket-line behavior intended to make the women's participation more palatable to Pikeville residents. The women were to present themselves as "ladies" on the picket line, and to pass the time by quilting, sewing, reading, cooking over barrels, and waving as people drove by. Men were usually assigned night picket duty because that was when the potential for violence was greatest. If men were on the picket line during the day, they were to appear supportive, chopping wood for the fires and carrying signs.

CWA also expected the women to help staff a strike office and to build support for the strike by appearing at events held around the country. Beyond these roles, the union was determined to minimize and control the women's activities. The union did not look to the women for input in strike direction. Nor did it see them as candidates for leadership development and future roles inside the union.

The union's attitude created a great deal of conflict for the women. They knew they needed a union to negotiate with the hospital and represent them in court and with the National Labor Relations Board, but they did not want to take a passive role in their strike. They believed the union did not understand the nature of their hometown opponents and that the union's strategies were misdirected and would not work. In particular, they were at fierce odds with the union over a decision to allocate time and substantial funds to a campaign to persuade the national offices of the Methodist Church to intervene on behalf of the strikers in Pike County. While groups of strikers were sent to meetings of bishops and church councils around the country, local support for the strike did not materialize, people crossed their picket line, and the hospital continued to operate.

Frustrated with CWA's strategy, the women devised their own tactics to influence the strike, including an elaborate behind-the-scenes campaign to pressure board members and people who did not honor their picket line. On many occasions they defied organizers, but they were not in the position to demand changes in strike direction. They depended on the union not only to bargain for them but also to supply the strike benefits that they needed to support their households. They did not have an autonomous base of operation. Nor did they have allies inside the ranks of the CWA leadership to pressure the union. The situation ultimately restrained their strike actions, and they struggled to keep their frustrations in check.[26]

Gender and the Collapse of Class Solidarity

In the early 1970s, Pike County was known as "UMWA country," a part of the coalfields where pro-union sentiment runs deep. The hospital strikers expected full, automatic, and substantial backing from their friends and neighbors, from area residents, and especially from coal miners and mining families. That support failed to materialize, and the strikers were stunned. Donations from unions and prolabor organizations poured into Pike County from all over the country, and national and international unions endorsed the strike. But locally, hundreds of people crossed their picket line to use the hospital for routine and nonemergency visits and even to go to work. One woman said, "Well, there was just a lot that went across our picket line and worked that really didn't need to. They didn't have to work. Some of our neighbors right around did that. They went across our picket line. You know, I wouldn't have done that to them for no kind of money. No kind of money would I have done that, and they done it to us."

This was one of the great disappointments of the strike. Fifteen years after their walkout, in interview after interview the women wrestled with the question of why people crossed their picket line. No one had reached a satisfactory answer. They were all confused and bitterly disappointed. One striker said, "I would have waited to see what we could have done with our union or with our working rights and things before I would run in there and take someone else's job."

Relations were particularly tense between strikers and neighbors or relatives who were not supportive. There were frequent confrontations, which, despite the union organizers' admonitions for female strikers to behave like "ladies," often happened at the picket line itself. One woman described such an incident:

> I had a first cousin that went in there to work. . . . He was a security guard. He come out there [on the picket line], and I guess he thought he was brave, slinging that black jack and that pistol on his hip. Taking that thing around and around. . . . Told him he ought to be ashamed of hisself. . . . It was awful. . . . He didn't have no business in there trying to work and us trying to better the community.

Other episodes happened out of sight of either the strike director or the public eye. Famous incidents of disciplining "scabs" have become the folklore of the strike. In their interviews many women told me about the "Tomato Queen," "Moonshine Girl," "that one from up at Jenkins," and "that one from up on Greasy Creek."

The "Tomato Queen" had provoked particular anger as she drove into the hospital to work, and the story unfolded in one group interview session:

First woman: Honey, she'd stick her finger up at us. She'd call *us* "scabs." She called us every name in the book. She'd make fun of us when she'd go in to work. And she'd come out, and she'd made fun of us. She'd throw things at us, and we got tired of it.

Several women then bought a bushel of rotten tomatoes:

First woman: We didn't tomato queen her on the picket line. We followed her after she come across the picket line. . . .They was four of us. . . .We all got in that car, and, honey, side by side we followed her about eighteen or nineteen miles, wasn't it?
Second woman: Well, we followed her all the way till she went in that trailer court where she lived, honey.
First woman: And, honey, we throwed a bushel of tomatoes at her.
Second woman: We'd hang out the car window and throwed it at her windshield till we—what we wanted, we wanted her out of there. We was going to whip her.
First woman: We tried every way in the world to stop her [car], and we couldn't get her stopped. We was going, we was going to give her a good one. We never did get her stopped. . . . And so we named her the "Tomato Queen." She never did come back to work.

The strikebreaking "Tomato Queen" filed charges and named several women in her complaint. To the union's dismay, these clandestine activities landed strikers in court:

Second woman: We had to go to court about the "Tomato Queen." Yes, honey, we did. Honey, to beat it all, we all went to court. Everyone of us got us a wig and dressed up, honey. And when we went in court that day, that girl couldn't identify the people that had done her like that.

The humor in these stories does not cover up the anger the strikers still feel toward those who did not honor their strike.

The hospital actively recruited replacement workers, or "scabs," from the town of Pikeville, the many rural communities along the tributaries that feed into the Levisa Fork of the Kentucky River, and even neighboring counties. Many were women attracted to the comparatively good jobs the strikers had risked. Others from the town's privileged families volunteered. And some were hired who had questionable "reputations" or were known as reluctant workers. As one striker said, "They come in droves. They honestly did. Women that wouldn't work in a pie factory showed up over there to work once we walked out. And that's the truth. They even picked up girls that walked the streets. And I knew it. I'd seen them on the streets . . . just walked the streets for a living. They ended up working over there."

Personally hurt by friends, acquaintances, and relatives who crossed the picket line, the strikers were mystified by people from UMWA families who became scabs. Several women tracked down one man who drove recklessly through the picket line and threatened pickets with violence. "We found out later that same man was a UMWA union man, honey!" one striker recalled. "His wife was working in there. She went in . . . was a scab." Another woman, who was married to a union miner, betrayed her striking friend by going inside to work: "We had one retired UMW girl that went in there and worked . . . wife [of] a retired miner, medically retired. Went in there and cooked. I still don't like her, because she was a friend of mine. I told her I couldn't understand a miner's wife—said that she wanted a job. That's all that she had to say about it."

Part of the answer to this puzzle lies in the gendered subtext to the strike. There was widespread sentiment that people who work in hospitals should not go on strike. Public criticism was often directed at the women for crippling a health-care institution. Caring for the sick, cooking for the sick, and cleaning up after the sick are considered women's work. To suggest that health-care workers should not strike amounts to saying that women should do this kind of work out of the goodness of their feminine hearts—not because they are workers who need jobs and have the right to organize and strike. In Pikeville women had the nerve to buck this ideology, go on strike, and hold out for years. But their union never challenged the gendered opposition to the strike. Unanalyzed and unaddressed, sexism split apart local support and devastated the strikers.

Class and the Failure of Gender Solidarity

While gender redrew traditional lines of class conflict and fractured class solidarity during the strike, class distinctions interfered with the potential for gender solidarity and mobilization around concerns many women at PMH shared. Women in professional, semiprofessional, and nonprofessional positions in the hospital all suffered from the broad disregard of caregiving as work. They were also all constrained by the severely segregated occupational structure that privileged working-class men in the region. And they all worked under the new pressures created by the merger and coercive management style at PMH. These issues could have united women across occupational categories and informed the union's strategies. But this did not happen. Instead, class divisions among hospital employees were rife.

The jobs women held at PMH can be positioned along a class hierarchy based on the amount of education and/or skills required. Nonprofessional and nonskilled workers in housekeeping and the kitchen were at the lower end, followed by nurse's aides and clerks or secretaries who had some formal training. Next were licensed practical nurses (LPNs) and certified technicians who had some advanced education, as well as bookkeepers and accounting staff. Registered nurses (RNs), who had the most formal education, capped the hierarchy.

The actual social distance between these tiers of occupations was not necessarily great. Women in any of these categories might be married to or the daughter of a UMWA coal miner. Any of the women might live next door to each other or might have gone to the same rural school or vocational education program. But wages, status, and authority inside the hospital varied across these occupational classifications. Important sorting and ranking occurred among these women, even within a region that seems at first to have few class differences beyond the distinction between dominant elites and working-class families. This hierarchy translated into split allegiances during the strike.

As a result, it was difficult to predict how someone with a long union lineage might answer the question in Florence Reece's famous labor song "Which Side Are You On?" As the strike unfolded, these distinctions helped keep the strikebound hospital functioning. They also created conflicts that are still very much alive in these communities and many families.

In the months leading up to the strike, most LPNs and some RNs signed union cards. On the night of the walkout, however, with few exceptions the LPNs, RNs, and other professional staff stayed on the job. LPNs were just a short distance above nurse's aides, and many aides were either taking vocational school courses toward LPN certification or had plans to do so. LPNs complained about serious barriers to quality care, and many worried about personal liability issues as working conditions deteriorated. Just before the walkout, however, LPNs were threatened with losing their state licenses, and they decided to stay on the job.

During the strike many of the LPNs served as a clandestine intelligence network. They provided inside information about operating procedures and poor patient care that strikers used in publicity campaigns to dissuade people from using hospital services. They also used the information in efforts, which ultimately were unsuccessful, to challenge the hospital's accreditation and to persuade the UMWA Health and Retirement Funds to drop PMH from its list of participating hospitals. Still, some strikers remained bitter that the LPNs did not risk their licenses and walk out. One woman who worked as a nurse's aide recalled:

> Some said they'd come out with us. They said, "You all won't be out long, we'll come out and support you all." But they didn't come out. They were too job scared. They said, "In two weeks, we'll walk out with you." Said, "If you all ever pulled a strike," said, "we'd walk out." Said it would take about two weeks. Said, "We'd get us a union." There'd been about five or six of them told me on the night shift. . . , "We'll walk out." But they didn't come out. They didn't stick to their word.

None of these inside informants was in a supervisory role, and all shared the strikers' hopes that a union would improve their working conditions and household incomes. In contrast, most RNs and all but one nursing supervisor opposed the strike from the beginning and actively tried to break the organizing drive. This group included women in UMWA households. One nursing supervisor drew particularly strong wrath from the strikers because of the tactics she used to oppose the union openly, even though she was married to a UMWA miner. As one striker who had worked under her recalled, "She'd say, 'I wonder when them old strikers, when are they going to have their strike? I just don't see why they want to strike the hospital. The hospital ain't no place to have a union.' All the time her husband worked for a big union mines. He was UMWA, honey!"

Women in supervisory positions were aligned with management; despite personal ties to unions via the men in their lives, their class allegiance followed their own occupational privilege. This stratification within eastern Kentucky's working class deeply divided the women at PMH and weakened the strike. For the public at large, it also contributed to the perception of the strike as an aberration, an unacceptable departure from familiar forms of class conflict between men.

Racial Lines Redrawn

In a surprising turn of events, the social arrangements of the past failed in yet another way to prepare the workers for their strike. In the past, strikebreakers in the central Appalachian coalfields were often African American men from the South, brought by train into a strike zone to mine coal. This strategy frequently backfired when these workers either joined the union effort or departed once they realized they were facing a strike situation. Further, since miners shared experiences of exploitation in both the workplace and the company town, racial collaboration eventually developed in support of the UMWA.[27]

The hospital strikers were a multiracial group. Most of the employees at PMH were white, but some African American women worked as nurse's aides and in housekeeping.[28] They all went out on strike and walked the picket line for the strike's duration. The president of the CWA local at the telephone company (which made the contact with CWA for the strikers) was an African American man married to one of the nurse's aides, and he was actively involved in strike support. The strikers and their union had come to terms with their diversity. They had talked about race and had planned in advance to stay unified if the hospital attempted to use racial differences to break the strike. As one striker said, "I thought we'd win if we'd all stick together."

But the hospital introduced a new form of racial-ethnic difference for which the strikers were unprepared. By importing LPNs from the Philippines to be strikebreakers, management confounded the workers' commitment to interracial solidarity. The hospital strikers simply did not know what to do when young Filipinas arrived in town to staff the strikebound hospital. One woman said, "I knew they couldn't use the colored people any more, because the colored people wasn't slaves any more. . . . I didn't realize . . . they brought Filipinas in. So they made slaves out of the Filipinas."

Here were displaced women, enticed from their home country with the promise of good jobs and a better life in the United States. They spoke very little, if any, English. They had no idea they were coming to the United States to work at a strikebound hospital. The hospital set them off from the strikers not at a coal mine but literally on the hospital grounds. Under the guise of addressing eastern Kentucky's housing crisis among poor people, the local elite arranged for the U.S. Department of Housing and Urban Development to send trailers to Pikeville. Officials connected with PMH then put the trailers on the hospital property and moved the Filipinas into them. Some were also housed inside the hospital and later in the former Methodist Hospital building in town. One striker remembered, "Lee Keene [PMH administrator] had them trailers moved up beyond the hospital, and had all them [in] trailers till they wouldn't have to come through that picket line and go through. . . . Then they carried them in and out in different cars."

Another woman described these developments this way: "I tell you what hurt us. See, they used to make slaves out of colored people, and now they made them out of the Filipinas. They brought all those Filipinas in here and set up those trailers in the back and housed them up. And then they housed them up on [the] eighth and seventh floor [of PMH] too."

Housed on hospital property, the only way these new arrivals to the United States could get in and out of the hospital grounds (for food, clothes, church, etc.) was to be transported across the picket line by people opposing the strike. They were unfamiliar with their new country and the small mountain town where they found themselves, and they were basically unable to speak the language. They depended on hospital officials for everything. They were not so much opponents of the strikers as captives of the hospital administration.

These were not the kind of "scabs" the strikers were prepared to face, to intimidate with threats of physical violence, or to entice to join the strike. Interviews indicate that the strikers understood that the Filipinas were victims; however, they were at a loss over how to respond to these foreigners. The traditional options for dealing with strikebreakers—chasing them out of town, beating them up, or signing them up—did not apply in this situation. The strikers restrained themselves from violence, but were not necessarily hospitable.

According to one striker, "We just wasn't nice to them." As one example of how strikers were not "nice," she described an incident on the picket line. A strike supporter who had served in the Philippines during World War II primed one of the strikers to threaten the women as they went in to work: "We was all over [at PMH] one night, and them Filipinas went through. [He] knew what he was telling [an orderly] to say. . . . [He] was captured three years and a half in the Philippines. He could talk to them, you know. And he would tell [the orderly] what to say to them. He would say it, but [the orderly] didn't know what he was saying. They were scared to death."

Another striker reflected, "You know, they [there] would have been murder in some places in the world. . . . I've studied about it. I don't know how they escaped. It was just that we was good people over there."

The historical experience with strikebreakers provided no guidelines, then, for handling poor women imported by the hospital from another country. The gender, race, nationality, and captive status of these replacement laborers confounded the strikers. In a fall-back position, the strikers just tolerated them. This allowed the hospital officials to build up the hospital staff and to keep the facility running. One woman said, "They brought the Filipinas in here, and that's what hurt us. If they hadn't got the Filipinas in here, we might have put them on their knees."

The region's labor history of "class over caste" did not repeat itself at Pikeville. Indeed, in some respects that history impeded the strikers' capacity to grapple successfully with the gender and race dimensions of their conflict. Management's racialized replacement worker strategy was successful; the hospital was able to stay open and operate at nearly full census.

Conclusions

In the final analysis, a collision of social class, gender, and racial divisions defeated the Pikeville hospital strike. Class solidarity was fractured by deeply embedded understandings of gender roles, women's economic status, and the work of caregiving. An expected broad base of working-class support did not develop as it had in coal strikes. Much to the dismay of the strikers and the union, hundreds of people in this part of eastern Kentucky did not translate their otherwise pro-union sentiments, developed in the context of the industrial history of coal mining, into support for the female strikers who were crippling their regional hospital. "UMWA country" did not mobilize as "working-class country." Sexism was the culprit.

Gender hierarchy also influenced the paternalistic relationship between the women and their union representatives, who limited the women's ability to use their knowledge of their opponents and the area, and to influence strike strategy and direction. Moreover, the union and the female strikers were not able to organize on the basis of shared gender interests. As a result, a potential gender-based alliance among hospital workers was circumvented by class divisions. Women opposed each other in the strike, even though their work situations and status in the region's economy and culture might have generated solidarity.

Further, the strikers and union were confronted with a new replacement labor strategy that left them confused and immobilized. Not only were neighbors, kin, and acquaintances crossing their picket line to use the hospital and take their jobs, but non-English-speaking women from the Philippines were imported and used as a captive labor force by hospital officials. Nothing in their received repertoire of strategies to deal with strikebreakers prepared them for this development. Gender and race combined in new ways in this dimension of the strike, which stands as a portent for future labor struggles throughout the South.

Gender, race, and class intersected in this labor struggle to challenge the legitimacy of the strike, undermine class solidarity, and prevent the development of a collectivity based on the regionally contextualized constraints of gender. The findings indicate that class relations are far more complicated than research focused only on the manifest markers of class position has suggested. Gender and race confound the relations of class, even as their significance is obscured by a historiography, both academic and popular, that features the genderless, interracial labor struggles of men. Using the critical localism of a case study, it is possible to mine the complex details of this matrix of inequality and bring them to the surface. This allows a deeper understanding of the exercise of power, the perpetuation of powerlessness, and the possibilities for collective protest in the Appalachian coalfields.

Notes

1. The case study is part of a larger project comparing women's participation in two nationally significant strikes, the hospital strike and a strike at a coal mine in Harlan County, Kentucky. Principal sources of data include structured in-depth interviews with twenty-four female strikers supplemented by fifteen interviews with male strikers, relatives of female strikers, members of the hospital administration and board of directors, and selected close observers of the strike. Additional data analyzed include archival material, arrest records, court hearings and trials, legislative hearings, the congressional record, newspaper and photographic archives, and strike documents. See Sally Ward Maggard, "Eastern Kentucky Women on Strike: A Study of Gender, Class, and Political Action in the 1970s" (Ph.D. diss., University of Kentucky, 1989).

2. Patricia Hill Collins, in *Black Feminist Thought* (New York: Routledge, 1991), p. 236, notes that the exercise of power and experience of privilege are based on intersecting race, gender, and class statuses, or a "matrix of domination" that is experienced as a local way of life and that functions to routinize and maintain relations of inequality.

3. A subregion within the larger federally defined Appalachian Region, central Appalachia consists of sixty counties in the coal-producing sections of Kentucky, Virginia, West Virginia, and Tennessee. See Appalachian Regional Commission, *Appalachia* (Washington, DC: U.S. Government Printing Office, 1964).

4. Sally Ward Maggard, "From Farm to Coal Camp to Back Office and McDonald's: Living in the Midst of Appalachia's Latest Transformation," *Journal of the Appalachian Studies Association* 6 (1994): 14–28; Maggard, "From Farmers to Miners: The Decline of Agriculture in Eastern Kentucky," in Lawrence Busch, ed., *Science and Agricultural Development* (Totowa, NJ: Allanheld, Osmun, 1981), pp. 25–66; John Gaventa, *Power and Powerlessness: Quiescence and Rebellion in an Appalachian Valley* (Urbana: University of Illinois Press, 1980); Ronald D. Eller, *Miners, Millhands, and Mountaineers: Industrialization of the Appalachian South, 1880–1930* (Knoxville: University of Tennessee Press, 1982); Keith Dix, *What's a Coal Miner to Do? The Mechanization of Coal Mining* (Pittsburgh: University of Pittsburgh Press, 1988); Daniel J. Curran, *Dead Laws for Dead Men: The Politics of Federal Coal Mine Health and Safety Legislation* (Pittsburgh: University of Pittsburgh Press, 1993); Barbara Ellen Smith, *Digging Our Own Graves: Coal Miners and the Struggle over Black Lung Disease* (Philadelphia: Temple University Press, 1987); Carol Giesen, *Coal Miners' Wives* (Lexington: University Press of Kentucky, 1995); Ann R. Tickamyer and Cecil Tickamyer, "Gender, Family Structure, and Poverty in Central Appalachia," in *The*

Land and Economy of Appalachia: Proceedings from the 1986 Conference on Appalachia (Lexington: The Appalachian Center, University of Kentucky, 1986), pp. 80–90.

5. Mary Beth Pudup, "Women's Work in the West Virginia Economy," *West Virginia History* 49 (1990): 7–20.

6. There are historical accounts of isolated women working in contract or family-run mines early in this century, during World War II, and in the 1950s, but coal mining employment remained blocked to women until the 1970s when a series of sex discrimination charges were filed against coal companies under Title VII of the 1964 Civil Rights Act. As late as 1975, 99.8 percent of all U.S. coal miners were men. See Betty Jean Hall, "Women Miners Can Dig It, Too!" in John Gaventa, Barbara Ellen Smith, and Alex Willingham, eds., *Communities in Economic Crisis: Appalachia and the South* (Philadelphia: Temple University Press, 1990, pp. 53–60); and Hall, "Background Paper on Sex Discrimination in the Coal Industry" (Jacksboro, TN: Coal Employment Project, 1977), paper in possession of the author.

7. Maggard, "From Farm to Coal Camp."

8. Eller, *Miners;* Joe William Trotter, Jr., *Coal, Class, and Color: Blacks in Southern West Virginia, 1915–32* (Urbana: University of Illinois Press, 1990); Ronald L. Lewis, *Black Coal Miners in America: Race, Class, and Community Conflict, 1780–1980* (Lexington: University Press of Kentucky, 1987).

9. For a detailed account of this labor recruitment process in West Virginia and the particular labor force recruited from the Asturias region of Spain to work in the zinc factories of Spelter, West Virginia, see Suronda A. Gonzalez, "Talking Like My Grandmothers: Spanish Immigrant Women in Spelter, West Virginia," (M.S. thesis, West Virginia University, 1991).

10. Trotter, *Coal, Class, and Color;* Kenneth R. Bailey, "A Judicious Mixture: Negroes and Immigrants in the West Virginia Mines, 1880–1917," *West Virginia History* 34 (January 1973): 141–61.

11. Trotter, *Coal, Class, and Color;* Lewis, *Black Coal Miners.*

12. Crandall A. Shifflett, *Coal Towns: Life, Work, and Culture in Company Towns of Southern Appalachia, 1880–1960* (Knoxville: University of Tennessee Press, 1991); Trotter, *Coal, Class, and Color;* David Alan Corbin, *Life, Work, and Rebellion in the Coal Fields: The Southern West Virginia Miners, 1880–1922* (Urbana: University of Illinois Press, 1981); Lewis, *Black Coal Miners.*

13. Corbin, *Life, Work, and Rebellion,* p. 61.

14. The Reverend J. I. Meyer, *Doors of Hope That Never Close* (Pikeville: The Methodist Hospital of Kentucky, 1972), p. 101.

15. Pike County business and civic leaders have had astonishing success in obtaining federal funding for their development objectives. Perhaps their most famous achievement is a $77.6 million "cut-through," a physical realignment of the Kentucky mountains and the Big Sandy River so that the town of Pikeville had room to expand. See Lee Mueller, "City Hails Cut-Through, Airport as Boon for Eastern Kentucky," *Lexington Herald-Leader,* October 3, 1987; "Dropping in on Pikeville," *Kentucky Monthly* 1 (1980): 49–51; "The Pikeville Cut Moves Forward," *Appalachia* 10 (1977): 16–24.

16. All quotations from strike participants and other informants are from the author's interviews. To protect their privacy, participants are not identified by name.

17. Gaventa, *Power and Powerlessness;* Maier B. Fox, *United We Stand: The United Mine Workers of America, 1890–1990* (Washington, DC: The United Mine Workers of America, 1990); Curtis Seltzer, *Fire in the Hole: Miners and Managers in the American Coal Industry* (Lexington: University Press of Kentucky, 1985); Corbin, *Life, Work, and Rebellion.*

18. Auxiliary interviews with strike observers indicate that one reason hospital officials never wavered from their opposition to the union was a fear that other groups of workers in Pike County would organize. This was a realistic fear. Pikeville city employees walked off their jobs on October 25, 1972, and indicated that they also wanted recognition of the CWA as their bargaining agent. The protest by Sanitation and Street Department personnel ended after four days, when about half of the employees returned to work after the city commission threated to fire the workers and sought an injunction to stop picketing and striking.

19. Maggard, "From Farm to Coal Camp."

20. Sheila Kishler Bennett and Leslie B. Alexander, "The Mythology of Part-Time Work: Empirical Evidence from a Study of Working Mothers," in Lourdes Benería and Catharine R. Stimpson, eds., *Women, Households, and the Economy* (New Brunswick: Rutgers University Press, 1987), pp. 225–41; Martha May, "Bread Before Roses: American Workingwomen, Labor Unions, and the Family Wage," in Ruth Milkman, ed., *Women, Work, and Protest: A Century of U.S. Women's Labor History* (Boston: Routledge & Kegan Paul, 1985), pp. 1–21; May, "The Historical Problem of the Family Wage: The Ford Motor Company and the Five Dollar Day," *Feminist Studies* 8 (1982): 399–424; Alice Kessler-Harris, *A Woman's Wage: Historical Meanings and Social Consequences* (Lexington: University Press of Kentucky, 1990); Kessler-Harris, *Out to Work: A History of Wage-Earning Women in the United States* (New York: Oxford University Press, 1980).

21. May, "Bread Before Roses"; Barbara F. Reskin, "Sex Segregation in the Workplace," in Women's Research Education Institute, ed., *Gender at Work: Perspectives on Occupational Segregation and Comparable Worth* (Washington, DC: Women's Research Education Institute of the Congressional Caucus for Women's Issues, 1984), pp. 1–11; Ronnie Steinberg and Lois Haignere, "Separate but Equivalent: Equal Pay for Work of Comparable Worth," in Women's Research Educational Institute, ed., *Gender at Work,* pp. 13–26.

22. Karen Brodkin Sacks, "Does It Pay to Care?" in Emily K. Able and Margaret K. Nelson, eds., *Circles of Care: Work and Identity in Women's Lives* (Albany: State University of New York Press, 1990), pp. 187–206; Sacks, *Caring by the Hour: Women, Work, and Organizing at Duke Medical Center* (Urbana: University of Illinois Press, 1988); Susan Reverby, "The Duty or Right to Care? Nursing and Womanhood in Historical Perspective," in Able and Nelson, eds., *Circles of Care,* pp. 132–94; Reverby, *Ordered to Care: The Dilemma of American Nursing* (New York: Cambridge University Press, 1987); Barbara Melosh, *The Physician's Hand: Work Culture and Conflict in American Nursing* (Philadelphia: Temple University Press, 1982).

23. Reverby, "The Duty or Right to Care?" p. 133.

24. Gene E. Layne, president of CWA Local 10317, to Communications Workers of America Local 10317, July 8, 1972; letter in possession of the author.

Dan Jack Combs was a key informant in the research. A Kentucky appeals court judge when interviewed by the author in Pikeville on July 9, 1987, and later a Kentucky supreme court justice, Combs represented many of the strikers in court hearings and trials during and after the strike. According to Justice Combs:

> It's common knowledge that these board members were all anti-union. Very, very much so. Ernest Elliott [the chairman] was perhaps the strongest of the members of the board, but all, including their counsel, were very anti-labor. . . . I always thought there was probable cause of action against the members of the hospital board for their intransigent attitude toward this strike. . . . When they assume positions as boards of directors of an institution such as the hospital, an eleemosynary institution, they are to consider the public welfare of the institution above and beyond their own personal views. . . . Had an action been brought by the people of this area—the beneficiaries of this institution. . . . the people who depend on it for their medical and hospital care and treatment—against those board members for the damages that the hospital had incurred by virtue of their arbitrary actions . . . there may have been some relief.

25. See, for example, the testimony given in the U.S. House of Representatives on January 15, 1973, by Congressman Frank Thompson, Jr., of New Jersey, describing this labor dispute as rationale for NLRA amendments in "Nonprofit Hospitals," *Congressional Record—Extensions of Remarks,* January 16, 1973, p. E232.

26. For a detailed analysis of the importance of this gender/class intersection for political mobilization, the routines of striking, the women's relationship with CWA, and the consequences of participating in the strike, see Sally Ward Maggard, "'We're Fighting Millionaires!' The Clash of Gender and Class in Appalachian Women's Union Organizing," in Kathleen M. Blee, ed., *No Middle Ground: Women and Radical Protest* (New York: New York University Press, 1998), pp. 289–306.

27. Corbin, *Life, Work, and Rebellion.*

28. Exact PMH employment data by race were not available, but census data indicate low nonwhite labor force participation in occupational categories that would have included hospital employment. In 1970 the African American population of Pike County was very small; only 390, or 0.6 percent, of the 61,059 residents were classified as "Negro." See U.S. Bureau of the Census, *Characteristics of the Population,* vol. 1, p. 19, *Kentucky* (Washington, DC: U.S. Government Printing Office, 1973). Of the 390 African Americans, 41 employed women were in the civilian labor force and only 9 of them worked in health services, cleaning, or food services. Of the 37 employed African American men in the civilian labor force, 12 worked in these occupations.

In this study, three black women were included as possible respondents; two had moved out of state and could not be located. Despite several informal discussions with the third woman, her frequently changing work schedules kept us from completing a taped interview. All principal respondents were white.

12

Southern Women
and Southern Borders
on the Move

Tennessee Workers Explore the New
International Division of Labor

Fran Ansley and Susan Williams

omen throughout the South, in big cities and tiny towns, work
in factories. Many companies originally came to this region
for a climate of minimal unionization, right-to-work laws,
lower wages, and weak environmental regulation. However,
increasing globalization has recently triggered waves of capital flight from this area to developing countries. Companies
have encouraged workers in the Southern U.S. to blame workers of the Southern Hemisphere for "stealing their jobs." At
the same time, several Southeastern states like Tennessee and
Kentucky have for the first time begun seeing significant numbers of Mexican and Central American workers arrive in their
communities as migrant farm laborers or year-round workers
in lowest-wage occupations.

In Tennessee, a community/labor coalition called TIRN,
the Tennessee Industrial Renewal Network, came together in
1989 to help communities and unions address the problem of
plant closings. Since 1991, TIRN has sponsored a series of
worker-to-worker exchange trips between factory workers in
Tennessee and Mexico. These trips, made up predominantly
but not exclusively of women, and including both whites and

African Americans in the Tennessee delegations, have provided powerful experiential education for TIRN members and Mexican workers
alike.

In the summer of 1996, TIRN convened three focus groups in different parts of the state, made up of past Tennessee participants in the program. These gatherings, which were recorded with the informed consent
of those involved, provided a welcome opportunity for the participants
to compare stories and analyze their different experiences. The following text was created primarily from the tapes of those focus group discussions, which have been dovetailed into one constructed (and substantially shortened) conversation. Occasional words and phrases were
added to help with transition and continuity. All contributors (including
ourselves) had an opportunity to edit, revise, or expand their own remarks as extensively as they liked, and to give feedback and final approval
on the whole, so the final reconstructed conversation seen below is the
fruit of our three initial discussions and of subsequent collaborative reworking.

Although we want this group of American travelers to speak primarily for them (our)selves, we also want readers to have what they need to
engage in effective listening and responding, and to see how this conversation fits into some of the unifying themes of this collection. Ac-
cordingly, we open with some background information, followed by a
brief introduction to each of the participants, before moving to the conversation itself. For readers who want a clearer idea of the sequence and
people involved with specific trips and other activities, a brief chronol-
ogy of the TIRN worker-to-worker exchange program appears at the
end of the conversation. A bibliography and resource list conclude the
chapter.

Background

The people whose words you are about to read speak from situations
marked by profound and rapid economic change. Characteristics of
global economic restructuring as it plays out in the United States include
an increase in capital mobility within and across national boundaries; a
decrease in real and perceived job security; a rise in "contingent" employment (that is, jobs in which workers are involuntarily in a part-time,
temporary, leased, contracted-out, or otherwise less-than-full-status relationship to the people or entities for whom they work); a decline in union
membership and union bargaining strength; an erosion of real wages
and job benefits for those toward the bottom of the wage scale; a pro-
nounced shift away from manufacturing jobs and toward service jobs; the

continued segregation and segmentation of "job ghettos" for many women workers and workers of color, especially those in low-wage occupations; a reduction of benefits and amenities accessible to the public through the government; a regressive drift in the tax structure; widespread privatization; increased concentration of ownership and control in key parts of the business and financial sectors; mounting evidence of environmental harms that threaten society in general but whose burdens fall disproportionately on the poor and on communities of color; well-financed and often effective attacks on legal rules that impose limits and responsibilities on corporate conduct; and of course the alarming and growing disparity between the rich and the poor.

TIRN began its life in 1989 with a focus mainly on deindustrialization, a single thread from this larger economic fabric. It described itself as a "plant closing organization," building the phrase "industrial renewal" into its very name. What quickly became obvious, however, was that the problems TIRN's members were experiencing were deeper, more multi-faceted, and more interrelated than TIRN's original idea had suggested.

Under the pressure of the life experiences of its members, TIRN's focus began to grow. First, the organization spawned a Temporary Employment Committee to address the problem of the rise in contingent employment. Soon, workers began telling TIRN stories about their jobs and products moving south of the border, to factories called *maquiladoras*. TIRN learned that special arrangements between the U.S. and Mexican governments were allowing U.S. companies to open wholly owned branches in Mexico; bring their components into that country duty-free; and assemble the final products for return to the U.S. market with Mexican workers who were paid rock-bottom wages and who were prevented from organizing in their own defense by repressive labor practices tolerated (and even facilitated) by the Mexican government. In response to this new information, TIRN formed a *Maquiladora* Committee. This group was later renamed the Fair Trade Committee to reflect TIRN's increased understanding that the forces at work were bigger than one program, and were associated with broader trends of globalization and the movement toward international "free trade." (The North American Free Trade Agreement, or NAFTA, is a trade agreement among Canada, Mexico, and the U.S. After being hotly debated beginning in the early 1990s, it became effective on January 1, 1994, and may end up expanding to the rest of the hemisphere within the next few years. It is only one example of the regional and global trade deals that governments around the world are currently rushing to enter, and it continues to be the subject of fierce debate among people who differ on questions of economic policy.) TIRN is still struggling with what it can do to address the broad array of developments and policies outlined above. On the one hand, these dynamics seem dauntingly far beyond the immediate ability of local groups to change. On the other hand, they are far too important and powerful to ignore.

The workers who have participated in the U.S.–Mexico exchanges, along with other members of TIRN, bear the unmistakable signs of these economic trends in the story lines of their own lives. Some of these stories will emerge in the conversation below. Others we should mention briefly here.

These workers have gone through plant closings and downsizing and contracting out. They have been forced into second occupations late in their work lives, for lower pay and radically reduced benefits. They worry about what their children and grandchildren can do to find jobs that will support them and their families.

They observe with rising concern the increase in racial tension and the numerous expressions of racial resentment and hostility they hear in their communities and at their workplaces. African American members in particular are apprehensive about the fact that some of the programs that have worked in recent years to create more opportunities for African Americans are now being cut back, as if there were no more need for counteracting racial bias in the labor market or in education. And yet they know quite clearly that their children still face many overt and subtle racial obstacles to an equal chance at a secure economic future.

People active in TIRN often need to spend precious energy keeping their ears to the ground. They try to figure out alternate survival strategies for themselves and their loved ones in a volatile economy where the industrial structure and vocational expectations are changing every day. They sign up for retraining opportunities that look helpful, and they blow the whistle on others that look like scams. They weigh the risks of putting their families further into debt. They are concerned about the future of the social security system and their company's retirement plan— or its lack of one.

These workers watch as some of the toughest and worst-paying jobs in the South are "changed to brown" for the first time, with the work now to be carried out (complete with declining wages and worsening conditions) by a new workforce of isolated and superexploited laborers from Mexico and Central America. They strive to untangle their complex reactions when the local antilabor newspaper publisher editorializes that Mexicans and Central Americans should be welcomed by local business because they have "a better work ethic" than U.S.–born workers, and when he makes sure to drape his argument with lofty words about the dangers of prejudice and the importance of international understanding. They hear racist and fearful comments about these developments from white neighbors, friends, and family members. They respond with letters to the editor about their trip to Mexico, and what they learned about the character and the struggles of Mexican working people. They observe their own desire to save money when selecting the casual farm labor they occasionally hire at home to help with cash crops like tobacco, which allow so many rural Southern working families to supplement inadequate wages. And then they struggle over how to harmonize their desire to economize with their belief in fair wages for all workers.

In the midst of negotiating with an employer for a new labor contract, these people have had companies threaten to move jobs to Mexico if Tennesseans do not agree to concessions. They have seen the fear and defeatism that can spread through a workplace as a result of such threats, and they have suffered the consequences when weakened unions agree to "two-tier" contracts with some workers at substantially reduced wages and benefits that divide a plant into embittered and unequal camps.

They carry a lot of anger about investments they and their spouses have made, the years of labor and the list of forgone opportunities, all now threatening to go up in smoke. It often seems to them that the rules are being changed, late in a very serious game, by players who have stolen half the cards and who apparently feel no qualms about walking off with the lion's share of the winnings.

In the midst of all this, TIRN members share another trait. For the most part, in one way or another, they are activists. Despite the many harsh economic trends that are working themselves out in their lives, these are people who don't give up. They volunteer to help with blitz campaigns at distant manufacturing plants where their union is trying to organize, and then volunteer again even if they lose in heartbreaking elections after the company lies and retaliates its way to victory. They join the PTA when their children are young, and spot fellow troublemakers there with whom they bond for life. They kick and scream when they find out their water well has been poisoned with industrial waste, and they get together with their neighbors to do something about it. They stage a community boot-burning when their footwear manufacturing employer of thirty years announces it is leaving for greener, cheaper pastures. They go on TV and give interviews to the newspapers, or travel to a fancy college campus to appear on a panel, or go to a strange church to present a slide show, although they never dreamed in their whole life they'd have the nerve to talk like that in public. They stand up in a meeting and tell their state representative he has sold out his constituents.

They remember how hard life was for their parents and their grandparents, with all they had to do just to keep body and soul together, and a lot of times that memory helps them to keep things in perspective. They go to their grandchildren's ball games rain or shine, season after season, and they bust their buttons when a teacher calls to say this eight-year-old grandchild has been explaining NAFTA to the rest of the class in Technicolor and four-part harmony. They spend untold hours trying to straighten out troubled communication between people who are not getting along—at work, or at home, or at church, or in some community organization.

They go to the Martin Luther King Day parade even when they are too tired and too busy and their kids are driving them crazy and their feet hurt. They don't let other people—even people whom they love—get away with bullying them. At least most of the time they don't. And they take in people who are sick or temporarily down on their luck. They hold their desperate sister together for six hard weeks by means of one thin telephone wire. They nurse their mothers or fathers at the last. They definitely don't go fishing nearly often enough.

They get scared and depressed and exhausted, and they feel overwhelmed by how things are going, and sometimes they think they are crazy because most people don't even see things that to them are screaming out to be seen. But they keep on going anyway, a lot because of the strength they gain from other people like themselves. And these patterns and feelings and responses are part of the restructuring economy too. Actually this energy is among our most precious resources in responding to the problems we currently face.

All these things that are happening to people, and all the ways that TIRN and its members are attempting to understand and act on them, are highly relevant to the major theme of this book: the complex relationships of Southern women to one another and, ultimately, to women throughout the world. In fact, the question of relationships has been a central focus of TIRN's exchange program at every stage.

In organizing and conceiving these trips, TIRN leaders made some initial decisions about the sorts of relationships they thought were important and why. From their inception, the trips were "worker-to-worker" in design. This characteristic implied some assumptions. First, it assumed that workers in Tennessee and Mexico shared important commonalities, that both were being harmed by the actions of their multinational employers and their respective growth-hungry governments, and that people in their position had much to learn from each other. Second, although in many instances participating workers also made contact with their own and other employers and with government officials, and although conversations with such individuals in the U.S. and Mexico have been an important source of insight and learning for TIRN members at every stage, the exchange program has displayed a clear preference for the civil sector, a clear preference for working with those "at the bottom." In TIRN's view, U.S. and Tennessee workers have many opportunities to hear the views of business leaders and elected officials, but very few opportunities to hear from their counterparts in Mexican civil society, and to develop networks with people whose economic position in the global economy is more structurally similar to their own. Organizers therefore attempted (sometimes more successfully than others) to give a strong priority to creating settings and encounters where U.S. and Mexican workers had the chance to learn from and teach each other about the trends and developments that they were experiencing.

We have learned that exploring and building these sorts of relationships is a complex proposition. At different points and in different settings on our trips, Tennesseeans have found sameness. We have connected with Mexicans around many kinds of commonality: on the basis of being fellow trade unionists, fellow women, fellow men, fellow singers, fellow industrial workers, fellow environmentalists, fellow employees of the same multinational corporation, fellow Christians, fellow watchers of sunsets, fellow people of color, fellow relishers of food and drink, fellow organizers, fellow opponents of racism and gender inequality, fellow mothers, fellow troublemakers, fellow humanists. Southern rank-and-file activists have had the deep pleasure of meeting people in Mexico who are like them in not giving up, who get angry about injustice, and who keep on meeting the challenges of each day with remarkable energy and resilience.

We have also learned that U.S. and Mexican workers and activists are often divided from each other in important ways: by language, by wealth, by race, by age, by the differences in the degree of political repression or economic retaliation likely to be visited upon them for the same activities. Workers and unemployed people in Mexico face conditions that often simply took our breath away. For many Tennessee participants in TIRN's exchange program, seeing those living conditions of Mexican workers up close provided a startling introduction to the gross disparities that characterize the global distribution of wealth.

Meanwhile it was clear to all of us that people in both countries have important gaps in their knowledge, as well as inaccurate preconceptions, about the lived realities of those "on the other side." Both U.S. and Mexican promoters of worker-to-worker exchange and cooperation still have much to learn about how we appear to each other, about what issues need to be surfaced and addressed, about what kinds of joint work can strengthen efforts on both sides. From the start, the TIRN trips were conceived as exchanges between peers. They were not about charity, we said, but about solidarity between U.S. and Mexican workers and communities. But TIRN members have learned that making such sentiments real and effective will take a lot more work.

As you read the conversation below, you will see signs of both connection and distance, sameness and difference. You will hear TIRN members struggling with our own ideas—those we have been taught by people we love, those that have been sold to us by strangers, and those we have more consciously chosen—about what identity categories, what loyalties, and what self-concepts are most appropriate in our changing and challenging environment, what kinds of relationships we want to have and with whom in the new global economy. You will see that the categories that feel right to people sometimes shift with the context. And you will see that sometimes one of us feels "stuck" between or across two categories that have power in our lives but that point in different strategic directions.

To be strong, friendships and alliances must take into account differences as well as commonalities. This is true whether the relationships are between U.S. factory workers and Mexican *maquila* workers, between factory workers and academic researchers who want to write about them, between black and white or male and female Tennesseans, or between people born in the U.S. and their new immigrant neighbors down the street. We are only just beginning to understand what it may mean to recognize our samenesses and differences simultaneously, and specifically how to do this in the context of border crossings, whether those borders are international boundaries or the invisible but very real lines of power and privilege that so often divide and structure communities and labor markets here at home.

TIRN is not alone in seeking ways that workers and their communities can connect to their counterparts in an increasingly globalized world. Labor, church, and community organizations in the U.S. are participating in tours and exchanges, and are building solidarity networks that can mobilize emergency support for grassroots and shopfloor efforts in Mexico and elsewhere in the world. Some groups and unions have taken the further important step of entering into longer-term organizing alliances with international counterparts, alliances that involve an explicit commitment to mutual respect and cross-border equity, including some transfer of resources from north to south. Increasingly groups in the U.S. are also working to build global bridges and alliances within our own country as well. For instance, a recent wave of labor-community organizing has targeted U.S. sweatshops that use and abuse immigrant labor. Organizing campaigns directed at low-wage job niches in the U.S. economy such as meatpacking, poultry-processing, and institutional and home-based nursing care have the potential to bring together immigrant workers with U.S.–born workers who—whether for reasons of race, gender, geography, culture, or otherwise—have all been relegated to sectors of the economy where conditions are harsh, worker power is severely curtailed, and wages are insufficient to support a decent life.

Make no mistake: most of these efforts are still small and emergent. They face great obstacles created by many things beyond their control, including physical distance, language barriers, racial prejudice, sexism, fear of retaliation, overwrought work schedules, narrow nationalism, and the sense of powerlessness shared by so many individuals about the state of the world today. The efforts are usually understaffed and underfunded, and often lack meaningful support from organizations at a national level, which means that by most measurable indicators, they are dwarfed by the magnitude of the corporate investment flows, burgeoning research networks, proliferating private infrastructure, and "top-to-top" bridge-building that are currently being undertaken by businesses, law firms, banks, think tanks, and elite educational institutions.

Nonetheless, these weedlike, bottom-up efforts are demonstrably happening, spurred on by the very trends that can sometimes make success appear so difficult. And in our view, this kind of horizontal transnational outreach and interchange represents a heartening development, containing seeds of more to come. We hope that many more Southern women and men, of all colors and from many settings, will have the opportunity to expand their horizons, deepen their self-understanding, and win greater levels of well-being and democracy for their own and other communities through taking part in the creation of this new grassroots, rank-and-file internationalism. We also believe that workers from the Southeastern U.S., although they face special obstacles and difficulties, can bring special gifts and insights to this task.

Participants

Fran Ansley teaches at the University of Tennessee Law School, in Knoxville, where she also does research on issues related to deindustrialization, economic restructuring, and globalization. She is a past member and officer of the TIRN board and a member of the TIRN Fair Trade Committee.

Bob Becker has been a community organizer for fifteen years; he works for TIRN. He lives in Knoxville, Tennessee, and is working with Knoxville-area groups to increase local democratic access to economic decision-making.

Ann Bishop worked at the Acme Boot Company in Clarksville, Tennessee, for over thirty years, until she was laid off in 1995. She was an active member of the United Rubberworkers Local 330 when Acme announced it was moving boot production to Puerto Rico. The local, with backing from the international union, undertook a major campaign to keep the plant open and to reduce federal tax breaks to companies that moved existing jobs to Puerto Rico. Ann still lives in Clarksville and now makes her living by caring for an elderly woman in her home. She is a member of the Fair Trade Committee. Ann recalled her feelings before leaving on the exchange program:

> My biggest problem about going on the trip to Mexico was the travel. I was sitting back really wanting to go, but yet I had a fear of riding an airplane— I never had rode one before [laughing]. But Bill promised to hold my hand all the way to Mexico, and I did it!

Luvernel Clark lives in Knoxville, Tennessee, where she has worked at an automotive seat-belt factory since 1971. The plant is now owned by Allied Signal Corporation. Luvernel is the president and an active member of Local 1742 of the United Needletrades, Industrial, and Textile Employees (UNITE!). A long-term member of TIRN's board and chair in 1994 and 1995, Luvernel is also a member of the Fair Trade Committee. As she remembered:

> I first heard about TIRN from my union. I was in the office one day, and somebody had brought a bunch of pictures from the *maquiladora* plants down on the Mexican border. He was showing me pictures of the Allied Signal plant—Allied Signal is where I worked—and those pictures got my attention.

In testimony Luvernel gave before the Office of the U.S. Trade Representative in 1991, after her return from Mexico, she described the situation at her plant as follows:

> A dozen years ago, our factory at Allied was a big, busy place. There were over three thousand workers employed there. We had contracts with GM, Ford, and other big car manufacturers. But in the early eighties, Allied started shutting down parts of our operation and transferring them to a nonunion facility south of here in Alabama. The jobs did not stay in Alabama long. Soon we learned that the work had been moved from there down to a place called Agua Prieta, Mexico. That was the first that a lot of us had heard about all these factories moving to Mexico. We had no idea what really was happening. I am still working now, but I never feel secure.

Dan Clemmons lives in Nashville, Tennessee, and has worked at the Ford Motor Company's Nashville glass plant since 1977. He is associate pastor at Mount Hopewell Missionary Baptist Church, and serves as a district committeeman for Local 737 of the United Auto Workers (UAW). He is a member of TIRN's Fair Trade Committee.

Jo Ann Greene worked for over thirty years in Morristown and Greeneville, Tennessee, making televisions, first for Magnavox and then for its successor, Philips Consumer Electronics, a multinational corporation headquartered in the Netherlands. Several years ago, a new contract with Philips was negotiated in the midst of rumors that the plant might move to Mexico. Jo Ann was bumped back to a newly negotiated "second-tier" status where she earned less than six dollars an hour. Eventually she took layoff status, and for some time stayed home and took care of her grandchildren.

Jo Ann lives in Morristown, where she is also active in a local environmental justice organization, Save Our Cumberland Mountains, with which she worked to organize against landfill operations that were polluting the groundwater. Through their efforts several inactive old landfills on the Tennessee Superfund list were cleaned up, and city water was provided to the community to replace polluted wells.

Philips Electronics recently decided to stop producing televisions in east Tennessee altogether. A smaller company has been created to continue television production for sale to Philips, and Jo Ann has been called back by that company. Her husband works at a local furniture factory. Jo Ann is co-chair of TIRN's Fair Trade Committee. She described her introduction to the group as follows:

> The way I got involved with TIRN is that I was working with Save Our Cumberland Mountains, and I was invited through them to go to the Highlander Center for a workshop. And at that time, someone heard me talking, and they came up to me, wanted me to meet somebody that was with the Tennessee Industrial Renewal Network. There I was, just raising hell about "them damn Mexicans." It was right after the contract my union negotiated with Philips, a contract that really shafted me royally. They had used the threat of taking our jobs to Mexico to get a rotten, two-tier contract, and I was mad.

June Hargis worked for over thirty-five years for the Palm Beach Company, a manufacturer of quality men's suits, first in Newport, Kentucky, and then in the cutting room of the company's Knoxville facility. After a period of the steady downsizing and closing of facilities in Knoxville, Palm Beach was acquired by a major competitor, Hart Schaffner & Marx. The company now contracts out a major portion of the work from June's factory to Mexican and Central American facilities. June is a long-time leader and member of Local 2494 of the United Needletrades Industrial and Textile Employees (UNITE!). A past member of TIRN's board, June is now a member of the Fair Trade Committee.

Ann Huggins worked with Ann Bishop at the Acme Boot plant in Clarksville, Tennessee, for eighteen years, until she was laid off as part of a radical downsizing. Like Ann Bishop, Ann Huggins was a member of Local 330 at Acme, and she was active in the union's campaign to resist the plant closing and to curb federal tax incentives for job export. She still lives in Clarksville, and she and her husband now make their living by sitting with elderly people.

Barbara Knight lives in Greeneville, Tennessee, and worked at Philips Consumer Electronics for almost nineteen years before the company pulled out. She served as a chief steward of Local 796 of the International Union of Electrical Workers (IUE). Philips has been shifting substantial production work from Tennessee to Mexico for a number of years. In a pattern seen frequently in industry today, Philips has sold its Tennessee manufacturing operations to a number of smaller companies that will continue to produce the old product, now with Philips as their major customer. As part of the transfer of ownership, it was agreed that the IUE will continue to represent workers hired by these entities. Philips's departure, however, leaves behind a cohort of workers whose average age is fifty-two; the majority have over twenty years' seniority with the company. Barbara, like Jo Ann Greene, is one of those who have found employment for now with one of the smaller successor corporations. She is a widow with grown children. Barbara is an active participant on the TIRN board and serves on the Fair Trade Committee.

Betty Malone, like Barbara Knight, has worked for many years making televisions in Greeneville, first for Magnavox and then for Philips. She is an active member of IUE Local 796, and she too has a job with one of the successor companies at present. Betty lives in Bull's Gap, Tennessee. With Jo Ann Greene, she has also been involved in struggles to solve local environmental problems. Her husband works at a local furniture factory where a recent round of downsizing bumped him from a job making over twelve dollars per hour to one that pays a little over six dollars per hour. Betty is presently a member of TIRN's board of directors and co-chair of TIRN's Fair Trade Committee.

Sherry McAmis lives in Afton, Tennessee, and worked for many years at Magnavox and Philips in Greeneville. Her husband also worked for the company. Together the two of them had thirty-three years seniority when Philips sold the operation in May 1997. Sherry was a chief steward with IUE Local 796. She now has a job at the successor company, represents her local on the TIRN board, and is a member of the Fair Trade Committee.

Janice Perkins is a team-development specialist at the Bendix Allied Inflator Company (BAICO) in Knoxville, Tennessee, which is closely affiliated with the Allied seat-belt plant there. Like Luvernel Clark, Janice is a member of UNITE Local 1742. Janice's mother worked at the plant from the late 1970s to the 1980s but was laid off when some production shifted to Alabama and then to Mexico.

Susie Putz was a staff member of TIRN from 1994 to 1996, working with the Nashville chapter. She is currently pursuing a graduate degree in education and plans to teach high school.

Shirley Reinhardt lives in Morristown, Tennessee, and was a founding participant in TIRN. From 1985 to 1997, she worked for the General Electric Corporation in Morristown and was active in an unsuccessful attempt to organize that plant. After the union lost the election, GE relocated one of its operations to a nearby town and refused to allow existing employees to transfer to the new facility. Shirley was laid off. When she and others started looking for new jobs, they learned to their surprise that the only factory jobs available to them were through temporary agencies, with substantially reduced wages, benefits, and job security. They soon organized a group called Citizens Against Temporary Services (CATS) in Morristown, one of the first groups in the nation to sound the alarm about the rise of the contingent workforce. After a period of being effectively blacklisted, Shirley found work as a sales clerk at a local outlet of a national retail chain that sells home supplies. She is a past member of the TIRN board and a member of the Fair Trade Committee.

> When I worked at General Electric they were talking about moving jobs to Mexico, and some of the managers were going and working in Mexico. So Fran Ansley and I and some others were having lunch at a local restaurant one day, and she said, "Well, wouldn't it be something if we could just go down there and see where all those jobs are going?" And eventually that's what we did. It was an experience I'll never forget: it educated me. I really respect the Mexican people. I think about that a lot, about what they endure every day, just to survive. And it kind of makes me feel ashamed when I hear somebody make a joke about a Mexican.

Virginia Smith lives in Morristown, Tennessee, and works at Lear Corporation manufacturing seats for automobiles. There she is a member and past officer of Local 1617 of the United Auto Workers (UAW). Virginia is presently serving as the chair of TIRN's board.

> My first experience with TIRN was when I went to an interview with Congressman Jim Cooper at the textile local. Me and my friend Kathy at our plant had talked about this issue of NAFTA, and we didn't like the looks of it. We were selected to go to the meeting with Cooper, and we wanted to be there. We showed him a little film on Mexico and asked him what the difference would be. And he didn't have the right answers at all to any of our questions. I was really, really disappointed in him. When he saw the

film, he didn't have any concerns about issues. It was very disgusting to me at the time. I was bent on retaliating against this person, removing him from his office.

Bill Troy is the director of TIRN and lives in Knoxville, Tennessee. He formerly worked with the Commission on Religion in Appalachia and helped to organize TIRN's founding conference in 1989.

Susan Williams formerly staffed TIRN's Fair Trade Committee; she now works full-time as a popular educator at the Highlander Research and Education Center in New Market, Tennessee. She is trying hard to learn Spanish.

We should note that despite the lively roster just outlined, there are people whose voices are missing from the conversation below. Several individuals who went on TIRN exchange trips to Mexico did not or could not, for one reason or another, participate in the focus groups convened in 1996. Each made important contributions to the ongoing work of the project, however, and each—like many others who have supported and helped this program over the years—are indirectly "at work" in the conversation that follows. We hope that those of them who read this chapter will feel their presence among us.

Finally, we especially regret that readers of this book cannot see and hear these speakers in the flesh. They/we are a lively group, with a wonderful array of accents, facial expressions, hand gestures, and body types. We/they enjoy each other's company. Imagine lots of laughter. . . .

Susan: So is it all right for us to videotape this?
Barbara: If you give me that bag.
Susan: What bag?
Barbara: If you give me that bag to put over my head!
Jo Ann: If I'd known we were going to be taped, I'd have gone to the beauty shop.
Barbara: I would have combed my hair again since 6:00 this morning.
Susan: I would have had my nose job done.

Crossing the Border

Susan: One thing we want to do in this conversation is give ourselves a chance to think back on the different trips we have been on, to think about what stands out for us: what were high and low points, what did we learn. Does anyone want to start?
Betty: Well, the trip to Mexico made me realize how bad off people really were. Nobody can really tell you, you got to look for yourself. You know my husband Delmus just took a $200 a week cut in pay. He went from

between $11 and $12 an hour to $6.41. He's been there about twenty-five years. That's the group they are going after. But he still has his retirement and his insurance, it could be a whole lot worse. We could have small kids and we could have big payments on a house or something. I get to thinking how bad it really is and feeling sorry for myself, and then I get to thinking about what I saw in Mexico, and I don't have any reason to complain whatsoever.

Jo Ann: Betty and I both went to Juarez. And I guess the word would be devastated. Me, growing up in the mountains of east Tennessee, growing up as poor as I was, we didn't have a bathroom, we didn't have running water. I mean, hell, we was dirt poor, let's face it. We carried our drinking water for almost three miles. Then to go down there to see people that are poorer than I was! I really turned away from Mexico with a respect for those people, a respect that I have tried to share with everybody that I meet. Those people may not have anything, by our standards, but they've got spirit, they've got dignity, they make it day by day by their faith in God. You just can't help but respect people like that.

Sherry: I remember that people treated us exceptionally well. The white people down there, the American managers, were condescending, very condescending towards the Mexicans, while they're down there living high on the hog. I found that very offensive. Made me very conscious of myself.

June: Once you've been there, you don't forget it. It's not like looking at pictures. You look at pictures people bring back, and you walk away; that's it. But once you've been down there, you can't walk away from it. I think what I remember the most was going through a *colonia*—one of those neighborhoods where a lot of the workers live, squatter camps really—and seeing these little children have nothing. And stagnated water all over the place. And you go, and they invite you into their home, they are so friendly.

The *best* thing that I think happened was when the group of us was standing out in front of this General Motors plant in Mexico. This man from America did not want to let us in. But we went in, and we were in the lobby, and that film crew that was with us from public TV, they were taking pictures.

Fran: I remember that well. This receptionist was there, and she kept telling the camera people to stop, that they must stop filming. And the film crew was very polite, very noncommittal. But they just kept filming her. There she was, telling them that they couldn't keep filming, and they just kept steadily on. She was treating it like, "This is the company's space, and I can tell you what to do." And the film crew was acting instead like, "No, this is public space, and we are recording news of public—of international—significance. It is definitely our job to keep filming, to document what you are doing." It meant that her telling them to stop was not an effective command; it became part of the story.

June: It was fun, wasn't it? Finally, after we stood around out there for a long time, the plant manager invites us in. I guess he figures this is not going to look good back in the U.S.A., if they wouldn't let us in their plant. So he let us in, and then he gives us this speech that he really *cares* for these people. Like he told us that GM burned up four pumps that they used to get water out of workers' homes after a big rain. Now, these are cardboard boxes that these people live in, little shanty shacks, with no sewers or sanitation. But the company, they love the people! And I mean, you go in there in the factory, and you could have eat off the floors.

So I looked at this man—because he's from up in Indiana, Kokomo, Indiana, and I'm from just across the river in Kentucky—and I asked him how he could say that he loved these people, when they treated them the way they did, and didn't pay them nothing. And I think that really done me good, to tell this man that I knew he had no feelings for nobody. Then I said, "Because the stuff you're making, you're paying them no money, but when it comes back to the U.S., you're charging me the same thing that I paid when it was made in the U.S." And he looked at me and told me I knew too damn much. Just to let that man know that we knew what was going on, I think was the best part of it.

Fran: That factory was huge. You looked out over it, and you could see what seemed like acres of shopfloor, and just hundreds of young people working.

Luvernel: And it was almost all women, and a lot of young, young kids, young girls.

June: Well, when you're twenty-five there, you are too old to work in those plants, they say!

Fran: Yeah, he said the average age was nineteen at that plant, didn't he?

June: The Mexican girls we met couldn't believe that we still worked. [Laughs]

Luvernel: It was *ancient* to be working at our age.

Fran: What about your second trip, Luvernel, when you got to go into one of your own company's plants down there?

Luvernel: Oh, yeah, I really remember that visit. But it was strange, too, because the Mexican workers was looking at you. You *know* they was saying stuff. I couldn't understand them, and they knew that, and they couldn't understand me. But I was just talking like they could! That was exciting to have the opportunity to do that. As soon as I walked in the door I saw the whole spring operation. That was the first job that I ever worked on when I went to Allied in 1971, is the spring winder.

Bill: I remember a similar thing that happened on our trip. We had a woman with us who worked at the Ford glass plant in Nashville, and we arranged for a tour of the Ford glass plant in Juarez. This woman was seeing parts and numbers, and she would walk around, and this engineer, this poor guy from Knoxville, sort of a nice fraternity guy, a West Knoxville, country club Presbyterian boy, was nervous as he could be. Here's this woman, walking around just smiling and beaming at him and writing down serial numbers on her wrist.

Susan: Every time he'd turn his back she'd write down a serial number!

Bill: It was hilarious. Another thing I remember well is a time we were in a van down there in that neighborhood by the Allied plant. And Janice, I remember you saying (you were looking at one of the houses, and they were built out of all this material, you know, that people had scavenged from different places), and I remember you saying that those black corrugated things . . .

Janice: They were the things that hold the skids at our plant, the gaylords!

Ann Huggins: I'd like to say this too. All of Mexico is not like that, with people building their houses out of scrap and being so poor and all. On our trip we went and visited this big group of fancy homes that belong to these other Mexican people—

Dan:—the ones that *run* the parks—

Ann Bishop: Yeah, the ones that *run* the industrial parks! And some of them had houses like the White House. Some of them would have been—here in the United States—a real expensive home. So, what I'm saying is, it's not altogether the American companies that's going over there doing all this stuff, it is also Mexicans and the Mexican government taking advantage of their own people.

Dan: They're allowing it to happen.

Susie: There's rich people on both sides.

Fran: And poor people on both sides.

Ann Bishop: That's right.

Bob: My favorite was actually the tour that some of us got to take of a Philips plant there in Mexico. We asked the U.S. plant manager, "What is your entry-level wage?" And he goes into this whole number, pulling up papers, and he's got a calculator. (We already knew the wage, we figured it out. It was pretty simple.) It was amazing, he had no concept of what his people made. It was like we asked him to convert from Russian to Chinese.

Susan: Do you think he didn't have a concept, or he didn't want to say?

Sherry: I think he truly didn't know, because he was looking, he was digging hard to try to find it. He would call in this woman who handled this, this woman who handled that. . . . (Notice I say, "This *woman* who handled this, this *woman* who handled that." That's just how it was.)

Barbara: Yeah, like, "Maria, come in here and tell me when was it we quit checking your sanitary napkins to find out if women were pregnant when they were hired in?"

Sherry: We asked him that!

Jo Ann: They *admitted* it, then?

Barbara: Yes. In August of '95, they quit asking.

Sherry: He was so proud of that!

Barbara: It had to do with the last time that the Coalition for Justice in the Maquiladoras met in Juarez. They put a stop to it, 'cause the Coalition brought it up and was making a big stink. In fact, at the plant they asked, "Who's that nun lady, is she still with them?" So Susan Mika's reputation precedes her. She ought to be proud! She was the reason that at that plant they no longer check for six months when you're hired in to see your dirty sanitary napkins.

Jo Ann: After the six months, do they check?

Sherry: No, after that the government pays for your maternity leave if you get pregnant, so the company doesn't care.

Susan: You know, I think about other things, too, other memories. Like the first trip when we went to visit Colonia Roma. Remember the woman and that family who showed us how high up the flood water had come in their house?

June and others: Yeah.

Susan: And she had this little bitty garden, and she was showing it to us, this garden that she had to carry water to. And it was just, it's sort of like this picture in your mind. The things that I remember from the trip are things that are very human and beautiful. Like that woman with the doily that she crocheted while she was waiting for us.

Fran: That doily was made of gold-colored thread. I remember it glowed like a star in that dark house of hers.

Ann Huggins: What struck me was for them to be so clean and neat—for what? I don't know how they go on like that.

Fran: You know, a lot of people on these trips have talked about that. Why do you think it is so remarkable to us for Mexican people to be clean and neat?

Ann Huggins: Well, take a look at our poorest neighborhoods in America. Have you noticed? They are not clean and neat. In our poorest. I mean I watch it on TV and all, and they are not clean and neat. They're just nasty. That's how they show it on TV.

Fran: So let me see if I am hearing you right: somehow the image that we Americans have before we go is that it's going to be dirty. So when people keep things clean, it is remarkable because it is different from our expectations?

Ann Huggins: Yes. And they are doing it with no water! No lights!

Janice: Do you remember when we went down into those houses behind Allied, and there was a woman down there, remember? She was washing clothes. And she was beating them with a rock. It was the whitest shirt I've ever seen in my life. And I thought, "Lord, I bleach my shirts, and they don't even come this white!" But here she was, she was beating this shirt. *Beating* it. With a rock!

Ann Huggins: We should really be thankful—

Ann Bishop: There's another thing I haven't figured out how they do there. They say when they set up their little huts, them little cardboard boxes—you remember they said they caught them stealing electricity—how do they get that electricity in them houses? Somebody's got to know something about it. How do they get them electricities in them cardboard boxes from a pole without getting electrocuted?

Susie: They've got somebody that knows more than me!

Ann Bishop: And another thing. I still haven't figured out how their groceries is just as high as our groceries. How are they buying? We went in the stores, and the prices are just exactly like our own here at Kroger's.

Susan: And that was before the peso got devalued. When the peso got devalued, they made even less, but the prices didn't necessarily go down.

Ann Huggins: They couldn't have much to eat.

Dan: The cost of living is not that low.

Ann Huggins: That makes me want to help a fellow.

Ann Bishop: Yeah. When they're clean and neat, and everything—

Susie: To me it also reminds us of what we carry around with us. Like you mentioned TV and images of poor neighborhoods in this country. And where do you get those pictures? They're from TV! And it's the same with Mexico, right?

Fran: I believe we need to think more about where we get these ideas from.

Susan: Well, we've been talking about a lot of stuff here, good and bad. But what if I asked you to focus for a minute on the worst thing, on low points of your trip?

Janice: The worst thing was learning how the Mexican people had to live and what they had to put up with just to keep a job.

Ann Bishop: I couldn't believe our country was letting companies, American companies, go down there, hire ten-year-old kids as security guards, pay them five dollars a day, and use those young boys, just work them. And to see those people live out there in those cardboard boxes.

One day we went to a place where these people were all standing out in this big open field. They had just gotten to Juarez from somewhere out in the country south of there, and they thought they had bought this land; but now they were told they couldn't stay. It was about a hundred and four degrees that day. I looked back out the van door, and saw this cardboard box, folded out. The bottom part was on the ground, and the top part was hooked to the fence. There was two Mexican people in this box. That's what stood out in my mind more than anything: they was trying to keep this land. They was trying to homestead this, and the law tried to run them off. That really stuck in my mind more than anything: those two bodies sitting in that cardboard box.

Susan: Any other low points?

June: The motel we stayed in was sort of a low point on our trip—

Fran: Oh, yes. [Laughs]

Shirley: It was low because we weren't prepared when we walked in the room for bugs to be there. We weren't prepared when we pulled the covers down for them to be in the bed.

Jo Ann: Well, that wouldn't have surprised me. Like I said, I grew up poor and I had lots of bugs.

Shirley: I did too, Jo Ann. And I would have laid down in that bed and slept that night if I'd died right there. But you know, everybody didn't feel that way.

Sherry: Was it a home or a motel?

Shirley: A motel—the best they had. The best they had. Some of the girls with us from Tennessee tried to pay somebody to take them back across the border.

Virginia: They *did?* They were actually going to leave?

Jo Ann: That would have been rude.

Betty: Those people, do you think they had never been around a place where there was any bugs?

Susan: No, I think they had been around bugs.

Fran: Don't you think that something like finding bugs in your motel room is likely to throw you for a loop when you are visiting a poor country? I think when Americans visit a country like Mexico, a lot of us feel vulnerable and strange.

Luvernel: 'Cause you're kind of scared anyway—

June: [Laughs] Well, maybe there's gorillas outside! I mean we didn't know whether to go to bed or not!

Fran: To me, it wasn't a low point because of the bugs, it was a low point because of trying to figure out how to react to our own delegation. I found myself wanting to get angry at the people who were upset.

Shirley: I *got* angry.

Susan: I wanted to strangle people! We were all tired too, because we had been driving and we were in the vans and we knew we had even longer days ahead.

Shirley: So I just said, "We're not going anywhere. We're staying right here, I don't care how we do it, we're not going anywhere." And we didn't. And after we kind of got mad at each other—let me rephrase that—after everybody got mad at *me!*—we kind of sat down and decided this was how we were going to handle it. And it worked out okay, didn't it?

   But see, you know what I looked at, as we opened the door, right across from where we were, were these Mexican girls. One of our Mexican hosts, Tere, her daughter was looking at me, and the look on her face was, "You think it's not good enough." It was there, it was there. That was what was on her face. And she felt honored to be in that place, and it broke my heart. They understood there was a problem, and the problem was the bugs. They understood that.

Jo Ann: No, the problem was the attitude.

Sherry: Well, I just want to say that if I had been on that trip, I would have stayed, but I would have still had an attitude. I would have had a problem with the bugs!

Luvernel: That trip was something that I never thought that I would be able to do in my lifetime. But here lately I've been doing a lot of things I never thought I'd do in my lifetime. [Laughter] Now to me, the worst thing was not the bugs. And it wasn't the attitude either. It was the day we were in Reynosa, and we drove into Colonia Roma. When we drove up, I don't think any of us knew what to expect when we made that right turn down in there. I can just *see* that. Some of the houses were in standing water. The kids were running around. It was just the conditions of those little *colonias,* I guess, that I never expected to see. I couldn't have dreamt it in a million years.

June: I didn't expect them to really have anything. But I didn't expect it to be underwater!

Shirley: It took me fifteen minutes to get myself to where I could even— I thought they had a disaster and we were stopping to look at it.

Sherry: On our trip to Juarez, we saw *colonias* too. One day we went through the Philips factory down there, and then we went down behind it, where workers were living. The plant manager said he didn't want to go any further, because this was a Communist *colonia* and he was afraid! But then he bragged that just recently there had been real bad storms, and seventy-five of these houses had been washed away, and the company had rebuilt them.

Barbara: He complained because the dirt from the *colonia* blew up all over their plant; their nice building was covered from the dust from the *colonias*. And I thought, "You lowlife! If you'd run that pavement you've got out here just a little further back, maybe their dirt wouldn't blow up here." You can't tell where there's street, where there's yard, where it ends and begins.

Sherry: I know one negative thing for me on our trip was about communication. I hated those earphones they used for simultaneous translation at the Coalition meeting we were at! And I got stressed out with the language barrier there. I just crashed one day: I was full-up, I could not absorb any more, that was the worst part of the trip.

Barbara: Yes. It really, really bothered me, that I couldn't talk to them. It was like if I wanted to talk to Bob over there, I had to have Fran sit here, then I would talk, and then she'd tell him. A long, drawn-out ordeal. I was thankful for the translators, but I'm ashamed that I don't know Spanish. Because I know how I felt before, one time when I went to Miami: I went to places that didn't speak English, like I went to a service station and they didn't speak English—

Sherry: —which I think should be against the law. This is America.

Barbara: And I thought, "This is the United States! Why don't you speak English!" So when I went to Mexico, this was their backyard and I still didn't speak Spanish. And it bothered me that I couldn't speak it.

Betty: Maybe the worst thing of all for me was knowing that our factories were coming from the United States to Mexico. They know the environmental laws, but they do these people the way they do, endangering their lives, not caring, polluting their land and the air. And it didn't matter how many people die, they could care less. And we're supposed to be people who care about everybody. Surely don't care too much, do we? We're Americans and we're supposed to care, yet we don't. It blows my mind.

Virginia: Well, corporations are not American, Betty.

Betty: They're not human, I don't believe.

Jo Ann: They let greed get in their way.

Bill: Another thing that struck me that I've never really thought about before: these corporations are paying hardly any taxes in Mexico. They don't! These multinational corporations, the richest entities in the whole world, make practically no contribution to the municipality that has to run the sewer and everything for these thousands of people who are flooding in to work in their factories. And a lot of these people don't have adequate water or electricity or sanitation or anything. It makes you furious, really.

Janice: Do you remember when we talked to the Allied plant manager? I asked him what would happen if he just brought their wages up to our American wage, which was like $4.25 then.

June: [Laughs] I bet he said, "Oh, no, no, no, no!"

Janice: He said, "Oh, the company would move to Guatemala first, before they would do that." They were making about nine dollars a day in Juarez at the time, bringing home about six or seven. And he said if they got forced to bring wages up, they would take it to Guatemala where they could pay people two and three dollars a day.

Ann Bishop: Yes, I remember that like it was yesterday. He made a comment and looked at us in the face and said American workers was going to eventually have to get down to the Mexican standard. If you didn't get down to the Mexican standard, you wouldn't have no jobs.

Susan: He lives beside a beautiful green golf course in El Paso.

Ann Huggins: If we did get down to their standards, we wouldn't have nothing here. I said, "Well, man, I couldn't pay my light bill on that!"

Ann Bishop: Somebody said something to him about organizing there, and he said if they did, the company could move on down to another country.

Susie: Well, he was candid!

Susan: He was very slick.

Ann Bishop: Yes, he said we was going to have to come down to the Mexican standards.

Susie: Maybe he could be the one to start.

Bringing the Lessons Home

Susan: Let's try to focus for a little while now on what we think we've learned: what we've learned about working together with Mexicans in the future, what we've learned about our other work. What does all this mean?

Susie: One thing I've thought about a lot was how some of us got to go to a meeting of Mexican people along the border. It was *their* meeting. It was conducted entirely in Spanish, and it was all these groups from along the border from Tijuana to Matamoros. Just like the images you have in your head about cleanliness, we also have images in our heads about, "Well, *we* have unions, and *we* have organizations, *I* know about those, and these poor Mexicans do not." But the meeting showed me how much work people down there are doing, and how much people are being strategic and imaginative, and organizing in really, really tough situations—they're doing some pretty amazing things.

One day we got to visit people in their homes, and then that night there was an organizing meeting at somebody's house, with all these people from one plant. It was great. An organizing meeting is pretty exciting no matter where you are, and it's sort of the same as here, you know? At first people are sort of shy, and then they start to talk, and soon everybody was connecting about what was going on.

Bill: We had something a little similar on our trip when we got to meet some labor organizers. These people at a GE plant were on strike. And I know now, since then, that they lost the strike, and a lot of people were critical of the way they handled some things. But for us, visiting the strike was really a big thing. They took us out to this little village. We all got out of the van and walked into this dark storefront, and here are these organizers, this small group of guys. And one of them, who's very good and charismatic, tells us what they are doing and what the strike is all about, and what management is up to. And when we got back to our hotel, people were buzzing. Especially Annie and Ann, who remembered organizing their plant in Clarksville in the fifties and having to carry guns because of getting threats. And they really picked up on what was happening, and they said, "This is what they need to do, they need a strike fund."

Ann Huggins: That's one thing I regretted about our trip. I had took me some money to shop with. When we visited that office where those guys were trying to organize, they told us about what they were doing. They had got fired from their jobs. And afterwards I regretted not giving those guys, those three guys, fifty dollars a piece. Because I could have done without the shopping. I've wished a thousand times I had. Twenty-five or thirty dollars would have been a whole week's pay to them, wouldn't it? See, I knew what it felt like, 'cause I had worked with organizing Frosty Morn years ago, and I got fired over it. And I knew how they felt, 'cause I lost my job. I still don't know why I didn't. I kicked myself. I would've loved to have told them I knowed how they felt because I had been there. I tried to talk to them, but they couldn't understand me and I couldn't understand them. But I wanted to talk to them so bad.

Bill: Do you all remember that we met the labor lawyer, Gustavo de la Rosa? A very interesting, smart guy, who sat there in his courtly kind of way, and wondered just why it was that the AF of L–CIO did not understand that it was in their self-interest to send some money down there to help do this organizing.

Luvernel: Which it is in their self-interest, it really is!

Fran: I wanted to ask all of you if you thought that your trips altered the way you look at your own life, the way you look at your job, the way you look at the global economy. Did it change your mind about what is happening in the world?

Ann Huggins: You know, I heard my mom and dad talk about "Hoover's day." But even in Hoover's day it wasn't as low as they have it over there. I mean my folks *did* have water. They did have kerosene lights.

Fran: Also in Hoover times most poor people were poor because they couldn't get a job. In Mexico you've got people living in those conditions and working four and five in a family for Fortune 500 companies.

June: You know, you feel like the Mexicans are taking your jobs away from you. And when I went on that trip and I came back, I realized that they weren't taking our jobs away from us—our government was, and the manufacturers was. So, I really had feelings for those people when I came back.

Jo Ann: When one of these groups of Mexicans came to the United States, they came to my house, they came to my community. And from my community, they realized not all Americans are rich. The Americans that are going down there with those companies are leaving this impression on Mexican people that all American people are wealthy. But those visitors saw that we're not all wealthy. I think that made a big impression on them; they saw that there are people . . . in the United States that are just like the people in Mexico. We're all the same.

Betty: I would hope that some of the people I met down there don't compare me to that plant manager we met. Just the thought that because he is American and I am American, they would compare me to him gives me the creeps.

Susan: I'm trying to think about how the trips changed my thinking. Especially because the big NAFTA campaign came right after our first trip, it really made me think about, well, there's us, and there's the government, and then there's these huge corporations. I was already sort of cynical about the government in many ways, but it really, really pushed me way beyond what I believed before about how much the government serves business and corporations versus serving the interest of people in this country or other countries. The *maquilas* were just an example of what the trade agreements are for, and it's basically to help increase profit. That was a really good little concrete example of something that helped me picture, that's helped me understand, what these big trade agreements are. To me, NAFTA will always be what I learned about in the *maquilas*.

June: Right. We need fair trade, not "free" trade.

Susan: But what I learned there wasn't enough by itself. It was the stories I heard from people here and the stories I heard there, put together.

Luvernel: I've learned that we both have a lot in common as far as the workers go, mostly everything in common, as far as jobs go. They're fighting, we're fighting. There's very little difference. To me.

Bill: Maybe it's because I've shown the video about that first trip in 1991 to church groups several times, but I always remember the point in the video when you all were sitting around in a meeting with the workers there. And this woman talks about how we're all children under God.

Others: Yes. That was Tere's daughter.

Bill: I think that you could talk to lots of people in our own unions, or our own community groups, or our own neighborhoods, who would put it just the same way. And it's really a powerful statement for these church groups. Because they're not expecting it at that point in the video. There's no particular "church" lead-up. And then socko, she just says that. It's a strong statement.

Betty: It made me realize how little faith I have, seeing people with no homes, who have nothing, tell me that they rely on the Twenty-Third Psalm to take care of them. It blowed my mind. It absolutely stayed with me, and it will always stay with me, how much faith those people have. I don't think I'll ever forget that. I asked, "What do you do? Where do you go for help? You have no social programs." They said, "We rely on the Twenty-Third Psalm." That should make anybody feel mighty little.

Susan: Another thing that the trip, especially in Juarez, did for me, was to help me think about why people immigrate here from Mexico. It's so much like people from the mountains here in Appalachia moving away for jobs. I see it more that way now than I see it as people sort of anonymously coming into this country, who knows why. It's the same way people here moved north for jobs for years, to places like Detroit, and now they move over to the Triangle area in North Carolina, or to Atlanta, looking for decent work.

Shirley: I think about immigration more too. I remember the little house we went in where the young mother was with her two children. She had a little boy, I guess he was six months old, and she handed him to me. I can just see his little face, he looked at my nose and just smiled. Her house was tiny, much smaller than this room. We were late getting there; she had made a little doily and she showed it to us, to let us know that she had been busy while she was waiting for us. Everything had a place and everything was in its place. It was so hot that day, she had a little bucket of water, she set that little boy in that water to cool him off. Her little girl squatted down beside him. I thought, "She's so much a better person than I am." Because if that had been me, every night I'd be out there on that river with a log and I'd take my two children across there. So I know why they come across that river, and when I look at them, I'm proud they made it.

Sherry: Before we went there, Bob asked if any of us were interested in meeting migrant workers up here and I said no. I had no interest because, quite frankly, the only migrant workers are the boys, the men. They run in a van-full at a time—"Chickie, chickie," they say. You go to any dance club up in this area around where I live, if I get asked to dance, it will be by a migrant worker every time. So I had a very biased opinion about these Mexican men. But I would be willing to meet with migrant workers now.

Shirley: I guess I'm fortunate that there's not a day go by that I don't meet a Mexican family. They come in the home supply place where I work.

Sherry: I meet a lot of Mexicans but they're not the whole family. In our area, you have the men only, there's not the families.

Betty: Where we get our tobacco plants, where they grow them for us, this year they had Mexican guys working. One of them could speak English, and I asked him, "Do you all cut tobacco for people?" He said, "Yes," and I said, "What do you charge?" And he said, "What do you pay?" I said, "We pay a lot more than minimum wage!" (Which we do, we really have to pay quite a bit.) I said, "Would you be interested?" and he said, "Yes." Well, then he goes on—he was a really young guy—and he sort of put his hand on his stomach—and said, "Beer?" I looked at him and said, "No beer." My husband said, "Hell, I can't cut any tobacco with him." The boy laughed and swaggered, but he was just extra nice. Tickled Delmus to death over it.

Jo Ann: Let me tell you something. You just simply cannot hire American people to get out in the garden or work in the tobacco or anything.

Shirley: It's hard work!

Jo Ann: That's right. I don't care who I am, if I'm going to hire somebody to do a job, I want somebody that's going to work and do the job right. Let's face it, Mexican people do the job right, they do the job well, and they work for less. Betty wasn't going to pay them less, but she couldn't find Mexicans or nobody. Betty was paying seven dollars an hour.

Betty: We are going to contact these guys to see if they can cut tobacco for us when we're ready to cut, and, like I told them, we paid six and seven dollars an hour last time. I'm not going to pay you six and them two. I'm just not that way.

Fran: Do you think some people are doing that?

Betty and others: Sure, yes.

Sherry: We have some Mexican workers in the plant now. The biggest turning point for me was, this guy done my job on night shift when I was on the line. And I got laid off. I went to the unemployment office, and he was in there. Actually, I was waiting on my husband to get his unemployment. He was there after my husband came out, and finally I went back and I asked him, "Can you read this?" He could barely understand English. I felt really bad. I thought, "My husband doesn't read, and I fill out his papers." I said, "Give me your papers and I'll fill out your papers." And so it hit me: he is human, he isn't these dirty little farm boys that go, "chickie, chickie," there is more to them.

There's a bunch that come in Winn Dixie, and I just about know all of them, because that's where we shop, and that's where they shop. They wave and say, "Hi, there," not the "chickie, chickie" stuff. They are more human; they aren't just dirty young guys trying to pick up on the American chicks. And, realistically they've got wives back home, and kids. When we went to Mexico, the men were being very respectful. None of them made any approaches, 'cause they're family men. Up here, they are probably lonely.

Shirley: In Hamblen County they are ripping them off big-time in housing. They are renting them trailers, and houses too, I think, and charging them by the head.

Barbara: I just wonder if my sons had gone somewhere with a bunch of their buddies, how well they would have survived, ten or fifteen guys living together. How would they have done?

Jo Ann: These hostilities—what is the word?—these discriminations, prejudices. You have to contend with it in your own families. A lot of times I've heard my kids say stuff, and I've had to get on them about it. They see the Mexican people as taking jobs.

Shirley: I'd say, by Christmas in Morristown, in the mall, in the stores, they'll be working at the outlet chain where I work. They aren't paying them a real good wage, so they can't afford to live any better than what they're doing. This young boy at work, he was talking about Mexicans being in Hamblen County, and he said, "What scares me is we're all going to slide a little closer to living like that." And that's true.

Susan: Well, it's getting close to time to stop. Shall we spend a little time talking about what TIRN should be thinking about for the future in its work on the global economy?

Luvernel: We need to get out and talk to people.

Fran: After our first couple of trips, the big campaign around NAFTA was happening, and so it was easy to figure out how to take all this energy and knowledge and information and put it out there into the campaign. We jumped right in. Three of us drove down to Atlanta and gave testimony to a group that was traveling around the country from the Office of the U.S. Trade Representative. (That was during the Bush administration, remember?) We had demonstrations. We had petitions. We had a big motorcade and a rally. We had speakers. We also ended up meeting and cooperating with other people around the country that were working on NAFTA issues. We recruited a lot of new members into TIRN based on our work on fair trade. But now with the NAFTA fight over, or in a different phase, I think it's a little harder to figure out.

June: We can talk, we can show pictures, and we can show films, but the people can walk away. Because they've never actually seen it. All they saw was this picture. They can see that on TV ads wanting you to send twenty-seven cents a day for this poor little child. They're not fortunate enough like we were to go and really see what it is. And a lot of people are really down right now. At my plant, they're sending so much work out, contracting it out, and it's going to Mexico. You go in there right now and say something like, "Let's help the Mexicans." You know what reaction I'd get? "Pow! June, you're dead!"

Luvernel: Still, I think people are more educated about these trade agreements than they ever were. There's a lot more exposure to sweatshops on television, a lot more than what we used to see. Like on "20/20," and with Kathy Lee Gifford.

Bill: They show people suffering, but they don't show anything on TV about people fighting back, trying to unionize in Guatemala or in Mexico or anything like that, do they?

Luvernel and June: Oh, no!

Susan: You know, TIRN has always thought it would be helpful if people who work for the same multinational corporation were able to talk to each other. For instance, Dan, you and Bobby Stockard are both Ford workers, and I know that you all talked to Ford workers in Juarez when you were there. I am curious what kind of things you talked about. Was there information you all exchanged?

Dan: Yes. Bobby is involved in health and safety at our plant, and he was trying to find out how he could help. They were talking about the different kinds of chemicals that they work in. We even talked about sending back samples so Bobby could send them to the lab and have them diagnosed. They have no hearing protection, no gloves—a lot of safety issues. Once we got back, he sent down gloves, and he sent down earplugs and masks to help protect them, give them something to work in.

Susan: Was it news to them, the salaries that people made at Ford in the U.S.?

Dan: Well, they understand. They understand that they're working for nothing. And they want information as far as union organizing. I think

Bobby even sent them a copy of our contract; how they interpreted it, I don't know. In the meantime, we got a copy of a tape that we were shown down there, where they were on strike at this one particular plant, and the policemen were brutalizing these people. One guy even got run over by a policeman while walking on the picket line.

Susie: And some of us in Nashville wrote letters about that. Emergency letters and faxes is another thing TIRN members can do.

Susan: It's good that we bought that fax machine for our friends in Juarez.

June: I think we need to build relationships with people that we already know in Mexico, that we already have connections with, building some kind of firm relationship there.

Shirley: I think we definitely need to continue the trips; it's so good to educate people. But when we come back, it seems like we end up talking to each other, and not enough to the outside.

Betty: I got my whole area at the plant educated. Everything I get, I pass it around. The company moved me, in fact. They've moved me kind of out of the way.

Barbara: You know they've done me the same way; they've got me off in a little room now, just like they did you. I have no intercom, no telephone, I have nothing. I'm isolated now.

Bob: How do you do that, educate all the people in your section?

Betty: Talk to them! See, I talked to all the repairmen so much they put me back in that little room.

Ann Bishop: One more thing I'd like to say before we stop. I can understand why the American people, some of them, are mad at the Mexican workers. I can understand it, that feeling. Because you sit here all your life, and you've dedicated your life to this one company. Very few days you've missed, unless it's something that's happened to your family or you're sick or something. And you get pitched out like a dog on the street, without a job. You don't never know if you're going to have a job or not. And I can understand how the American people feels against the Mexican people, because they feel like they're coming across the border, and we're paying some of those people welfare. They come across the borders, and some people say, "Well, they're taking our jobs." Well, per se, some of them *are* taking our jobs.

And I can understand those Mexican people's side of view, too. Why are they taking our jobs? Because they want to better their life.

Fran: What are you going to do to survive now, Ann?

Ann Bishop: I'm sitting with a lady right now, home care.

Fran: And how much are you making?

Ann Bishop: I'm making seven dollars an hour. I clean up, and I cook.

And I guess I'm kind of a counselor. I talk to her. She's kind of down, she lost her husband. But here I am, I'm making a dollar and forty-three cents less than what I was making after thirty-one and a half years at the boot factory. (So you can see they weren't paying me any great shakes either.) But see, I've been to Mexico, and I can understand those people's feelings, but I can also understand my fellow workers here.

I say we need to go down there and help those people. I truly believe that. But I can also understand that people got a right to be bitter on both ends. I feel like we as American people should take care of our homeland and get our homeland straightened out. *Then* let's venture off to help our neighbors. I don't see taking food out of *our* children's mouth.

Fran: Do you feel that's why the companies are going down there—to help our neighbors?

Ann Bishop: No. No, I don't! I don't think our companies are going down there and helping our neighbors, I think our companies are going down there to help the big man's pocket. The Mexican people would truly be better off if the United States, the American companies, would stay out of there. Because I really think the big dogs is going down there and taking advantage of the little dog.

Dan: It's more or less that some people here are going through the same thing those Mexicans are going through.

Ann Bishop: That's what I'm saying.

Dan: And nothing is being done about it.

Ann Bishop: Nothing is being done right here. I think our people, we should stand up for each other. Whatever it takes for us to join together. *Then* after we get joined together and help our people, then we need to venture off and help. Because there's poor people here in the United States and kids are starving.

Dan: Labor's issues there are that if we can get the Mexican workers better wages, then the American companies, corporate America, will quit going to corporate Mexico.

Ann Bishop: OK, they'll go to Mexico. I don't believe their standards will ever—I might be looking at it wrong—but I don't think their standards will ever get up equal enough to keep the American companies from going down there and using them people.

Dan: Some people thought the same thing back in the thirties and forties here.

Ann Bishop: If we get Mexico up, then they're going to have to go to Guatemala, or they're going to have to go to Honduras. There is not enough time in the world.

Fran: So what should we do about it?

June: We've got to stop and think. If the Americans don't start sticking together and fighting, we're going to be in the same shape that Mexico's in today. And our government is doing it to us! We think they are in poverty, what are we going to become? What is my grandson going to grow up to have? We talk about sticking together and solidarity and all that, we're going to have to do it against our own government! Otherwise, we're going to be the way they are.

Fran: June, what you are saying reminds me of things that TIRN people said back in 1991 when some of us went down to testify in Atlanta. There were public hearings down there, organized by the Office of the U.S. Trade Representative. Remember this was back when NAFTA was first being proposed by George Bush and President Salinas of Mexico. Bush was about to send off negotiators to work out a deal with Canada and Mexico, and TIRN was upset about it because of what people had seen in the *maquiladoras*. In fact, we will be involved in another debate about this pretty soon, because there is going to be a push to expand NAFTA to Chile. Anyhow, back at that time Dianna Petty, a factory worker and union member, was one of the people who went on TIRN's first trip; she couldn't go to Atlanta, but she sent a paper down there for the hearings. Here is some of what she said:

> Our American companies are telling us that in order to keep our jobs, we must compete with Mexico, or the rest of our jobs will be moved. If they really mean we are supposed to compete with Mexican workers on the basis of wages, then they must be assuming it is perfectly fine for U.S. workers to live below the subsistence level, like so many Mexican workers do. Well, that is NOT just fine by me.
>
> The people we met in Mexico were very gracious. They were proud to have us. But I did not feel pride, I felt shame: shame and guilt that corporations from my country were causing these people to live in such poverty for the sake of cheap labor. People who defend the *maquiladora* program say that it is a success because it is making money for businesses and providing jobs in a country that has a serious unemployment problem. But can it be a success when there is gross pollution and when the jobs are unsafe and pay wages that are below subsistence? Who do you think is going to buy all these wonderful products that our American companies are making in Mexico? One thing is for certain: it won't be Mexican workers. They will still be struggling every day just to keep beans on the table, just to keep something over their families' heads.
>
> It's not just because of this trip to Mexico that I have strong views on the subject of corporations taking responsibility for their actions. I grew up in southwest Virginia, in the heart of the coalfields. My father was a coal miner. But when I was just a child, many coal companies decided to

close down their mines and leave Virginia behind. Whole communities were devastated.

Like many others, my father moved north looking for work. He got a job in a steel mill in Chicago. After that, when boys we knew back home would graduate high school, many times they would come north and move in with us for a while until they could get a job and a place of their own to stay. And of course, they would also be sending money back down home. I can remember times we had eight or ten people staying in a three-bedroom apartment with one bath. I thought of those days when I saw people piled in on each other in the *colonias* near the *maquiladora* factories, and when I heard them talk about moving there from other parts of Mexico, looking for work.

I wonder: in all these years have we learned anything? Look at the coal counties in Virginia today, and you will see what happens when outside corporate interests are allowed to take a region's resources and work the people sometimes literally to death, and then move on as they please. . . .

If people have no say in the economy of their own home, if government demands no accountability from major economic powers, then the land and people will simply be abandoned when they are no further "use" to those who profited from them. Nowadays, many places besides Appalachia are finding out what it means to be left behind. Those Chicago steel mills are closing down now.

To me it looks like a sure thing that the U.S. and Mexico are going to continue to grow closer together economically. We will share more and more common ground, and the gap between our countries will narrow. But what direction will this change take?

So I urge you negotiators: first, remember who you represent. You should be negotiating for all the American people, not just for the powerful few. And second, your goal should be healthy, balanced development for both countries, geared toward the welfare of the majority.

It makes me proud when TIRN members come back from Mexico and talk like this about what they've seen. More people in power should be listening.

Others: Amen.

Selected Chronology of TIRN Exchange Activities

1990: TIRN began exploring the possibility of a worker-to-worker exchange trip. The organization made contact with the Border Committee of Women Workers, or *Comite Fronterizo de Obreras* (CFO), a grassroots group of women employed in *maquiladoras* along the U.S.–Mexico border, supported by the U.S.–based American Friends Service Committee.

February 1991: Two former *maquila* workers from the Matamoros/Reynosa area, who are now activists with CFO, visited east Tennessee.

They spoke to labor and community groups and attended a workshop with Tennessee women factory workers who were interested in visiting Mexico.

July 1991: A delegation of nine women from TIRN paid a return visit to Matamoros/Reynosa, hosted by the Coalition for Justice in the *Maquiladoras* (CJM) and CFO. CJM is a coalition of church, labor, and community organizations in both the United States and Mexico that presses corporations to subscribe to a voluntary code of conduct, publicizes problems in the industry, and builds support for improved living and working conditions for *maquila* workers and communities. (On that trip were Fran Ansley, Luvernel Clark, June Hargis, Shirley Reinhardt, and Susan Williams.)

1991–93: Growing directly out of its work on the 1991 exchanges, TIRN began to learn about NAFTA and to become active in campaigning to block its passage unless it was significantly changed to provide strong protection of labor rights and the environment. As NAFTA negotiations were completed and the associated legislation came to Congress, TIRN—along with many cooperating groups in Tennessee—held public events such as forums, rallies, and a memorable motorcade designed to criticize the free trade model that NAFTA represented. In July of 1993, TIRN organized NAFTA forums across Tennessee that featured representatives from labor-related fair trade groups in both Canada and Mexico.

March 1994: TIRN sent representatives to a workshop in Ciudad Juarez on occupational health and safety for *maquila* workers. (On that trip were Fran Ansley and Luvernel Clark.)

August 1994: A delegation from TIRN visited El Paso and Ciudad Juarez, meeting with community and labor activists on both sides of the border. (On that trip were Ann Bishop, Jo Ann Greene, Ann Huggins, Betty Malone, Janice Perkins, Bill Troy, and Susan Williams.)

December 1994: A return delegation of five *maquila* workers and activists from Juarez came to Tennessee. The delegation met with church groups, community organizations, and union locals, and visited factories, union halls, and neighborhoods.

June 1995: TIRN sponsored an After NAFTA Tour with a Mexican border activist and a representative of the main Mexican fair trade network; they talked about NAFTA and the peso devaluation that was then ravaging Mexico on stops in Nashville, Knoxville, and Morristown. Also speaking on the tour was Sarah Anderson from the Institute for Policy Studies, in Washington, D.C., who focused on what had been happening in the United States since the passage of NAFTA.

November 1995: A delegation from TIRN attended a meeting of CJM in Reynosa. (On that delegation were Susie Putz and Virginia Smith.)

March 1996: A delegation from TIRN attended another meeting of CJM, this time in Ciudad Juarez. They heard from trade unionists, environmental justice groups, human rights activists, and community health educators from the Juarez area. (On that trip were Fran Ansley, Bob Becker, Dan Clemmons, Barbara Knight, and Sherry McAmis.)

December 1996: TIRN helped convene and coordinate a U.S. Gathering on Trade and Globalization in Jemez Springs, New Mexico. The meeting brought together a broad range of U.S. groups that had been active on issues of fair trade. Participants discussed ways of building a network that was more integrated with and connected to work on domestic economic justice issues in the United States, and was based firmly in people's experiences at work and in their neighborhoods.

June 1997: Two TIRN members took part in a Mexican tour organized by the Southwest Network on Environmental and Economic Justice. They visited factories and communities at the border and in some industrial towns further into the interior of Mexico. (On that trip were Jo Ann Greene and Susan Williams.)

July 1997: TIRN hosted a visit to Tennessee by a worker from the border town of Ciudad Acuna, who had been fired from his *maquiladora* job for helping to organize an informal committee that tried to meet with management to discuss improved wages and working conditions. The plant where he had worked was a subsidiary of Alcoa-Fujikura, an international joint venture that happened to be headquartered in Brentwood, Tennessee. TIRN was able to help arrange a meeting with managers of the parent company and also to set up visits with trade unionists and community activists in the area, including members of a United Steelworkers local that represents workers at an Alcoa Aluminum plant in Alcoa, Tennessee.

Fall 1997: As the authors finish the manuscript for this chapter, TIRN is once again joining in the fierce social debate around free trade. The issue is heating up because Congress will soon be asked to vote on whether to grant the executive branch "fast-track authority" covering the extension of NAFTA to Chile and other upcoming trade deals as well. Through fast-track authority Congress delegates significant power and responsibility to the executive branch by voluntarily agreeing to accept severe constraints on the normal congressional process for developing, drafting, debating, and voting on legislation. This delegation has become increasingly controversial, especially as trade agreements have come to cover subjects much broader than mere "trade." TIRN recognizes that NAFTA is only one part of a much larger economic picture, but it has decided to join the NAFTA debate once more because it sees the vote on NAFTA as an important opportunity for ordinary people to raise questions about the wisdom of the economic model upon which NAFTA is based and which NAFTA helps to institutionalize.

Selected Resources

The list of books, articles, videos and other resources that focus on (and argue about) economic globalization is long and growing. Many organizations and projects are trying to develop strategies that can effectively intervene in the interest of those who are being hurt by the type of globalization now taking place. Given our space limitations, we cannot include a sizable bibliography or mention all the potentially helpful materials and groups we know. We hope instead to signal a few available entry points for readers who would like to go further in learning about—or taking action in—the global economy. We have tried particularly to include resources and organizations that focus on industrial workers, on the southeastern U.S., and/or on bottom-up strategies and perspectives. We have also included resources that document or deal directly with TIRN's own program described above. We have excluded articles in publications not readily accessible. But even after having limited ourselves in these ways, we have still had to exclude many items because of the restrictions of space.

Print Resources

American Federation of Teachers. *Child Labor: A Selection of Materials on Children in the Workplace.* Washington, DC: AFT, n.d. Suitable for use in high school classrooms.

Nick Alexander. "Missing Pieces: How the Nike Campaign Fails to Engage African Americans." *Third Force,* July–August 1997, pp. 12–16. Raises important questions and problems about the relationship between current anti-sweatshop campaigns and the African American community.

Fran Ansley. "The Gulf of Mexico, the Academy, and Me." *Soundings* 78 (1995): 68-104. Describes the TIRN worker-to-worker exchange program and considers how the author's work on that program relates to scholarly work and standards.

———. "North American Free Trade Agreement: The Public Debate." *Georgia Journal of International and Comparative Law* 22 (1992): 329-468. Reprints the testimony of Fran Ansley, Luvernel Clark, Dianna Petty, and Shirley Reinhardt before the Office of the U.S. Trade Representative.

———. "Standing Rusty, Rolling Empty: Law, Poverty, and America's Eroding Industrial Base." *Georgetown Law Journal* 81 (1993): 1757-1896. Briefly discusses the author's trip to the *maquiladora* region in the context of a larger look at deindustrialization in the United States.

———. "U.S.–Mexico Free Trade from the Bottom: A Postcard from the Border," *Texas Journal of Women and the Law* 1 (1992): 193-248. Reprints the script of a play that TIRN members performed for Mexican workers in the town of Miguel Aleman in 1991.

Jeremy Brecher and Tim Costello. *Global Village or Global Pillage: Economic Reconstruction from the Bottom Up.* Boston: South End Press, 1994. 237 pp., $14. Features examples of pro-active responses to globalization. A related video is currently in production.

David Brooks. "The Search for Counterparts: A Labor-Community Agenda Must Cross Borders as Well." *Labor Research Review* 11 (1) (Fall 1992): 83–97.

John Cavanagh, ed. *South-North Strategies to Transform a Divided World.* San Francisco: International Forum on Globalization, 1995. Pamphlet.

Allen Hunter. "Globalization from Below? Promises and Perils of the New Internationalism." *Social Policy* 25 (4) (Summer 1995): 6–13.

Thalia Kidder and Mary McGinn. "In the Wake of NAFTA: Transnational Workers' Networks." *Social Policy* 25 (4) (Summer 1995): 13–21.

Abby Scher. "Coming in from the Cold in the Struggle for Solidarity." *Dollars and Sense* 213 (September–October 1997): 24–28. Describes examples of new cross-border activity by U.S. trade unions and other organizations.

Films and Videos

Dirty Business (15 minutes). Story of the Jolly Green Giant shifting jobs from Watsonville, California, to Irapuato, Mexico, and the responses of workers and communities in both locations. Available from: Migrant Media Productions, P.O. Box 2048, Freedom, CA 95019; 408-728-8949.

From the Mountains to the Maquiladoras (20 minutes). Shot on the 1991 TIRN trip to Matamoros and Reynosa, Mexico. Available from: TIRN, 1515 E. Magnolia, Suite 403, Knoxville, TN 37917; 423-637-1576.

Global Assembly Line (60 minutes). A documentary look at export processing zones in Mexico and the Philippines. Available from: New Day Films, 863 Broadway, Room 1210, New York, NY 10003; 212-477-4604.

Indonesia: Islands on Fire (25 minutes). Presents labor conditions, struggles, and rights in the overall context of intense political repression. Available from: Global Exchange, 2017 Mission St., San Francisco, CA 94110; 415-255-7296 or 415-255-7698; http://www.globalexchange.org.

Mickey Mouse Goes to Haiti (20 minutes). Critiques Disney's role in the Haitian garment industry. Offers good material on the argument that low wages are acceptable because the cost of living is lower. Available from: National Labor Committee in Support of Worker and Human Rights in Central America, 275 12th Ave., 15th Floor, New York, NY 10001; phone 212-242-3002; fax 212-242-3822.

Nike in Vietnam (20 minutes). A segment of the "48-Hours" television show, reported by Roverta Baskin and aired October 1996, that exposes conditions for women in Nike factories in Vietnam. Includes interviews with workers and company officials. Available from: CBS Video, P.O. Box 2284, South Burlington, VT 05407; 800-338-4847.

Tomorrow We Will Finish (26 minutes), by UNICEF. Focuses on girls in the rug-weaving industry in Nepal and India. Available from: Maryknoll World Productions, 800-227-8523.

Zoned for Slavery: The Child Behind the Label (23 minutes). Looks at *maquila* workers in Honduras. Interviews workers and families. Available from: National Labor Committee in Support of Worker and Human Rights in Central America, 275 12th Ave., 15th Floor, New York, NY 10001; phone 212-242-3002; fax 212-242-3822.

Organizations and Projects

The best source of information on organizations and projects working to build equitable and productive links between labor and community groups in the United States and Mexico is a three-part directory called *Cross-Border Links 1997*. It includes information on labor, the environment, and fair trade/sustainable development. It is available from Interhemisphere Resource Center, P.O. Box 2178, Silver City, NM 88062; phone 505-388-0208; fax 505-388-0619.

Games and Activities

The New Global Economy. A simulation game with video segments, a facilitator's manual, and discussion exercises for six sessions. Available from: Resource Center of the Americas, 317 17th Avenue SE, Minneapolis, MN 55414; phone 612-627-9445; fax 612-627-9450. The same company publishes a very helpful newsletter, *Working Together,* that focuses on international labor rights and labor solidarity.

13

What's Sex Got to Do with It, Y'All?

Mab Segrest

Thanks to Laura, for hearing this through.

"Civilization behaves toward sexuality as a people or a stratum of its population does which has subjected another to its exploitation. Fear of revolt by the suppressed elements drives it to stricter and stricter precautionary measures."
Sigmund Freud

"The erotic is a resource within each of us that lies in a deeply female and spiritual plane, firmly rooted in the power of our unexpressed or unrecognized feeling."
—Audre Lorde

was a virgin until I was twenty-one, the night a guy from Dartmouth came down to Montgomery, Alabama, with his rowing team and got me drunk as a skunk, and I stripped naked with him behind the country club and we fucked, me alternately exclaiming, "I am the Earth Mother!" and "I am not an easy lay!" I retrieved my grass-stained dress, the only thing I had to wear to church the next morning in Tuskegee as I repented as best I could through a headache that started at my shoulder blades and scrambled the syntax of the Doxology and the Apostles' Creed.

I did not know how to masturbate until I was twenty; I had figured anything that had "master" in it was only for men.

This is not to say that I was not in love with girls and women since I was at least about four, beginning with my Mama and my next-door neighbor Judy. One of my early memories is of Judy riding her bike on the sidewalk across the street while I was standing in a new dress getting my picture taken, a photo that failed to show my little heart snapping out of my chest toward Judy's churning legs and the spinning spokes. Preadolescence was the perfect cover; females are not yet expected to have matured into heterosexuality. But by thirteen, all my girlfriends had shifted their emotional allegiance to boys, leaving me exposed. They spent their spare time groping with the most uninteresting males on the plastic seats of old cars, while I practiced the piano, wondering if there was something about me that would always keep me from love.

It didn't help that I was butch. My mother spotted me early on; she later said that she could tell I was a lesbian when I was five by the way I "strode across the floor with a pistol on your hip, cried when you had to wear a dress to school, and bossed everybody around." The main male I remember being interested in was Elvis. I cried when he got shot at the end of *Love Me Tender* and decided I was in love with him. But I was not quite sure whether I *wanted* Elvis, or wanted *to be* Elvis. That was 1956, and I was seven. I would come home from school in the afternoon, shut the door of my parents' bedroom, slick back my hair with a wet comb, and practice flicking my hips against an imaginary guitar, crooning, "Never let me go."

By the third grade, my uncle-doctors put me on a diet, since I was "too fat," whatever that means for a nine-year-old. So at the beach while they were eating fried mackerel, I would eat broiled hamburger; their ice cream to my cottage cheese. The memory is one of deprivation measured in calorie counts that registered as punishment, but for what? I would stand next to my blond cheerleader/homecoming-queen cousins and know that all the cottage cheese and tomatoes in the world would not make me like them. My body was betraying me.

One memory is from a bulletin board in a ninth-grade English classroom that showed a very femme woman looking back over her shoulder in horror at the bottom of her dress: "Your slip is showing," the letters cut out of construction paper proclaimed; it was a poster about the embarrassment of bad grammar. But I felt a rush of shame seeing the display, a flash that people were probably seeing/reading my "gender slips" behind my back.

I was not so much out of sight as out of language. I didn't know the word "homosexual" until I read it when I was eleven or twelve, in the early 1960s, in an article in *Life* magazine, one of the first treatments of the urban gay subculture in the mainstream media. In the back corner of my brain in which I allowed such conversations, it occurred to me that the word might explain a lot. My problem, at nine and thirteen and twenty, was not that I was not seen but more that I was not named—or that the names available carried such lethal stigma. Queer: alone, outside community, outside family, outside love, the only one. Genuine invisibility would have been a relief; instead, I had my painfully visible efforts at invisibility, my futile efforts to suck all my energy back in: a child of the universe, trying to be a black hole. I had little means to figure the "*curious abrupt questions [that] stirred within me*," as the great faggot poet of democracy Walt Whitman wrote, questions of how "*I had received identity in my body,/that I was I knew was of my body, and what I knew I should be I knew I should be of my body.*"[1]

So the struggle to fix elusive language to the slippery category of sexual identity has been a central preoccupation of my life, as it has been of many lesbians and gay men of my generation. It is one that I enter again with the drafts of this text, long overdue in some finished form but now littering my study as I shuffle through them in the early hours of the morning, trying to remember what it was I meant to say. This morning I pull out Eve Sedgwick's *Epistemology of the Closet* and recall that I had wanted to extend her project of developing an "alternative analytical axis—call it sexuality."[2]

My task here is to look at sexuality as a dynamic of power, a shaper of identity and culture; and at heterosexism and homophobia as part of the tangled intersection of race, class, gender, and sexuality in Southern and U.S. culture. The Southernness of this project is its particular conjunction of sexuality and race; its femaleness a similar nexus of sexuality and gender. Sedgwick observes that "not all oppressions are congruent, but . . . differently structured and so must intersect in complex embodiments."[3] To me, the slippery complexity of the embodiment is both its congruence *and* dissonance, intersection *and* simultaneity.

Locating sexuality as an "axis" or function of power is not only a theoretical question. I want to draw on some of the insights about sexuality of Queer Theory, but shall attempt to ground them in political practice. Paulo Friere defined "praxis" as an alternation of action and reflection.[4] I think the proliferation of academic "theory" in the past twenty years has produced a dangerous split between the two. Organizers have too little money and time to reflect adequately on their activism. And academics proliferate theory insufficiently grounded or tested in practice. You can write books about "social construction" up the kazoo, but how do we also help people deal with rapid shifts in racial, sexual, gender, and class identities? The survival of whatever "democracy" we have depends on answers to such questions.

Forces such as globalization, structural adjustment, privatization, downsizing, automation, and new information/computer technologies are propelling us into the next century through decisions made by a minuscule segment of the population, the ultrarich and the CEOs of multinational corporations. The results—a declining economy and cultural deterioration—are blamed on the most vulnerable among the rest of us, with sexuality at the core of scapegoating mythologies about welfare, crime, and gay rights. Clarity on the question of sexuality is a requirement if we are to create a qualitatively different human interaction going into the next millennium.

In this essay, then, I work to place thinking about sexuality firmly in contexts of political practice, drawing on twenty years of experience as a lesbian organizing in local, regional, and national contexts. How homophobia and heterosexism intersect with, overlap, or repel racism, sexism, and class oppression happens in particular historical and political contexts, so it makes sense to look at political practice, both movements and their discourse, to see what generalizations might emerge. (In other words, intersecting praxes make more sense than intersecting axes.) I will look at paradigms of civil rights and historical materialism with attention to how gay and lesbian people particularly and sexuality generally are and are not included, and what implications this has for transformative political movements.

Race and the Invisible Dyke

Sedgwick distinguishes sexuality ("an array of acts, expectations, narratives, pleasures, identity-formations and knowledges . . . that tends to cluster most densely around certain genital sensations") from gender ("rigidly dichotomized social production and reproduction of male and female identities and behaviors"), into which it easily slips.[5] My difficulty, I realize, is to distinguish sexuality from race (a rigidly dichotomized social production and reproduction of white and "colored" identities and behaviors), a particularity of my location as a Southern woman born circa 1949.

As an adolescent, with no one available to translate for or with me the language of my body, I began to translate it myself into the language of race. African Americans all around me were rising against ontological erasure as much as they were against Jim Crow. When I was thirteen in 1963 I lay on my belly underneath some shrubs to watch several black children my age walk across the breezeway at my high school, surrounded by hundreds of state troopers sent by George Wallace to keep my school from integrating. I have circled back many times to my moment of identity with the three black children inside the circle of force, my "queer" empathy with their aloneness. It has since occurred to me that they might instead have felt a huge sense of power and pride at having braved the troopers, after the president of the United States had threatened to federalize the

National Guard in their behalf. But to me, they were lonely because I was lonely, and we were all surrounded by mirrors of hard, distorting glass.

I saw also, clearly, how race and sex and white people's confusions about both were hopelessly intermingled. Even from my segregated family, I could see that the black uprising all around me was deeply spiritual in its challenge to the morality of white supremacist culture. But I heard white people defending that culture by attacking the sexual morality of the civil rights movement. The Selma to Montgomery March of 1965, one of the great ethical pilgrimages of the twentieth century, was dismissed as an occasion for white nuns to have sex with black men on the state capitol grounds, leaving used condoms in the bushes. Viola Luizzo, the white woman from Detroit who was murdered by Klansmen while driving marchers back from Montgomery, was dismissed as a whore. Even at thirteen, it was clear to me that part of the struggle was over contending views of righteousness: a prurient and constrictive sexual ethic that could be used to justify murder against an expansive ethic of liberation that was challenging deep violence in the culture.[6]

In the years that followed, as a generation of lesbians and gay men have gained our own acknowledged presence and language, I have found myself puzzled and frustrated at how the movement against homophobia and heterosexism and for gay and lesbian liberation could grow up so seemingly separate from the movement against racism and for the liberation of people of color. Indeed, there is a vocal presence in both communities conniving to maintain this separation. For example, recently Andrew Sullivan, editor of *The New Republic* and latest poster boy for the clichéd affluent-white-gay-male, wrote, "The truth is, our position [as gay people] is far worse than that of any ethnic minority or heterosexual women," a sentence whose syntax makes gay and ethnic minorities mutually exclusive and whose content shows his oblivion to any reality that is not white. On the other side of the barricade, the Reverend Marvin McMichol, a black minister in Cleveland, asserts, "It is our fundamental, reasoned belief that there is no comparison between the status of Blacks and women, and the status of gays and lesbians," the former being "an ontological reality . . . a fact that cannot be hidden"; the latter being "a chosen lifestyle . . . defined by behavior." Reverend McMichol likewise obliterates the womanness of lesbians and the existence of lesbian and gay people of color, illustrating his oblivion to the gay reality he presumes to define.[7]

The Christian right's "wedge strategies" feed such definitional schisms, most viciously in the video *Gay Rights/Special Rights,* which uses such devotees of black freedom struggles as Mississippi senator Trent Lott and Ronald Reagan's attorney general Ed Meese (who did as much as he could to dismantle affirmative action) to argue that since gayness is behavior-based, gay people do not deserve or need civil rights protections. These are instead reserved for minorities whose identities are based on "immutable characteristics." The video uses black spokespeople to reinforce the white message that gay people have "hijacked" the civil rights movement, which has in fact been subjected to decades of terrorist attack by the likes of Lott and Meese, who are not so thrilled with black behavior either, truth be known.[8]

I am puzzled, as always, by the opposition of blackness and gayness: "the fact [of skin pigment] that cannot be hidden" (McMichol) versus "*the* open secret" . . . the epistemology of the closet (Sedgwick).[9] Of course, it's not so simple. Blackness signifies much more than dark skin, given the sexual history of slavery, when any slave master had sexual access to black women and any offspring "followed the condition of the mother" into slavery, however light the child's skin. Passing as white under a regime of white supremacy was every bit as much a temptation and strategy as passing as straight under heterosexist regimes, and neither comes without cost.

Nor is "invisibility" a category of gay life only. Ralph Ellison begins his classic novel in my hometown of Tuskegee, Alabama, with a metaphor I totally understand: "I am an invisible man." Racism, like homophobia, is predicated on ontological erasure, an invisibility located not so much in the "biochemical accident of my epidermis," as Ellison's narrator explains, as in the eye and consciousness of the racist (or homophobic) beholder, "a matter of the construction of their inner eye": "I am invisible, understand, simply because people refuse to see me. . . . When people approach me, they see only my surroundings, themselves, or figments of their imagination—indeed, everything and anything except me."[10]

Like Ellison, as a child in Tuskegee I knew there was something about me, elusive as fog, that people around me acted out of but never explained. We wondered "whether [we weren't] simply a figure in a nightmare which the sleeper tries with all his strength to destroy." People bumped against me, and my aching need to convince myself that I "existed in the world, part of all the sound and anguish" of having and of being a body.[11]

Racism in the gay community and homophobia in the black community are realities, as are the deliberately divisive tactics of the Right. But is there also something in the category of "civil rights" that causes confusion and disjunction about the complexity of "having and being a body"? Have the praxes of our movements—their political discourse of civil rights and related strategies of legal protection—somehow hijacked us all?

Civil Rights: Life, Liberty, and the Pursuit of . . . ?

It is no accident that the civil rights movement gave me ways to understand my sexuality. Civil rights is the dominant discourse—which is to say
the most complex embodiment of identity, intersection, and disjunction—for translating among race, gender, and sexual orientation in the
twentieth-century United States. (Class does not fit so well in this
discourse, as I shall discuss later.) The civil rights movement was the mid-
twentieth-century incarnation of four hundred years of freedom struggles of African people on this continent. The struggle against slavery—
the racism that generated it and that it in turn generated—encompassed
slave resistance and rebellion; the abolition movement; the Civil War; the
brief period of Reconstruction when there was a glimmer of a possibility
of racial and economic democracy; and the reinstitution of white supremacy with Jim Crow segregation, voter disenfranchisement, and the
racist terrorism of lynching and the Klan at the end of the nineteenth
century. *Brown* v. *Board of Education* in 1954 challenged the school segre
gation legalized with *Plessy* v. *Ferguson* in 1896, and campaigns across the
South targeted segregated public facilities such as buses and restaurants
and hotels. Highly visible campaigns in Birmingham and Selma resulted
in the two Civil Rights Acts that by 1965 had opened up the vote and eliminated the legally enforced systems of segregation put in place at the beginning of the century.

When I encountered the civil rights movement looking out from be-
neath the bushes at the age of thirteen, its impact to me was revolutionary. Not that this movement was monolithic. We knew that King and the
Southern Christian Leadership Conference were leading the demonstrations in Selma; that young workers in the Student Nonviolent Coor-
dinating Committee were attempting to integrate our churches and were
registering poor black voters out in rural areas of the county, a strategy
at odds with the more middle-class black emphasis of the Tuskegee Improvement Association; that the Black Panthers were rumored to be stealing weapons out of the National Guard Armory, stockpiling them, we
feared, for open warfare. But it was all "radical" to me, because it shook
my culture and my family to the root, because our racism went that deep.
I left Alabama after undergraduate school, fleeing the racism as much as
the (still unnamed) homophobia and heterosexism. I went to graduate
school, came out as a lesbian, and in the 1980s started a "career" in political organizing.

Second-wave feminism had given me the context to finally come out
as a lesbian; and I learned how women's struggles grew up within, alongside, and at times in opposition to black struggles. Now, in the 1980s and

1990s, were gay people like myself "hijacking" the civil rights movement? I didn't think so, but how to explain it when *Gay Rights/Special Rights* was so good at propagating that distortion?

Lesbian and gay movements from the 1970s to this day, in fact, do make claims using civil rights laws and other legal concepts that emerged from antiracist struggles. The movement against hate violence, in which I participated for much of the 1980s, offers one instance of the efforts to extend civil rights to include sexual orientation. During the 1980s, a group of us with North Carolinians Against Racist and Religious Violence documented an epidemic of racist and homophobic violence, worked in communities under Klan siege, and pressured law enforcement officials to bring perpetrators of hate violence to justice. The Center for Constitutional Law pioneered a legal strategy against white supremacist groups and racist attackers using the anti-Klan statutes and the Fourteenth Amendment.

All of the federal protections that existed, such as they were, applied to race, and none to sexual orientation. In 1983, moreover, national civil rights groups generally did not include homophobic violence in discussions of hate violence, a discourse that was emerging as the Reagan administration's effects became more deadly. However, fascism tends to call forth united fronts. As we built a coalition against hate violence in North Carolina, we could handily document hundreds of brutal acts perpetrated against blacks, Native Americans, gay people, and Jews. Violence was the bloody common thread among stigmatized identities. A profusion of white supremacist groups, marching throughout the state with their pedagogy of hate, explicated the links among queers, kikes, niggers, commies, and so forth, in case we didn't get them.

During these years Kevin Berrill was doing his groundbreaking work on antigay violence with the National Gay and Lesbian Task Force (NGLTF), compiling the documentation that would lead the Reagan Justice Department to conclude, then censor the conclusion, that homosexuals were the most frequent victims of hate crimes. The Center for Democratic Renewal was able to link homophobia to the range of hate crimes,[12] and other national monitoring and response groups followed suit. In 1990, a civil rights coalition in which the NGLTF played a major role lobbied Congress to pass the Hate Crimes Statistics Act. "It was the first measure to put the federal government on the record as opposing violence against gay men and lesbians in any way," Urvashi Vaid, then director of NGLTF, explained.[13] It was an important victory but largely only a symbolic one, since being counted for a hate crime was not the same as being protected against one, and, over the long term, it has had the negative effect of putting the definition of the problem into increasingly conservative federal hands.

In the wake of the civil rights movement and attendant federal legislation, in the 1970s national gay rights organizations lobbied to get a gay rights bill introduced into Congress; its passage would have given lesbians and gay men protections against homophobic discrimination that was similar to gender and race regarding employment, public housing, access to public facilities, and hate violence. Most recently, gay lobbyists have whittled this down to a bill outlawing job discrimination based on homophobia or heterosexism (which came within one vote of passing in the House in 1996). Gay civil rights strategies have moved more successfully at the municipal level, where many cities have passed ordinances including gay people as a protected class. It was these successes that the Right targeted in a series of ballot initiatives pioneered in such places as Oregon and Colorado, with the argument that since gayness was a "behavior-based lifestyle," any rights we might gain were "special rights."

The Right has been effective in denying gays and lesbians access to civil rights protections in part by playing on important distinctions between discrimination based on race and on sexual identity. The civil rights paradigm fits gay experience at the points where it intersects with the experience of women and people of color as expressed in the Fourteenth Amendment. Equal protection arguments for lesbians and gay men can apply to freedom from discrimination in housing and jobs; from hate violence; and from police brutality and political repression, all of which are also tactics used against people of color. Sodomy laws in half the states (and all the Southern states) make lesbians and gay men second class-citizens, which by my way of thinking is a violation of equal protection, although these laws were upheld in 1986 in *Hardwick* v. *Bowers,* a case from Georgia.

Gay experience does not fit the historic experience of the African American community relative to the Thirteenth and Fifteenth Amendments. Gay people as gay people did not need the Thirteenth Amendment, through which African Americans won their centuries-long struggle to abolish slavery. Although many white lesbians and gay men are subjected to employment discrimination, being born into straight families has protected us from being ghettoized as a superexploited class over decades and generations, as had often happened with people of color, so that there is less of a case, in my opinion, for affirmative action for gay people. Gay people likewise did not need the Fifteenth Amendment's protection of voting, since gay people as such have never been legally prohibited from voting, although lesbians as women have and lesbian and gay African Americans and Native Americans have as people of color.

The Supreme Court's decision in *Romer* v. *Evans* (1995) finally acknowledged the Fourteenth Amendment rights of lesbians and gay men, declaring that they are not "strangers to the law." Justice Anthony Kennedy wrote, "We find nothing special in the protections Amendment 2 withholds. These are protections taken for granted by most people either because they already have them or do not need them; these are protections against exclusion from an almost limitless number of transactions and endeavors that constitute ordinary life in a free society."[14]

Constitutional experts were quick to explain that the ruling did not necessarily challenge the current policy on homosexuals in the military or the question of gay marriage, nor did it provide affirmative rights for gay people. However, it could prove useful in constitutional arguments against proposals to keep the children of "illegal aliens" out of public schools.[15]

Vaid argued that the shift to a "rights-based" gay and lesbian movement from the earlier "liberation-based" movement was an inherently conservative, mainstreaming strategy aimed at winning acceptance on heterosexual terms. Vaid saw this civil rights strategy as moving gay and lesbian liberation away from a more radical integration of gay people into the broad movements for social change that emerged from the 1960s, ironically the very movements that had birthed the terms of such a strategy. Civil rights strategies consolidated gay people as an identity (read "minority") group rather than looking, as the early liberation thrust did, at sexuality as a shaper of various and fluid sexual identities.

Lesbian and gay movements made claims using many laws and legal concepts that emerged from antiracist struggles at the same time that increasingly conservative courts were reshaping their premises. Simultaneously, legal scholars of color began to seriously challenge the reigning legal ideologies about race built in the 1960s and 1970s. "Critical race theorists" such as Derrick Bell, Richard Delgado, Mari Matsuda, and Kimberle Crenshaw started to chart the co-opting of the radical legal tradition of the civil rights movement:

> Racial justice was embraced in the American mainstream in terms that excluded radical or fundamental challenges to status quo institutional practices in American society by treating the exercise of racial power as rare and aberrational rather than as systemic and ingrained. . . . Along with the suppression of explicit white racism (the widely celebrated aim of civil rights reform), the dominant legal conception of racism as a discrete and identifiable act of prejudice based on skin color placed virtually the entire range of everyday social practice in America—social practices developed and maintained throughout the period of formal American apartheid—beyond the scope of critical examination or legal remediation.[16]

Not coming from contexts of struggle, many middle-class white gay people did not realize how contested these civil rights discourses were, or how fragile the gains to people of color given a virulent racist backlash and a declining economy.

Civil rights will remain a powerful paradigm for ameliorating the effects of systemic discrimination based on race, gender, and sexual orientation in the United States in the foreseeable future. Movements for civil rights and against hate violence will remain places where coalitions of people from various racial, ethnic, gender, and sexual communities will come together to get to know each other and figure out how to join efforts in the work to dismantle institutionalized oppression. We can hardly expect communities subjected to brutal attack not to use legal defenses with the only Constitution available.

While it is absolutely essential for progressive people to defend the Fourteenth and Fifteenth Amendments from the concerted assault by the Right, civil rights is also a limited paradigm for social transformation for gays as for other oppressed people. The limits of civil rights are the limits of classical nineteenth-century liberalism, which posited a solitary individual that existed prior to relationship or community. The seventeenth-century British philosopher John Locke formulated a theory of the social contract by which this individual entered into alliance with other individuals, agreeing to give up certain freedoms to a government.[17] Revolution, a rearrangement of the social contract, was necessary when that government no longer expressed, as Thomas Jefferson explained in the Declaration of Independence, the "consent of the governed." Human nature within this framework was seen as essentially rational, universal, and unchanging. Rights belong to the basic social unit of the individual, not to groups. This view of human nature accompanied the rise of capitalism, with individual as consumer or as worker in competition for jobs. An individual's motivation was to get as large a share as possible of available resources, thus maximizing self-interest. In this world view, the state is a neutral mediator among individuals and can intervene only in the "public" sphere.[18]

No wonder, then, that such a philosophical tradition, encoded in civil rights law, cannot comprehend or address the processes whereby groups are systematically privileged or oppressed. No wonder that the demand for group rights, as in aggressive affirmative action, has been so denounced by liberals and conservatives alike. It is the individualism of this tradition that enables the Right to condemn gay and lesbian sexuality as individual choice, the repercussions of which are thereby beyond the scope of civil rights protection.

In perhaps its most fundamental limitation, the rights paradigm of the U.S. Constitution gives primacy to the right to own property over the right to what Karl Marx called "unalienated labor." Economic justice is not much of a constitutional consideration; class exploitation is not a violation of civil rights. The Fourteenth Amendment guarantees due process of law to protect "life, liberty, or *property*," and in that last word, property, there's a Constitutional rub. The Declaration of Independence declared the inalienable rights to "life, liberty, and the *pursuit of happiness.*" In this passage from happiness to property, much is lost. So much of the spirit of the law in the United States is still constrained by this idea that turned humans, including one's own children, and sacred land into private property operating for profit. In challenging slavery, the abolition movement disputed the classification of human beings as private property by using classic rights discourses, and thus was radical in its challenge to capitalism and the foundations of the U.S. political system, as I rightly perceived as a child. However, when property was reinscribed in the Fourteenth Amendment, part of this radical potential was stymied.

After the Fourteenth Amendment was ratified, the Supreme Court ruled, without hearing arguments, that corporations were "persons" within the meaning of the amendment and thus able to claim due process and equal protection of the law.[19] At a time when robber barons were amassing huge fortunes, corporations gained more protection as bodies under the Fourteenth Amendment than the freed slaves, who were still incredibly vulnerable to the white supremacist system that was reconstituting itself in the wake of Reconstruction.[20] The interpretation of the Fourteenth Amendment that gave corporate bodies more protection than black or brown bodies at the end of the nineteenth century did not bode well for gay bodies in the twentieth.

In the 1970s, when emerging gay movements began to argue within the rights framework, one result was to reify sexual orientation as a static identity category, rather than keeping the focus on sexuality as a category for shaping identities. So it keeps the straight gaze on us as a receptacle for heterosexuals' peculiar sexual projections. Within the range of "everyday social practice in America" that lies beyond race- and gender-based antidiscrimination law are most parts of the messy question of sex, the two-thirds of the celluloid lying beyond the rights arguments in *Gay Rights/Special Rights.* How can we persuade people to pass a federal law protecting our civil rights when they are wondering whether we eat shit and rape children, as right-wing videos suggest? How do we have that conversation in any public way, on our own terms?

The rights framework also requires us to prove our belonging by proving our victimhood. We gain strict judicial scrutiny (to use the legal language) in Fourteenth Amendment cases by establishing ourselves as a special (discriminated) class. Many gay people responded to *Gay Rights/Special Rights* by clamoring to prove we are a "real (read: 'persecuted') minority," thus distracting us from rights held as the preserve of the majority, variously constituted as white, male, propertied, and straight. With these victim arguments, we could persuade a good many people that we should not be mutilated, tortured, or brutally attacked, thereby barely asserting our right to life. Liberty and the pursuit of happiness, which in biblical terms some of my friends call the "fullness of life," are quite another matter.

Historical Materialism . . . but What About the Orgasms?

Historical materialism is a second major paradigm for bringing together race, class, gender, and sexuality in the United States. It emerged from Marx's theory that described and challenged a virulent industrial capitalism and the undergirding view of rights and self in the nineteenth century. "With the change of the economic foundation the entire immense superstructure [of natural science, and the legal, political, religious, aesthetic, or philosophic] is . . . transformed," Marx explained in the preface to the *Critique of Political Economy*.[21] Socialists and communists set to work to transform society and human behavior by changing economic, or material, conditions. How have issues of sexuality been fit into this paradigm, how is sexuality illuminated by it, what is missed and what remains for us to understand? In other words, what are the possibilities that an understanding of sexuality brings to transformative movements based in class? How have those movements shaped and challenged gay and lesbian organizing, and how does gay and lesbian organizing challenge movements based on class?

Radical gay and lesbian liberation movements emerged, as Vaid explained, in the late 1960s and 1970s, arguing for a materialist view of sexuality as constantly shaped by economic and other cultural forces, and offering gay sexuality as a positive alternative to the constraints of heterosexual monogamy under capitalism.[22] But these insights did not fit into the line of most Old Left organizations, which at best considered homosexuality a form of bourgeois decadence that would wither with the capitalist state. "Homosexuality is like heroin," one straight commie explained to me in the mid-1980s. ("Tell her it's much cheaper to be gay," a friend advised.) Much of the New Left in the 1960s and 1970s failed to understand the emerging gay liberation movement, because left-wing movements had contested the "private" in private property and counterasserted "public" need without drawing on feminist insights regarding the obfuscating fiction of this public-private split. Even socialist feminists failed to perceive the radical implications of their own critique; they tended to define the private sphere of families and relationships as nuclear heterosexual, with Gayle Rubin being a notable exception.[23]

Lesbians were infuriated with the homophobia of the Left and the sexism of gay men, and evolved a lesbian feminism that initially depended on universal notions of women's nature and condition. (The more progressive wing of this movement, led by lesbians of color and working-class white dykes, evolved a more complex view drawing from antiracist socialism.)[24] The "sex wars" over pornography and S&M challenged unitary lesbian feminist assumptions about female sexuality. Then along came AIDS, which upped the ante on questions of sexuality and brought closer alliances between lesbians and gay men. The rise of the Religious Right brought organizing that formed around the defense of democracy within the liberal rights framework. Queer theory emerged, consolidating the thinking around sexuality but often skimming off the social construction and anti-essentialist portions of historical materialism, leaving the class and race analysis behind. Its praxis, when it had one, consisted of ACT-UP or Queer Nation, both predominantly middle class, white, and male. Marketing specialists discovered the "gay market," and gay culture became commodified, with gay people organized as consumers rather than as a community. Civil rights often became the strategy for white and middle-class gay people to get our piece of the American pie.

In response, the gay Left began to counterorganize in the 1990s. The OUT Fund of the Funding Exchange sponsored two gay Left dialogues, bringing together activists (with majority representation by women and people of color). The National Gay and Lesbian Task Force added a Race/Class/Gender Institute to its annual Creating Change conference, which has also served as a gathering place for the gay Left. Gay presence in unions has increased (see the video *Out at Work*), as have coalitions with unions on antigay ballot initiatives. Historian Allan Berube researched models of solidarity, rather than visibility as organizing metaphors for gay life.[25] Leslie Feinberg helped to bring transgender liberation to the center of queer organizing and consciousness, drawing on hir experience of class solidarity from hir union background in Buffalo and hir decades in the Workers World Party.[26] Gay and lesbian organizations emerged to embody this vision: Esperanza, a peace and justice center in San Antonio, drew on the Marxist-feminist analysis of Chicana lesbians. The Audre Lorde Project in Brooklyn began to address the needs of gay/lesbian/bisexual/transgendered (GLBT) people of color. Southerners on New Ground (SONG), initiated by six Southern lesbians, specifically focuses on these intersections and prioritizes issues such as welfare and popular education on the economy in GLBT communities. Vaid's *Virtual Equality*, Suzanne Pharr's *In the Time of the Right*, Susan Raffo's *Queerly Classed*, and Laura Flanders's *Real Majority/Media Minority*, all by participants in one or more of the gay Left dialogues, extended a lesbian/feminist/Left analysis.[27] This is a sample of the gay, lesbian, and transgender work being done all across the country in the search for a more coherent analysis of the relationship of sexuality to power in the United States.

This analysis will come increasingly from more coherent movements that bring together seemingly disparate communities to meld consciousness, share struggles, and form more inclusive understandings. This essay is another such attempt at consolidating my own experiences over the past five years in situations of deepening relationships, challenging conversations, and teachable moments to try to push toward a deeper synthesis, my personal cycle of action and reflection. Again, as in the work on civil rights, I have run up against what feel like ideological barriers to more comprehensive understandings, and it is those that I am trying to reach beyond here.

In 1992, I began working out of the Durham, North Carolina, office of the Urban-Rural Mission (URM) of the World Council of Churches, a program that brings together community organizers, liberation theologians, and activists from the church to promote transformational organizing in local contexts all over the world. I found myself excited and stimulated by the new framework, which is grounded in a critique of capitalism and colonialism within international contexts. URM emphasized community- and relationship-building. In organizations like URM and its sister group, the Southeast Regional Economic Justice Network (REJN), I got a crash course in the economy, a view of the shifting economic terrain in what is being called "globalization." I learned, for example, that privatization is the process by which public resources such as schools, hospitals, libraries, and government-controlled industries such as the oil industry in many Third World countries, are increasingly either sold or contracted to private corporations to run for profit. Since the early 1980s such "structural adjustments" have been required of Third World countries that want loans from the International Monetary Fund and the World Bank. Within the United States they have been sold to voters with the ideological justification that the government should not be meddling in people's private affairs. The effects are the same here and abroad: lowered wages, deteriorating working conditions, slashed social spending, rapid environmental degradation, and an increased police state.

In 1992 I attended a special gathering of the Southeast Regional Economic Justice Network that had as its theme "Building Just Relationships for the Next 500 Years," as part of the quincentenary of Columbus's arrival in the Americas. One hundred participants from grassroots groups working on economic justice throughout the Southeast were joined by guests from Mexico, Canada, Central America, and the Caribbean to discuss the globalization of the economy and the North American Free

Trade Agreement (NAFTA), which would come to a vote in Congress the following year. As far as I could tell, however, I was the only out homosexual in sight. I faced a nagging question: how does the lesbian part of me fit in? How does homophobia intersect with these issues of gross capitalist exploitation? "What," I pondered, "is a dyke to think about NAFTA?" In retrospect, what I was asking was this: how can a lesbian, shaped by "private" experiences of sexuality, have an opinion on something so public as the economy?[28]

Marx's diatribe against free trade in *The Communist Manifesto* as "naked, shameless, direct and brutal exploitation" is as applicable going into the twenty-first century as it was in the middle of the nineteenth.[29] NAFTA and the General Agreement on Tariffs and Trade (GATT) represent a tremendous repudiation of national boundaries. Under "free trade," goods and capital move freely, but people are constrained. Consolidated multinational corporations increasingly pursue massive profits across borders at the expense of national economies and in the name of private enterprise. Globalization, then, plays into continuing public/private sphere mystifications and personal/boundary confusions in ways that are easily manipulable by demagogues who would lead people into rigid, authoritarian family and social structures, as reflected in the politics of Pat Buchanan in the 1996 Republican presidential primaries.

This public/private split is one of the barriers to understanding the connections of sexuality (defined as private) to class (defined as public), and of integrating gay/lesbian/bisexual/transgendered people into a broader social justice movement. The split is evident in Marx's own writings and in the praxis of most class-based activism. An acute observer of emerging industrial capitalism, to Marx "difference" meant class difference as it played out in the public sphere. In 1848 he described how class differences in Europe over the past one hundred years had been reduced primarily into "two great hostile camps, into two great classes directly facing each other; Bourgeoisie and Proletariat."[30] Although his language of "bourgeoisie" and "proletariat" may seem antiquated in the post-Soviet era or in a period when some economists predict the end of work due to automation, his predictions of a gross and increasing inequality between rich and poor and his condemnation of the depredations of capitalism seem extraordinarily timely. His revolutionary vision of an "association, in which the free development of each is the condition of the free development of all," remains resonantly appealing.[31]

However, Marx's emphasis on wage labor and public action left women in the private sphere, outside the means of production, and therefore outside history and the possibility of transformed conditions. Feminists have refused to ignore the systematic domination of women by men, which is as great a divide as that between capital and labor. In the twentieth century, as Alison Jaggar explained, socialist feminists have mainly tried to deal with Marxism's theoretical inadequacy by retheorizing production and reproduction to break down the dualism of public/private spaces. They have located women's role in human reproduction and sexuality as basic to the structuring of society's resources and relationships.[32] Socialist feminists have also elaborated on Marx and Engels's notion of the "sexual division of labor" (that is, the differentiated economic activity of women and men, which preceded class divisions) within both production and reproduction.[33] This analysis is increasingly relevant in this latest period of globalization, as a new international division of labor has put women of color at the front of the global assembly line.

Feminists also broadened Marx's concept of alienated labor by exploring alienation from bodies as well as masculinity and femininity themselves as alienated conditions. If the goal of Marxism is the free development of human potential through the free activity of labor, this should involve "free sexual expression, freely bearing children, and freely rearing them."[34] (John Locke's fiction that the isolated individual exists prior to community and relationship is quite remarkable to any woman who has ever given birth or to any person who has assisted in this process. Any feminist attention to reproduction and child-rearing puts the lie to the alienating premise of liberal individuality.)

Perhaps this gender/feminist unrest was part of the initial struggle I experienced as I listened to discussions of NAFTA at that Southeast Regional Economic Justice Network gathering in 1992; it finally took on words in a conversation with a fifty-year-old black man who organizes the homeless in Atlanta, whom I will call Pete. During a break, he sang a song about all the "mean things" down here on earth, like homelessness, crime—and women wanting to be men, men powdering their noses and similar "abominations." As the succeeding verses sank in, my palms began to sweat and my heart began to pound. I considered jumping up to interrupt him, or stomping or slipping out of the room. I decided, instead, to try to open a dialogue. First, I approached the singer privately and shared with him my thoughts and reactions. He explained, among other things, that the song had been inspired by the presence of a good number of gay street people in Atlanta's Piedmont Park, many of whom he said (and I believe him) were his friends. Then, working with the conference planners, we carried this discussion into the larger group, where I began to clarify for myself the questions I had framed earlier. It was a moment of deepened articulation in my emerging queer socialism. What I said went something like this:

First off, given the forces we are up against, who decides to powder his nose is pretty inconsequential.

Second, in some cultures, the male and female principles are not so at war as they are in this culture, and people like the *berdache* in American Indian societies were considered holy people. Perhaps those street queers in Piedmont Park are our holy people, cast out by both black and gay communities.

Anyway, if most women acted like women are supposed to act, we would be completely passive, just lay down and die.

Next, people of color have suffered for five hundred years from the European/Christian war between mind and body, soul and body, projected onto cultures that often had more holistic worldviews. The same mind/body split that led the one hundred white men owning poultry plants in Mississippi to tell the workers "we only want your bodies, not your minds," also defines gay men and lesbians in this period as only perverse bodies engaged in sinful/sick/illegal physical acts, as "abomination."

We gay people know that we humans are not only "means of production," however much capitalism seeks to define us that way. Our needs include not only the survival needs of food, shelter, health care, and clothing, but also dignity, pleasure, intimacy, and love. But all gay men and lesbians also need to understand more clearly (as some of us do) how we are also workers, means of production; and the same way we are defined by an obsession with our bodies and our sexuality, black women in Mississippi poultry plants and Mexican women in *maquilas* are also defined as only bodies, to be used and discarded, machines without feelings and souls. We need to understand more fully how our fates are implicated in theirs in order to deepen our own political vision and the possibilities of our own eventual freedom.

We had about thirty minutes for our exchange (during which Pete said he would not sing the song again) and questions, before the agenda turned back to free trade. But I felt in that brief time the possibility of a entirely different kind of conversation about homosexuality, sexuality and power, and gay and lesbian politics, given the collective history of struggle and the spiritual and political grounding of the people in the room. But how could we get back—or forward—to that space?

In this essay and elsewhere, I set out to explore how sexuality was included or omitted from historical materialism, and what gay and lesbian experience might have to offer transformative political movements based in class. I have gradually come to see that sexual intimacy between same-sex partners places sexuality beyond the realms of production or reproduction, and that sex for its own sake opens up a path beyond the public/private split. While most heterosexual sex does not end in conception, it could. Sex between two men or two women has nothing to do with procreation. It is more obviously for its own sake: for pleasure, intimacy, co-creation. That's what makes the Puritans so crazy.

Same-gender sex (and heterosexual eroticism separate from procreation) also moves us beyond the public/private fiction. The devastation of the genuinely private (which is deeply transpersonal) by the privatized has created profound confusions all across the culture, in terms of what psychologists call "boundaries," by disrupting the relationship of the self with itself and with other humans, the natural world, and the realm of the spirit that is transpersonal and transcendent. In fact, what we have been taught to think of as the private sphere is not private at all, in the sense of being isolated and individualized, but more intimate, in the sense of providing the ground on which genuine transformation, community and relationship occur. Sexual intimacy is intensely personal, and ultimately transpersonal, and sexual practices are highly cultural. A clearer discerning of the creative and destructive potentials of sexuality is central to figuring out how to reclaim the intimate from the devastated, the private, the public, and the privatized. There is nothing private about multinational control. There is nothing intimate about the drive for profit.[35] What people long for is not privacy, but intimacy; not individualism, but a capacity for autonomy-within-community.

Sexuality for itself also prioritizes being over doing in a way difficult for Marxist theory. "Praxis" derives from the Greek word for "to act" or "to do"; in Jaggar's terms, it is "conscious physical labor directed toward transforming the material world so that it will satisfy human needs."[36] But when Marxism locates our human worth in labor (whether production or reproduction, grinding away within capitalism or at dismantling it), does not this just reproduce another form of Western alienation? Doesn't transformation involve as much how we are with each other as what we do together? That's a strong lesson learned from whatever experience I have had across the police-enforced racial boundaries of my childhood. Praxis can allow little room for states of being; sexuality again puts this question of consciousness back on the table as re-creation, as intimacy, as transcendence. Sexuality brings us into the realm of spirit, of which neither Marx nor Freud had much apprehension. What I have at times experienced with people of color has been struggle beyond praxis that incorporates both being and doing, with a profound spiritual undergirding.

The brilliant African Caribbean lesbian poet and activist Audre Lorde explained the power of sexual being and the stakes of incorporating the power of the erotic in our political practice. In her essay "Uses of the Erotic: The Erotic as Power," she cuts through both the public/private obfuscation and the peculiar notion articulated by Sigmund Freud that desire is antithetical to culture. Lorde explained: "The erotic is a measure between the beginnings of our sense of self and the chaos of our strongest feelings. It is an internal sense of satisfaction to which, once we have experienced it, we know we can aspire. For once having experienced the fullness of this depth of feeling and recognizing its power, in honor and self-respect we can require no less of ourselves."

She goes on to claim "an erotic root" for satisfaction in our work (and, by implication, its loss is one of the primary factors in what Marx called the "alienation of labor"). Labor is not the sublimation of desire: labor is desire, and desire is deeply spiritual: "the deep and irreplaceable knowledge of my capacity for joy comes to demand from all of my life that it be lived within the knowledge that such satisfaction is possible, and does not have to be called marriage, nor god, nor an afterlife."[37]

I had Lorde in mind a year after the dialogue with Pete at REJN, when I went back to help staff their annual meeting. I came out from the get-go this time. After the meeting, I caught a ride to the airport with the folks from the Mississippi delegation—representatives from the A. Philip Randolph Institute (APRI), a national organization of black trade unionists. I had another dialogue, this one (in retrospect) a gloss on the pronouncement by Marx and Engels that the "sexual division of labor" was "originally nothing but the division of labor in the sexual act."[38]

Driving was Bill, an African American man who is president of the Mississippi APRI chapter; beside me was Fran, a Jewish woman from New York making a documentary on the textile strikes of 1934; and in the back seat were Lena, a black social worker from Mississippi, and Mary, a black woman who organizes Mississippi catfish workers. (These are not their real names.) I happened to mention to Fran that I would be happy to get home early to see my partner Barb and our daughter Annie (whose birth was NOT a result of the heterosexual "division of labor in the sexual act," but that's another story). She asked to see pictures, and I passed them around the van. Lena, from the back seat, began to ask questions, clearly from the perspective of having participated in custody decisions involving lesbian parents in Mississippi (she opposed taking the children away, in spite of believing that the lifestyle was morally wrong): how can gay parents bring children into the world when they will suffer so much for their parents' sexual orientation? How can the parents endure the extra burden?

I explained that my partner and I have a supportive community of straight and gay friends that was a strong part of our decision to have a child. As to burdens, it's the sweetest burden I ever had. The problem is in the culture, not in the parents. For instance, I refuse to blame black mothers for the racism from which their children suffer. Deliberately having any child is, admittedly, an act of hope. Different children will have different issues through which to struggle.

"Well," she moved on, "will you want her to be homosexual when she grows up?"

I was ready for this one. "What gay people know is the terror we felt of losing our parents' love when they find we are gay. What I want Annie to know is that I love and support whoever she is as she unfolds. I want her to be able to have intimate relationships in which she fully gives and receives love, and to know that she never ever deserves to be abused."

Mary, beside Lena, began to nod.

"I don't feel that I had a choice to be heterosexual," I elaborated, "just not to lie. I just got one life, and I decided I could not waste it pretending. I believe those spirituals, 'Before I'll be a slave I'll be buried in my grave. . . .' "

Lena cut to the chase. "You know, never in my wildest imaginings— and I have fantasized a lot—could I imagine having sex with a woman. I mean, I have had a lot of experience, but I could never imagine—"

She asked for a Kleenex from the front seat and wiped the perspiration off her brow.

"Well," I countered, "you have a lot of help from the culture in not imagining it. Just look at how much propaganda for heterosexual eroticism comes out of Hollywood, out of movies and TV."

Fran, bless her heart, joined me on this one, sharing her close friendships with lesbians in New York and describing how seeing their beauty allowed her to think about the possibility of sexual relationships with women, although she knows that what holds her back is the social burden, the having to explain it to her mom.

"Well," Lena persisted, "maybe this is too personal, but . . . what about the orgasms?"

About this time, I noticed that Bill was circling the airport for the second time, past the north and south terminals. We were all laughing a lot, and everyone was intensely focused on the conversation.

I got the strong feeling that Lena was asking for instruction, and I got the strong feeling I could give it to her, talk her through it, like phone sex, like she is in a plane circling above the Atlanta airport and the pilot just died and I have to talk her down. But Bill was at the Delta Dash, and I chickened out.

I took the easier route: "You start from the context of both having women's bodies, of understanding sensations from within and without. There can be a depth of emotional, physical, and intellectual connection. Just think of what you get from your women friends—the depth of support and interaction, and add sex to that. It's not off the map; and think of some of the difficult power dynamics with heterosexual men."

Mary was nodding even more vigorously.

Lena didn't let me off the hook: "But what about the orgasms?"

"Don't worry about that! You've got your vagina, your clitoris, your hands, your mouth, your knees, or any object you want to use," I said rapidly, "but, hey, I got to go."

"You okay up there, Bill?" I asked, "We notice you been circling."

"I just wanted to see how many orgasms we got," he replied.

"You know, I never heard a gay person talk like that," Mary said.

"Maybe you never gave them a chance," I said.

I piled out of the van to general merriment, giving Lena the assignment that between now and next year's gathering, she was to imagine making love with a woman. She agreed.

Postscript

We are in a period of global reorganization. For some, the principle is maximizing profits and power. For others, it is using this most recent crisis to reach, once again, for more just human arrangements: "an association in which the free development of each is the condition of the free development of all," development that assumes our sustainable participation in the natural world, our kinship with the animals and plants, the minerals and water and air, with all the whirling molecules. This is the very old way of love, and it calls us to find new paths. Many of us are reaching for new connections and new ways to explain them. This no longer invisible dyke, trying to be true to her thirteen-year-old self, knows that our sexuality is basic to our interconnection, and that sexuality can help us move beyond the rift of praxis and being, to a practice of being.

Freud articulated the central problem of sexuality in Western culture: "Civilization behaves toward sexuality as a people or a stratum of its population does which has subjected another to its exploitation. Fear of revolt by the suppressed elements drives it to stricter and stricter precautionary measures." The root issue on the question of sexuality and power, I am coming to understand, is that of how we nurture or construct cultures in which desire is integral to culture. Desire, Audre Lorde teaches us, is, after all, desire *for* something or someone, and the ability of people to experience autonomous sexual desire is linked to our ability to desire health, decent jobs, safe neighborhoods, all the things we consider fullness of life. Before we can get what we want, we have to know what we want; to feel it physically: the desire for another person . . . for justice . . . for God; perhaps, after all, they are all the same longing.

Notes

The epigraphs are from Sigmund Freud, *Civilization and its Discontents,* James Strachey, trans. and ed. (New York: Norton 1989), pp. 10–11; and Audre Lorde, "Uses of the Erotic: The Erotic as Power," in *Sister/Outsider: Essays and Speeches* (Freedom, CA: The Crossing Press, 1984), p. 54.

1. Walt Whitman, "Crossing Brooklyn Ferry," in Richard Ellmann and Robert O'Clair, eds., *Modern Poets: An Introduction to Poetry* (New York: Norton, 1976), p. 4.

2. Eve Sedgwick, *Epistemology of the Closet* (Berkeley: University of California Press, 1990), p. 32.

3. Ibid.

4. Paule Friere, *Pedagogy of the Oppressed* (New York: Herder and Herder, 1968), pp. 119–20.

5. Sedgwick, *Epistemology,* pp. 29, 27.

6. For earlier versions of this narrative, see my "Southern Women Writing: Towards a Literature of Wholeness," in *My Mama's Dead Squirrel: Lesbian Essays on Southern Culture* (Ithaca, NY: Firebrand, 1985), p. 20; and *Memoir of a Race Traitor* (Boston: South End, 1995), pp. 21–25.

7. Both are quoted in Barbara Smith, "Blacks and Gays: Healing the Great Divide," in Chip Berlet, ed., *Eyes Right: Challenging the Right-Wing Backlash* (Boston: South End, 1995), pp. 264, 276.

8. For a longer analysis of *Gay Rights, Special Rights,* see my essay "Visibility and Backlash," in David Deitcher, ed., *The Question of Equality: Lesbian and Gay Politics in America Since Stonewall* (New York: Simon & Schuster, 1995), pp. 83–122.

9. Smith, "Blacks and Gays," p. 276; Sedgwick, *Epistemology,* p. 22.

10. Ralph Ellison, *Invisible Man* (New York: Vintage, 1972), p. 3.

11. Ibid.

12. See Mab Segrest and Leonard Zeskind, *Quarantines of Death: The Far Right's Homophobic Agenda* (Atlanta: Center for Democratic Renewal, 1988).

13. Urvashi Vaid, *Virtual Equality: The Mainstreaming of Gay and Lesbian Liberation* (New York: Anchor Books, 1995), p. 11.

14. *Romer v. Evans,* 517 U.S. 620 (1996), p. 631.

15. Linda Greenhouse, "Gay Rights Law Can't Be Banned, High Court Rules," *New York Times,* May 21, 1996, pp. 1, 19.

16. "Introduction," in Kimberle Crenshaw, Neil Gotanda, Gary Pellar, and Kendall Thomas, eds., *Critical Race Theory: The Key Writings That Formed the Movement* (New York: The New Press, 1995), pp. xiv, xv.

17. In 1690, Locke wrote in the chapter "Of the Beginning of Political Societies" in his *Second Treatise of Government* ([Indianapolis: Hackett, 1980], p. 52):

> Men being, as has been said, by nature, all free, equal, and independent, no one can be put out of this estate, and subjected to the political power of another, without his own consent. The only way whereby any one divests himself of his natural liberty, and puts on the bonds of civil society, is by agreeing with other men to join and unite into a community for their comfortable, safe, and peaceable living one amongst another, in a

secure enjoyment of their properties, and a greater security against any, that are not of it. . . . When any number of men have so consented to make one community or government, they are thereby presently incorporated, and make one body politic, wherein the majority have a right to act and conclude the rest.

The sexism of using "men" for "humans" sets the stage for the greater sexism of assuming that adult "men" emerge on their own as "free, equal, and independent," rather than through a process of the gradual emergence to a separate self that begins in their mother's womb. Western democratic theory builds on this masculinist alienation.

18. Alison Jagger, *Feminist Politics and Human Nature* (Sussex, England: Rowman & Allanheld, 1983), chapter 3, "Liberal Feminism and Human Nature," pp. 27–50.

19. See *San Mateo County* v. *Southern Pacific Railroad Co.*, 116 U.S. 138 (1885); *Santa Clara County* v. *Southern Pacific Railroad Co.*, 118 U.S. 394 (1886).

20. See Richard L. Grossman and Ward Morehouse, "Minorities, the Poor, and Ending Corporate Rule," *Poverty and Race Research Action Council Newsletter,* September–October 1995, pp. 1–2: "By 1904 corporations controlled four-fifths of the nation's industrial production, had begun to perfect a corporate system of finance, industry and governance, and had brought about what Morton Horowitz calls the 'transformation of American law.' Corporations actually turned themselves into de facto persons able to participate in elections and the process of self-governance—well before indigenous peoples, women, African Americans and other persons of color, well before most people without property." In *Coppage* v. *Kansas,* 236 U.S. 1 (1915), the Court ruled: "Since it is self-evident that, unless all things are held in common, some persons must have more property than others, it is from the nature of things impossible to uphold freedom of contract and the right of private property without at the same time recognizing as legitimate those inequalities of fortune that are the necessary result of the exercise of those rights."

21. Karl Marx and Friedrich Engels, *Selected Works* (New York: International Publishers, 1968), pp. 182–83.

22. In *Eros and Civilization: A Philosophical Inquiry into Freud* ([Boston: Beacon Press, 1966], pp. 35–36), Herbert Marcuse wrote: "Free gratification of man's instinctual needs is incompatible with civilized society: renunciation and delay in satisfaction are the prerequisites of progress. Happiness must be subordinated to the discipline of work as full-time occupation, to the discipline of monogamic reproduction, to the established system of law and order. The methodical sacrifice of libido, its rigidly enforced deflection to socially useful activities and expressions, is culture."

23. Gayle Rubin, "The Traffic in Women: Notes on the 'Political Economy' of Sex," in Rayna R. Reiter, ed., *Toward an Anthropology of Women* (New York: Monthly Review Press, 1975), pp. 157–210.

24. See the Combahee River Collective's "Combahee River Collective Statement," in Barbara Ellen Smith, ed., *Home Girls: A Black Feminist Anthology* (New York: Kitchen Table Press, 1983), pp. 272–82. This essay was influential on Sedg-

wick's discussion of sexuality in *Epistemology of the Closet,* although Sedgwick's applications, in terms of developing a "queer theory," are cultural/literary rather than materialist/economic.

25. Allan Berube, *Coming Out Under Fire: The History of Gay Men and Women in World War Two* (New York: McMillan, 1990).

26. Leslie Feinberg, *Stone Butch Blues* (Ithaca, NY: Firebrand, 1993).

27. Suzanne Pharr, *In the Time of the Right: Reflections on Liberation* (Berkeley: Chardon, 1996); Susan Raffo, ed., *Queerly Classed* (Boston: South End, 1997); Laura Flanders, *Real Majority/Media Minority: The Cost of Sidelining Women in Reporting* (Monroe, ME: Common Courage Press, 1997).

28. For an essay based on a keynote address urging gay opposition to NAFTA, which I gave at NGLTF's Creating Change conference in Durham in 1993, see "A Bridge, Not a Wedge," in *Memoir of a Race Traitor,* pp. 229–46.

29. Karl Marx and Friedrich Engels, "The Communist Manifesto," in David McLellan, ed., *Karl Marx: Selected Writings* (Oxford: Oxford University Press, 1988), p. 223.

30. Ibid., p. 222.

31. Ibid., p. 238.

32. Karl Marx and Friedrich Engels, *The German Ideology,* quoted in Jaggar, *Feminist Politics,* p. 68. Jaggar points out that Gayle Rubin also took on gender and heterosexism. Within an historic materialist analysis, socialist feminism aims to "abolish the social relations that constitute humans not only as workers and capitalists, but also as women and men." Gay experience begins to enter this paradigm. In Jaggar's words, "Normative heterosexuality must be replaced by a situation in which the sex of one's lover is a matter of social indifference, so that the dualistic categories of heterosexual, homosexual and bisexual may be abandoned."

33. Karl Marx and Friedrich Engels, *The German Ideology,* ed. C. J. Arthur (New York: International Publishing, 1970), p. 51.

34. See Jaggar's chapter "Socialist Feminism and Human Nature" in *Feminist Politics,* pp. 123–68.

35. But moving issues politically out of the silence of that privatized sphere is fraught with difficulties, a classic double bind. For example, on questions of reproductive rights, the choice movement makes the argument that women should have access to abortions as a protection of their private right to choose, but these are public arguments about public policy—laws and judicial decisions. For lesbians and gay men, the sodomy laws in half the states make our sexual acts illegal—in many places felonies—but our attempts to organize against such laws in the public sphere can reinforce the stereotype that we are only sexual beings or are obsessed with sexuality, rather than showing that we are having to learn how to negotiate questions of sexualty in the public sphere because the way our sexuality has been criminalized intrudes on our capacity for genuine relationships or could land us in court or in jail—two very public places. Racist and sexist stereotypes against welfare mothers put these women in a similar bind. I remember vividly the response of a welfare rights union organizer to a proposal to have a cross-cultural discussion at a URM meeting of what constitutes a family: their

people could not publicly discuss who was in their families—which is to say, with whom they lived and ate—because they could then be arrested for welfare fraud, so great was the level of surveillance they were under in the process of public assistance.

36. Jaggar, *Feminist Politics*, p. 54.
37. Audre Lorde, "Uses of the Erotic" p. 57.
38. Marx and Engels, *The German Ideology*, p. 51.

About the Contributors

Cynthia D. Anderson is an assistant professor of sociology at Iowa State University, Ames. She is co-editor of *Feminist Foundation: Toward Transforming Sociology* (Sage, 1998), and the author of numerous journal articles. Her current research interests include labor markets, single mothers' vulnerability to poverty, and structural obstacles to transitions from welfare to work.

Fran Ansley is a professor of law at the University of Tennessee-Knoxville and is faculty director of the University of Tennessee-Knoxville's Community Partnership Center. She works collaboratively with local groups and individuals to explore and document the impacts of globalization on local communities in eastern Tennessee and Mexico, and to make the results of that research accessible to blue-collar and low-income people.

Monica Kelly Appleby, a FOCIS member and former Glenmary sister, is the program director of a micro-enterprise organization in southwestern Virginia. She works with women who want to start home-based businesses.

Patricia D. Beaver is the director of the Center for Appalachian Studies and a professor of anthropology at Appalachian State University, Boone, North Carolina. Her research is focused on community, gender, ethnic diversity, and class in southern Appalachia and the U.S. South, as well as the impacts of economic reform on family and gender in China. She is the author of *Rural Community in the Appalachian South* (University Press of Kentucky, 1986), co-editor of *Cultural Diversity in the U.S. South: Anthropological Contributions to a Region in Transition* (University of Georgia Press, 1998), and author of numerous other publications.

Gemma Beckley is the director and chair of the Social Work Program at Rust College in Holly Springs, Mississippi. She has conducted research on the rural poor in the Delta for over ten years. In addition, she works with foundations and community organizations in the Delta to evaluate work and development

271

programs. With support from the Fulbright program, she takes scholars and leaders from the rural South on exchange programs in China, India, Egypt, and Israel.

Cynthia M. Duncan is an associate professor of sociology at the University of New Hampshire in Durham. Her forthcoming book, *Worlds Apart: Why Poverty Persists in Rural America* compares opportunities for mobility and community change in three remote rural areas. Her current research examines how families and communities have adapted to changes in the North Atlantic fisheries of Maine and Newfoundland since 1950. She also works with community development groups and foundations to encourage programs that support families and economic development initiatives.

Mahnaz Kousha is an associate professor of sociology at Macalester College, Saint Paul, Minnesota. She is a member of the board of directors of *Critique: Journal for Critical Studies of the Middle East,* and organizes an annual conference on Life and Politics in the Middle East. Her recent research focuses on the changing status of women in Iran, life satisfaction among Iranian men and women, and women's position in the Iranian family.

Patricia B. Lerch is a professor of anthropology at the University of North Carolina at Wilmington. She has published articles on the Waccamaw Indians of North Carolina, Umbanda spirit possession of southern Brazil, and women and tourism in Barbados. She is a past president of the Southern Anthropological Society.

Sally Ward Maggard is an associate professor of sociology and anthropology, adjunct associate professor of history, Regional Research Institute faculty research associate, and women's studies faculty associate at West Virginia University in Morgantown. Her research centers on the social and economic development of coal mining regions, including the intersections of social class, gender, and race as they shape social institutions and social change. She is editor of the *Journal of Appalachian Studies.*

Ann M. Oberhauser is an associate professor in the Department of Geology and Geography at West Virginia University, Morgantown. She has conducted research on industrial restructuring and regional development in France, South Africa, and the United States. Her current work focuses on the impact of gender and economic restructuring on households and communities in central and southern Appalachia.

Michael D. Schulman is a professor of sociology at North Carolina State University, Raleigh. His publications on the textile industry have appeared in *Social Forces, The Sociological Quarterly,* and in *Hanging by a Thread* (ILR Press, 1991), which he co-edited. His current research includes projects on rural restructuring, sustainable community development, agricultural health and hazards, and youth work and injury.

Mab Segrest is a writer, teacher, and organizer who lives in Durham, North Carolina. She is the author of *My Mama's Dead Squirrel: Lesbian Essays on Southern Culture* (Firebrand, 1985), and *Memoir of a Race Traitor* (South End, 1995). She is currently working on a third book, a collection of essays in which a version of the chapter in this volume will appear. Segrest has been doing political and cultural work on issues of racism, sexism, homophobia, and classism for twenty years.

Barbara Ellen Smith is the director of the Center for Research on Women and an associate professor of sociology at the University of Memphis. She has been an activist and writer on labor, civil rights, and women's issues in the South for the past twenty-five years. Her works include *Digging Our Own Graves: Coal Miners and the Struggle over Black Lung Disease* (Temple University Press, 1987), and, with co-editors John Gaventa and Alex Willingham, *Communities in Economic Crisis: Appalachia and the South* (Temple University Press, 1990).

Carol Stack is a professor of women's studies at the University of California at Berkeley, where she holds a joint appointment in the Graduate School of Education. She is the author of *All Our Kin* (Harper and Row, 1974) and *Call to Home: African Americans Reclaim the Rural South* (Basic Books, 1996); the latter was awarded the Victor Turner Prize in Humanistic Anthropology. She is currently working on a book dealing with youth in the low-wage labor market in Oakland, California.

Anne-Marie Turnage is a doctoral candidate in geography at West Virginia University in Morgantown. Her dissertation examines gender and the informal economy in rural northern Appalachia.

Loida C. Velázquez is the project director and principal investigator at the Southeastern High School Equivalency Program, an adult basic education project that serves migrant and seasonal farmworkers in Georgia, South Carolina, North Carolina, and Tennessee. She is interested in rural populations and has done extensive research within Hispanic migrant communities.

Margaret M. Walsh is an assistant professor of sociology at Russell Sage College in Troy, New York. She studies poverty, education, and family structure, and is currently working on a book about single motherhood in a rural community. She also does applied work with social service organizations.

Susan Williams grew up in eastern Tennessee, and worked for years as an organizer for the community-based environmental group Save Our Cumberland Mountains. She is now a popular educator at the Highlander Center in New Market, Tennessee, where she does economic education with grassroots groups.

Darlene Wilson has completed the course work for a Ph.D. in history at the University of Kentucky in Lexington. She currently serves as the director of Institutional Planning and Research at Southeast Community College in Cumberland, Kentucky.

Index

acculturation, 128, 129–37; definition of, 129, 137n. 4; and language, 130

Acme Boot Company, 215, 218

ACT-UP, 258

affirmative action, 150, 253

AFL-CIO, 230

African American men: and African American women, 15; as coal miners, 186–87; imagery of, 23; as patriarchs, 22; as strikebreakers, 199–200; and white women, 15

African Americans: class differences among, 141–42, 156, and community control, 18; in the Delta, 138–59; discrimination against, 187, 210; emancipation of, 20, 21; employment of, 140, 206n. 28; and gender relations, 15, 22, 31n. 26; and land ownership, 146; leadership among, 144; middle class, 17, 141–59, and political power, 144–45, 157–59; and racial resistance, 18, 24, 139–40, 248–49; return migration of, 161–69; and role models, 156; and skin color discrimination, 38; in the textile industry, 102–4. See also African American men; African American women; blackness

African American women: class relations among, 22; and community-building, 7, 149–59; 163–69; 175–77; as domestic workers, 22, 77–89, 102; employment of, 22, 80, 145–49, 165; feminist politics of, 21, 22, 23; as hospital workers, 200; leadership among, 149–59; middle class, 16; as professionals, 22, 145–59, 163; as slaves, 16; and white women, 13, 23

agriculture, Southern: activism in, 19; crop diversification in, 60; labor force in, 17, 39–40, 138–39, 211; among Waccamaw Sioux, 59–62; women and, 20, 31n. 27, 62. See also migrant workers; planters; sharecroppers

AIDS, 258

Aid to Families with Dependent Children (AFDC), 165, 166. See also social welfare programs

Alcoa-Fujikura, 241

Allied Signal Corporation, 216, 219, 223, 229

American Friends Service Committee, 239

Ames, Jessie Daniel, 24

Anderson, Sarah, 240

Anglo-Americans. See whites

Ansley, Fran, 215, 219, 220–41

A. Philip Randolph Institute, 264

Appalachia, 8n. 1, 15; central, 203n. 3; class structure of, 28n. 4, 185; community-based organizations in, 177–79; community building in, 171–81; constructions of, 7, 8, 34–35, 50, 185; elites in, 189–91; history of, 39, 112–14; hospital strike in, 185–203; informal economy in, 109–22; racial mixing in, 34–51; social inequality in, 185, 186. See also Appalachian studies; coalfields; Kentucky; Tennessee; West Virginia

Appalachian by Design, 117–18

Appalachian Family Ministries, 176

Appalachian studies, 2, 3; emphasis on class in, 185

Appalachian Women Empowered, 175

apparel, production of, 5, 118

Appleby, Monica Kelly, 171, 174, 175, 180

arts and crafts: marketing of, 116, 176; production of, 110, 176

Association of American Indian Affairs of New York, 67

Audre Lorde Project, 258

automation. See technological innovation

275